# The American Family

Also by Dan Quayle

*Standing Firm*

# The American Family

## Discovering the Values That Make Us Strong

Dan Quayle
and
Diane Medved, Ph.D.

HarperCollins*Publishers*
Zondervan

FIRST EDITION

*Designed by C. Linda Dingler*

ISBN 0-06-017378-5

96 97 98 99 00 ❖/HC 10 9 8 7 6 5 4 3 2 1

To the De La Rosa, Wallace, Burns, Cowden, and Burtin families
and to all the families
across America
whose values make us strong

# Contents

# Acknowledgments

In writing about the American family, I thank God for my wonderful family: Marilyn, Tucker, Benjamin, and Corinne. I am strengthened by their love and support. I've also been blessed with special caring parents, Jim and Corinne Quayle, as well as talented siblings, Chris, Mike, and Martha.

In acknowledging those who contributed to the book, I begin by thanking the people from HarperCollins and Zondervan who attended the first meeting at which the book's concept was discussed and determined: HarperCollins publisher Jack McKeown; editor Rick Horgan, who once again provided wise counsel and editing along the way; and Zondervan's John Sloan and Scott Bolinder, who gave me strong and early encouragement to travel America and interview a cross section of families.

My dearest friend for twenty-three years, Marilyn, was a great editor and gave me constructive, insightful comments throughout the production of this book.

My close friend, John McConnell, was invaluable in helping me to complete this book. A special friend Les Lenkowsky, the talented president of the Hudson Institute, delivered excellent comments, and my longtime confidant, Bill Gribbin, also made keen suggestions.

Laura Minter was indefatigable in transcribing interviews and organizing my trips. Anne Hathaway, Aaron Levenhagen, Jennifer Gagel, Candy Griner, and Tom Fleener made important contributions.

Book handler Bob Barnett did his usual superb job.

My coauthor, Diane Medved, was instrumental in helping to select and interview the families I profiled. Her contributions as a writer and a psychologist have been invaluable, and both of us have built warm friendships with these families. She was assisted in her efforts by transcribers Jackie Lugo and Kristy Montgomery, her longtime agents Richard and Artie Pine, and friend and researcher Lissa Roche of Hillsdale College.

Diane could not have completed this task without the love and support of her family, including her three adorable children, Sarah, Shayna, and Danny, and her beloved husband of eleven years, Michael Medved, who is her full partner in all of life's endeavors.

Finally, I owe special thanks to the five families I interviewed and wrote about: the De La Rosas, Wallaces, Burnses, Cowdens, and Burtins. I have developed a special fondness for these families and now consider each of them part of the Quayle extended family. Ultimately, this is their book as well as mine.

—DAN QUAYLE
*February 1996*

# The American Family

# 1
# The New Consensus

AMERICA HAS REACHED A NEW CONSENSUS ON THE importance of the traditional family—a consensus unthinkable just a few years ago. Ideas now considered part of conventional wisdom were considered hugely controversial as recently as 1992. No one knows that better than I do.

Nothing I said or did during the four years I served as Vice President of the United States generated more protest, anger, or ridicule than a few comments I made about a popular TV sitcom in a speech to the Commonwealth Club of California in San Francisco in May 1992.

The speech that caused all the controversy was about the "poverty of values" and the denigration of fathers and their importance in the lives of their children. The sound bite that raised the roof was this: "It doesn't help matters," I said, "when prime-time TV has Murphy Brown—a character who supposedly epitomizes today's intelligent, highly paid, professional woman—mocking the importance of fathers by bearing a child alone and calling it just another 'lifestyle choice.'"

No matter how you view the television character, the debate

that followed changed our country. However unwittingly, Hollywood became the catalyst for a national conversation on family values that continues to this day.

Yes, I suggested that the model family was an *intact* family. At the time, many considered this a debatable proposition. Since then, however, things have turned around. Bill Clinton, then a candidate for President, attacked the speech, saying we shouldn't be talking about family values but about "valuing families." Today, as president, he frequently punctuates his speeches and comments with the term *family values*. He's even gone so far as to say I was right and to declare that intact families should be considered the model.

America has truly reached a new consensus—an understanding that when families are happy and healthy, communities thrive; and when families are battered and children neglected, communities fail. Now voices at all points on the political spectrum, from Bill Clinton to Bill Bennett, are calling for strong families. National events, such as the October 1995 Million Man March, are staged by people who, though not my political allies, make the very arguments I raised in May 1992. Fathers *do* matter. Families *are* the basis of our society. We *must* support the unified model of father, mother, and child. On this, we're all allies. *Strengthening families should not be a political issue.*

## Putting Family First

I admit that I have a passion for politics. I served in Congress for twelve years and as Vice President for four. I've interacted with world leaders and with Americans from all walks of life; I've traveled to over fifty countries.

But my most treasured moments are those spent with my family. I've been blessed with the stability and love of Marilyn and our three children. I grew up with loving, supportive parents and caring siblings. It's relatively easy for me to prefer my own home to anywhere else. I delight in the company of my wife and children. I'm thrilled when my children make a goal in lacrosse, score points in basketball, or get an A on a school report. I feel uplifted when I come out of church and proud when I hear the National Anthem. That may sound corny to some, but to me, it's just normal life.

When I left the vice presidency, it was natural that I'd want to return to Indiana. Since coming home I've written a vice-presidential memoir, *Standing Firm,* founded BTC Inc., and joined the boards of the Hudson Institute and several corporations. I write a weekly nationally syndicated column and make speeches to audiences across America, political and nonpolitical alike. Though I still travel a great deal, my time isn't consumed by crises like those in the Persian Gulf or in Panama or by government shutdowns. Things can still be hectic, but the Quayle family's home life is more normal than it's been in twenty years.

Still, the issue of family values stays foremost in my mind. Now that those two words are accepted and our national attention is focused on encouraging the *values* that help parents and children thrive—*do we really know what they are?* How do healthy American families define and live out their values? To answer these questions, I embarked on this book.

An early decision was to not emphasize *my* ideas on family values—which are well known—but to let American families speak for themselves. Accordingly, this book is based on interviews and in-depth discussions with families across the country, from the hills of Virginia to the beaches of Hawaii. I found that ordinary working Americans rather than Washington officials or political pundits are the *experts* in creating healthy families.

Too often Americans are talked down to by the news media, entertainment elite, and politicians. Like many people I've met across America, I get tired of all those talking heads on television interpreting for me what I just heard. The media decision makers give the impression that the American people can't understand what is happening without constant analysis and interpretation by the media elite themselves.

You'll find none of that condescension in this book. Much of the material comes directly from the families interviewed. The wisdom is in *their* words, not those of a professional clarifier. They discuss marriage, parenting, outside influences, challenges, and values. And the children, who were equal participants in the interviews, offer their special insights.

In writing about the American family, I considered it essential to acknowledge our nation's diversity. I hoped to include a single mother. I wanted urban residents and a rural family; people from the north, south, east, and west; people of diverse ethnic origin. I sought a range of economic levels.

One criterion was paramount. The families would not be dysfunctional—that's all we seem to hear about these days. Rather, they'd be normal, healthy families—the very kind that don't get much credit in our tabloid culture.

On the other hand, I didn't expect to find a "perfect" family, nor did I want to. In fact, some of the most admirable families I talked to made it a point to say they did *not* have *Ozzie and Harriet*– or *Leave It to Beaver*–style homes. Several of the adults had parents who were alcoholics. Almost all had suffered major setbacks in their lives. They encountered—and overcame—such challenges as a child's debilitating accident, a painful divorce, infertility, the decay of their neighborhood, unemployment, learning disabilities, racial prejudice, and geographical isolation. Like all families, these are real people with real problems, not immune to disappointments and frustrations. But the encouraging truth is that they live real lives and implement real solutions for the problems that families face.

One issue that did *not* concern me was politics. I did not ask the families their political beliefs or even hazard a guess along that line. Of the five families I interviewed for this book, only one told me they had voted for the Bush-Quayle ticket. Putting politics aside, my coauthor, Diane Medved, and I found five families that would fit more relevant criteria—and would reflect, in their own ways, the real America.

I met Diane after being interviewed by her husband, film critic and author Michael Medved. After that meeting Diane sent me her third book, *The Case Against Divorce,* and I liked its message: Couples should use every possible means to make their marriages strong and keep their families united rather than succumbing to the prodivorce messages that permeate our culture. Together, Diane and I bring complementary perspectives to this book: As a clinical psychologist and journalist, she's well versed in probing what makes families tick; with my background in politics, the law, and journalism and years spent working with people and understanding their circumstances, I can tie our findings to policies and the broader picture. We both have wonderful marriages and three children, mine a little older than hers. We're both religious; I'm a Christian and she's an observant Jew.

## Discovering the Values

Prior to my intensive family interviews, I conducted an informal survey. My "focus groups" were some of the audiences I spoke to in 1995. I asked them to take a few minutes to fill out a card headed "Help Dan Quayle Identify Family Values." The locations included college campuses in eight states and national conferences of professional groups. Participants at those national conferences gathered from all parts of the country, so the responses have wide geographical representation.

The two items on the questionnaire were: "What do you think is the most important ingredient in maintaining a healthy family?" and "Tell us any other ideas you have about the most important family values." Then I inquired about a few demographics: occupation, age group, and gender.

I was pleased with the enthusiastic response. Almost a thousand cards were tallied, and boxes more were received after the calculations. The respondents were not shy about expressing their opinions. Most people continued their answers on the back of the cards, eager to share thoughts they considered important.

Here are a few samples of responses to my first question regarding "the most important ingredient in maintaining a healthy family."

From a 19-year-old female student: "Support and encouragement of the children's ideas. Also including the children in the decision-making process of things of the home."

From a male sales manager in the 35–50 age group: "Leadership of father, giving role model of husband and father who is loving, dedicated and supportive of the wife and children no matter what happens."

From a female teacher, in the 25–35 age group: "Discipline coupled with love and respect for each other."

From a male U.S. Marine in the 35–50 age group: "A healthy family is the product of the lifelong guidance from one parent who remains home during a child's critical years of cognitive and moral development."

From a retired Baptist minister in the over-66 age group: "Active religious faith, a family togetherness, share business knowledge and have family recreation."

With varied answers such as these, the task of categorizing responses was difficult. Ultimately, it came down to organizing stacks of questionnaires, looking for common themes. Here are the values that emerged and the percentages of the total each received. The values are ranked from most often mentioned to least often mentioned:

1. Religion, 38 percent
2. Teaching morals, 38 percent
3. Family unity, 36 percent
4. Communication, 26 percent
5. Love and affection, 24 percent
6. Respect, 24 percent
7. Time together, 21 percent
8. Responsibility, 16 percent

This was an informal survey. It was not scientifically selected to be nationally representative, since volunteers filled out the cards. But this exercise did allow me to take the pulse of national feeling about important family values. It gave me a useful place to start since the answers *came from the respondents themselves* and weren't planted by polltakers, whose word choices can influence people's answers. Further, the results hinted at some of the themes I could expect my five families to talk about when I interviewed them.

## Five Functional Families

My goal was to examine *healthy* families—those who are functional and by most standards "successful." I established three criteria:

1. They had to be recommended by a reliable third party, whose endorsement would indicate that from the *outside* they appeared to be healthy.
2. The family members themselves had to define themselves as happy and functional—an *internal* confirmation of outward appearances.
3. Finally, I chose families based on what they were *not.* I looked for the absence of major problems, such as drug use, gang involvement, school dropouts, fighting, separations, and out-of-wedlock births. I was looking for the kind of family where the mom can say of her children, "They all turned out okay."

Four of the five families I ultimately chose are intact; the fifth experienced divorce, and now the mother is raising her five children alone. There's a white rural family from Virginia, an African American family from Chicago, a Latino family from East Los Angeles, and a multiracial family from Hawaii. The single mother is white and from Indianapolis.

To discover the values that made these families strong and healthy, Diane and I separately traveled to their homes and interviewed them. Diane handled the first round of questions. After receiving her transcripts, I would then visit and usually ask different questions or follow up when necessary.

We developed a list of topics to cover, touching on marriage, parenting, work, life's highs and lows, and family philosophy—but we decided to keep to a conversational mode rather than a more structured format. We wanted to go where the families wanted to take us. It was a process of discovering not just their characteristics but their interests.

As you become acquainted with these five families, you will quickly learn why I feel honored to know them.

*The De La Rosas of East L.A.* Carmen and Tony De La Rosa, ages 58 and 60, came to my attention when my friend Peter Ueberroth, chief architect and superb handler of the 1984 Summer Olympics in Los Angeles, referred me to their son-in-law, real estate developer Tony Salazar.

Tony De La Rosa retired recently as a cable splicer for the telephone company, and his wife is a retired church secretary. During the interviews they made it clear that their primary occupations have always been parenting. Tony coached his children in sports and continues to coach the neighborhood kids; Carmen was "always there" for her children. Everything seemed fine until a tragic night nine years ago when Anthony, who had just graduated from college and was engaged to be married, suffered a near fatal head injury. His miraculous recovery and the values the family upheld—reflected in their belief that "a De La Rosa never gives up"—testify to the power of family devotion and faith.

*The Wallaces of Indianapolis.* Kathy Wallace, 40, divorced her husband of ten years after she discovered he was having an affair. She was four months pregnant with their fifth child. She has raised Sarah, 19, Gabriel, 16, Donovan, 13, Katelyn, 12, and Molly, 10, by herself, in a house on the same block where she grew up. Living in an inner-city neighborhood that partly takes its name from their Catholic parish, Holy Cross, the family's slogan became "Never forget where you came from." I met Kathy when, as Vice President, I toured Holy Cross School, a model institution thriving as a result of a school-choice program sponsored by a local businessman. Kathy was one of the parents who told me of the importance of that assistance in making her children's education possible.

Kathy supports her family by working for Eastside Community Investments, a community development corporation that acquires abandoned and boarded-up homes and helps low-income buyers refurbish them. Sarah, a student at a local college, works part-time as a department store cashier to help out. Kathy tells a poignant story of financial hardships, disappointments, and even abuse but has nevertheless built a loving home with respectful, well-adjusted children. With a positive attitude and a natural talent for household management, plus the crucial support of her close-knit community, Kathy demonstrates the praiseworthy competence of many single mothers.

*The Burnses of Honolulu, Hawaii.* Rob Burns, 42, thought he'd follow in the footsteps of a Hawaiian hobo uncle, since he was never much of a student and spent his time surfing, paddling canoes, and playing tennis. But at age 23, with no business expertise and a loan of $3,000 from another uncle, he began Local Motion, a surf shop that grew to a seven-store, multimillion-dollar firm before he sold it to a Japanese company and retired in 1991. His work ethic and simple strategies reflect his family's theme of responsibility, as presented in his mother-in-law's maxim, "It's not what you *want*, it's what you *ought*." He met his wife, Annie, now 40, while she was still in high school, and except for a break for her college studies in Washington, D.C., they've been together ever since.

Their hopes for having children were dashed by infertility. The adoption of their daughters, Natalie, 11, who is Filipino and Japanese, and Jennifer, 9, who is black and Caucasian, created the family to which both now devote their energies.

Annie and Rob are concerned with family issues, and it was at a college-sponsored symposium that the Burnses met my coauthor two years ago. Their Christian faith is central to their lives, providing the backbone for the values that allow them satisfaction in their newfound wealth.

*The Cowdens of Bath County, Virginia.* John and Caryl Cowden left their home in Dayton, Ohio, as newlyweds to make a go of a 3,200-acre farm in the Allegheny Mountains that had been in John's family. Dissatisfied with their success raising crops and cattle, they looked at the land and decided that its best use was for recreation. During the years they had their three children—David, now 14, Kelly, 11, and Josh, 9—they built, by hand, Fort Lewis Lodge, a country inn that hosts visitors eager for the fishing, hiking, hunting, biking, and solitude of their isolated locale. Diane Medved and her husband had visited Fort Lewis Lodge and knew well its hidden beauty, but they hadn't known the Cowdens before this book.

John, 44, and Caryl, 45, share insights on the forces that allowed them to prosper. Theirs is a story of independence—of creating a self-sufficient life where the family's needs and the desires of an ever-changing array of guests are intertwined on a twenty-four-hour-a-day basis. The methods, strategies, and values they use to function smoothly and contentedly hold lessons for the rest of America.

*The Burtins of Chicago.* Dan and Jackie Burtin and their two children, Darnell, 21, and DaToya, 17, are an African American family living in the inner city on a very special block that fronts the Eisenhower Expressway. We found them through Hillsdale College and a recommendation by Dr. Paul Adams of Providence–St. Mel, the private school with tough academic standards and strict discipline where DaToya is completing her senior year. Dan, 46, a computer specialist for the city of Chicago, and Jackie, 45, a substitute teacher, raised their children with assistance from their extended family, as well as the family-like protectiveness of their neighbors. Both Dan and Jackie's parents have been married nearly fifty years, live nearby, and play an active part in the lives of all their grandchildren.

The family, articulate and educated, has strong views about education, the proper way to raise children, the false image of

African Americans, the prison system, illegitimacy, welfare, and community. But it always comes back to family. "Family is the world," Darnell says.

Each chapter has a similar structure. First, I briefly describe my visit to the family's home. An *introductions* section provides an overview of the family's characteristics and the values that emerged from our conversations. Sections on *marriage*, *parenting*, and *cultural influences* follow, with subheadings relevant to the family's circumstances and lifestyle. Finally, under the heading "Making It Work" comes a summary of the lessons each family's story discloses, offering a list of concrete actions the reader can apply to his or her own situation.

Although there's no lack of news these days about families, much of what we hear and read is bad. Daily reports tell of urban fears, economic anxieties, high divorce rates, and children suffering from abuse and neglect. The tabloid culture searches endlessly for deviant behavior, unhealthy relationships, hate-filled marriages, and families near collapse, eagerly exposing television audiences to a steady stream of the pathetic, the shameless, and the sick.

Yet many Americans have sensed that all this negative news is not the reality of most everyday families. They know, from experience, that families still pull together and support one another; that marriages are more durable than statistics might suggest; that neighbors do band together to create enclaves of unity and safety.

This book offers the unreported news about the American family. The news that, for all the poundings it's taken over the last few decades, the family is still a resilient force and a shield against adversity. The news that successful families can be found in every part of America—and, though different in many ways, they still have a great deal in common.

Now that we've reached a new consensus on the importance of family values, let's discover the values that make our families strong.

# 2
# The De La Rosa Family of East L.A.

For Mother and Dad:

*In all the years I've known you both*
*You've planned and strived for me*
*Through sacrifice of everything*
*That could a pleasure be.*

—From a plaque hanging in Carmen and Tony De La Rosa's kitchen

AMERICAN CITIES ARE EXPERIENCING UNPRECEDENTED social problems. While it's undeniably true that city life has much to offer, it's also true that cities, with their population density, have a way of magnifying such social ills as crime, drugs, illegitimacy, and dysfunctional families.

In the city of Los Angeles, the bizarre seems to happen routinely. While residents are rightfully proud of their resilience in the face of such natural disasters as earthquakes, mud slides, and wildfires, they've recently had more than their fair share of man-made problems—from gang warfare to racial tensions and, sadly, riots.

Though the city has been jolted from time to time, its citizens are determined that L.A. will regain the luster it enjoyed when it hosted the 1984 Summer Olympics. A book on American families wouldn't be complete without a story line from L.A.

## In Transit

On a beautiful autumn day my flight to L.A. from Indianapolis arrives late. Though I have specific written directions, I have a hard time finding Boyle Heights, the area in East L.A. where the De La Rosas live.

Realizing I'm not making much progress, I look for a gas station to ask for directions. I can't find one, but I come across a police station that is most helpful. At the station, I meet Officer Sundstrom of the Los Angeles Police Department, who is positioned in a booth outside of headquarters, and he gets me headed in the right direction. When I step out of the car and introduce myself, he's a bit startled. Apparently, not too many former Vice Presidents have visited his station.

On my way out, I notice a bullet hole in the window of the police booth. It's a reminder of the risks the police take on a daily basis. Too often, the men and women in blue are underappreciated.

With new directions in hand, it doesn't take me long to find the De La Rosa home, which is located on a quiet middle-class lane in Boyle Heights. A chain-link fence borders the family's meticulously kept yard; inside, I notice a statue of the Virgin Mary. After I enter the house and meet the family, I recount my circuitous route to their home. Their warm and sympathetic nature is immediately apparent.

The home is comfortable and immaculate, and, thinking about

it later, I'm sure the spotlessness isn't due solely to my arrival. The tidy surroundings are a clear reflection of Carmen and Tony De La Rosa's personalities—very organized and disciplined. As in many homes, an arrangement of high school graduation pictures is proudly displayed in the living room.

We sit around the dining-room table and indulge in a splendid Mexican lunch of tacos, enchiladas, rice, and beans. I'm not bashful about diving in for seconds. I've loved Mexican food ever since I was a kid, when I spent eight years in Phoenix, Arizona.

## Introductions

Tony De La Rosa, 60, a newly retired telephone cable splicer, and his wife of thirty-four years, Carmen, 58, a retired secretary, raised their children on the same East Los Angeles street where both of them grew up. Denise, 33, Anthony, 32, Michael, 30, and Manuel, 18, attended Catholic schools and then college in the University of California system. Denise, an educational policy consultant, is married to real estate developer Tony Salazar, 43, a divorced father of two teenage girls, whom she met when both worked for the Latino social action organization, La Raza. They own a home in Whittier, and are the new parents of a daughter.

Eight years ago, the second De La Rosa child, Anthony, married Mary Luna, now 33 and working as a university financial aid officer. Their wedding was an emotional high point following a terrible ordeal: In 1986, just after the couple graduated from UC Santa Barbara and became engaged, a tragic automobile accident left Anthony with head injuries so severe his organs were designated for transplant and life support was about to be withdrawn. However, a glimmer of brain activity delayed that action—and after surgery described as "scraping his brains off the operating table" and two months in a coma, he began the arduous process of recovery.

Younger siblings Michael, a Los Angeles city budgeting director, and Manuel, a UCLA sophomore, are unmarried. Michael owns a home in West Covina, a short distance from his parents; Manuel lives in an on-campus dorm room. The eleven-year age gap between them makes for a generational difference, yet the entire family keeps in close contact, trading frequent phone calls and often attending the English Mass together at their local parish.

---

During and after lunch, I interview the De La Rosa family for several hours. At times, individual members grow animated and almost interrupt each other. However, their politeness is noticeable and the undertone is one of deep respect for Tony and Carmen. It's a relaxed, enjoyable afternoon, and each speaks forthrightly about what makes this family work.

Carmen's life has been her family. Now that the children are "out of the nest," the demands on her time have changed. Since his retirement, her husband has much more time to drive her places. Tony's main mission, like hers, has been to care for their family. For the first thirteen years of their marriage, Tony worked at International Paper Company constructing corrugated-board boxes. When it looked like the company was downsizing, he looked for a more stable job. At age 30, when his family was still young, he took a job splicing cable for Pacific Bell. It lasted until his retirement nearly thirty years later. Tony is still getting used to being retired; he finds it strange that he doesn't have to be somewhere. "I keep thinking I'm on vacation, that I'll have to get back to work on Monday," he says, chuckling.

The four children resemble their parents. Denise clearly has her mother's smile. She and her husband, Tony, are a serious and happy married couple. They've done well for themselves and now live in a very comfortable home.

On this day Anthony is in Tempe, Arizona, and I speak with him via telephone. Anthony speaks haltingly and through a relay system called TTD. His goal, like most young adults, is to secure steady employment. Though he's disabled, he has an attitude and a determination that would make any employer feel lucky to have him. He and his wife, Mary, are fiercely protective of each other. They're an inspirational combination.

Second son Michael is forceful and opinionated, but in a thoughtful, articulate way that I find impressive. Youngest son Manuel, a striving student, has an abundance of energy. His thoughts are appropriately filled with school, sports, personal development, and decisions.

As we talk, several family themes begin to emerge. First there is the importance of the De La Rosas' *neighborhood*, which is infused with Latino culture—a Mexican backdrop for an American identity. And enhancing the family's sense of community is the existence of *extended family*, a wide web of people with whom there is daily interaction. Two of Carmen's seven siblings still live at Carmen's birthplace, just a block away from her home of thirty-four years. This geographical closeness remains an important underpinning of a continuing system of support and values.

Another strong theme is the belief that *education* is the means to success, a process to be honored and taken seriously. Linked to that is the significance of the local *church*. Together, school and religion provide the standards and values the De La Rosas exemplify and pass on.

Finally, the family's character has been shaped by *events* that overtook it. Foremost is the nine-year struggle following Anthony's car accident and the subsequent rehabilitation and employment discrimination. To a lesser degree, a mugging experienced by Manuel two years ago has shaken the family's sense of well-being. But there've been deeply rewarding moments as well: Anthony and Mary's wedding, Denise's new life with her "one and only," and the poignant renewal of vows Carmen and Tony shared on their thirtieth wedding anniversary.

## Marriage

The De La Rosa family boasts three successful marriages, each representing a different stage of life. Carmen and Tony have been wed thirty-four years, have completed stable careers, and have raised a family just a few blocks from where each was born. Two of their children, Denise and Anthony—married four and eight years, respectively—face adulthood at a time when computer literacy, fast-track occupations, and wider personal options complicate the simple scenario their parents experienced.

### *Carmen and Tony*

The primary model of a strong and loving marriage is presented by the parents. Their story is one of durability, a feature not at all uncommon for Mexican American marriages, which, in the words of one study, have shown a clear "stability advantage."*

Carmen and Tony met as youngsters. As a schoolgirl, Carmen, the youngest of eight surviving children (three had died in Mexico before the family came to America in 1925), acted as housekeeper and homemaker in the predawn and after-school hours. When she was only seven months old, her mother, then 42, died. From early childhood, Carmen began each day making tortillas by hand and packing them into burrito lunches for her father and brothers. The men all worked construction, one of the few occupations open to immigrants at the time.

Carmen never thought to question her hard life. "You ironed the curtains and you hung them back up," she recalls. "And you polished the floor—on my hands and knees I'd take the wax off and put it back on again. Having so many men in the family, I had to iron all of their clothes for work. I had to iron the sheets because in those times we didn't have permanent press, and they were all

*W. Parker Frisbie, Wolfgang Optiz, and William R. Kelly, "Marital Instability Trends Among Mexican-Americans as Compared to Blacks and Anglos: New Evidence," Social Science Quarterly 66 (September 1985): 587–601.

wrinkled—everything had to be ironed, ironed, and more ironing."

It was through the housework that she and Tony first met. "I knew she was cleaning her house and making tortillas," Tony explains. "The houses were this far apart—see that garage over there?" He points to a structure about twenty feet away. "I could hear her early in the morning making tortillas."

Carmen picks up the story: "His mother complained to my father that I didn't let her son sleep. He worked night shift, and I used to open the door because it got so hot making the tortillas. I was up at quarter to five, and he was just going to sleep a few hours before. My father told his mother, 'He's not her boyfriend yet!'"

Later, Carmen's father pointed in Tony's mother's direction and wisecracked, "There goes your mother-in law!" Carmen laughs at the recollection. "I said in Spanish, 'Oh, Pop, she's not going to be my mother-in-law.' Well, she *did* become my mother-in-law!"

Tony first casually dated Carmen's sister. "Her friend had a brand-new car and I'd get to drive it," he remembers. "I'd take them to the dance and then I'd have the car myself. I was the chauffeur." He began dating Carmen when they were in high school, and after he completed his military service, they became engaged. Later they were married and settled in the old neighborhood.

Carmen admits she got the itch a few years ago to move to a "nice clean neighborhood" like her two sisters, one of whom lives in Pico Rivera, the other in Whittier. She'd felt a little stifled, spending her entire life within a radius of a few blocks. "I'm not an outgoing person—I'm not a traveler," she confesses. "I'm just a simple everyday housewife. I just wanted to see something different in my life, and now I guess it's too late for me," she sighs. "My children moved away—they wanted to move away. Thank God they have bigger homes."

Before the kids left, Carmen did admit her restlessness to Tony, but he was emphatic about staying put. As Carmen tells it, he said, "'We're not going to move out—you wanted to stay here, in "the barrio" as you call it, and we're not going to move out.' He got stubborn so here we are."

His one concession has been to remodel the kitchen and bathroom for Carmen. She is appreciative, especially since she knows Tony's retirement is straining their finances. "Anyway, she deserves it," Tony says with pride.

Between the time she graduated from nearby Roosevelt High School and their marriage, Carmen worked as a secretary. Her first job at a downtown accounting firm ended abruptly. "As I got to know my co-workers, they told me, 'Carmen, watch out for the boss. He gets fresh with the young girls.' I didn't believe it because I'd never had that kind of experience. And one day he did get fresh. It was the first and only time—I told myself I won't go back to the job. I had to go to the stockroom with him—and I was afraid to go there anymore with him after what he did. My husband was my boyfriend at the time, and he said, 'Oh, I want to kill him!'

"I called up the boss and told him 'I won't go back to work for you. I don't like what you did to me.' And he said, 'I won't give you a recommendation. I'll see to it that you don't get a job anywhere in town. You won't be able to get a job because you left without notice!'

"A week or so later I went to Occidental Life Insurance Company," Carmen recalls. "I got the interview, I had the test, and I told them what happened—'I quit my job without notice'—and why. And I got hired. I was there for about seven years before I got married and had my daughter Denise.

"I worked through my pregnancy, up to the last moment that I was allowed to," she explains. "And my boss said I could have my job back after the period of time you need to recuperate. But my husband said, 'You're not going to work anymore. You're going to stay home and take care of our child.'"

Was this a case of a dictatorial husband overruling a woman yearning for career fulfillment? "Oh no, I wanted to be with my child," Carmen insists. "If I wanted to go back, I'd have gone back. I wouldn't have thought of leaving my baby with anyone." She explains that while Tony lets her know his desires, he never really pressures her.

After Denise, Anthony and then Michael were born a year and a half apart. "Every time I gave birth Tony took two weeks' vacation to take care of me," Carmen says. "He wouldn't let me do anything. He would say, 'Don't do anything until I get home and I'll do the heavy work.' The mopping, the vacuuming, hanging the clothes, going to the market—he took over for those two weeks."

Their family-centered life was a gratifying one. "At 29 I already had my three children, and I didn't have any more for eleven years. And people said it was a mistake. All I could think of was: 'What's the mistake?'" Tony winks as he interjects that the couple had long been "trying" to conceive their fourth child.

"During that period of time that I had my three little ones together, I didn't work," Carmen continues. "I was happy to stay home and keep the kids clean and read to them and play with them—show them how to play. Show them their ABCs, play school with them out in the back yard. I'd buy them coloring books, or books about Jesus, about Easter—about whatever it took to learn. And as they went on to kindergarten I helped them with their schoolwork."

Carmen describes another factor she finds essential to the union: "Your faith, your religion, going to Mass together every Sunday. We have our ups and downs, we're not a perfect couple. We don't pretend that we get along great every day of the week. We have disagreements, but we *don't* say we're going to have a divorce. He doesn't abuse me; he doesn't have another woman as far as I know. That's very important, because I feel if he did, I'd leave him. I wouldn't take it. So I say, religion is the first [ingredient]."

Tony adds that communication is crucial. "If you don't talk then you're going to split up," he says. "She may have as much say about the family as I do; you always hear the fifty-fifty thing. We always think we're the man of the family, but I gave in a long time ago—it's a woman's world. This is a woman's world. Basically, they run it. We kind of direct it."

Anthony describes his parents: "My father and mother always had a good sense of humor. Sometimes he could make her laugh so hard she cried. Yet you could also see the other end of the spectrum. I've always said this: 'In marriage you love one another but sometimes you just don't like each other.' My family values were taught growing up. My parents set the example; I am a part of my parents, figuratively and literally. *They've made me into someone my wife could love.*"

Tony and Carmen have endured the bad times, notably Anthony's accident. Carmen says, "Tony told me, 'When you feel you can't do it anymore, hold my hand and I'll give you strength.' That saw me through it, his strength. And his strong belief in the Lord."

And at other times they've rejoiced. When their "big" twenty-fifth anniversary approached, "I wasn't in the mood for celebrating," Carmen says, since Anthony was still seriously debilitated. But five years later, in September 1991, things had changed. Denise had met Tony Salazar, and plans for their October wedding were intensifying. In the midst of this excitement, the parents' thirtieth anniversary seemed to be a small occasion.

Carmen recalls her experience that September 16: "My older son said, 'Pop, Mom, I want you to get dressed up. We're going to lunch at twelve o'clock.' We said 'okay.' Then my daughter-in-law and my son Anthony showed up from Santa Barbara. That was the first surprise.

"Then my daughter called me on the phone and said, 'Mom, what are you doing?' She was supposed to be in D.C., and I told her, 'Oh, Meha, remember that Michael invited us all to lunch, and Anthony and Mary are here! We're going to a fancy restaurant.' She said, 'Okay, I'll be talking to you.'

"Well, when it was time for my son Michael to come—here comes my daughter with him! I about fell off of my feet. I said, 'Denise, where were you when you called me?' She said, 'I came last night from D.C. and I stayed over at Michael's house. I didn't let you know anything.' So that was another surprise.

"We still believed we were going to lunch," Carmen goes on, "so we got in the car, and my son said, 'First I want to take you to Father Greg Boyle.' Father Greg Boyle is a Jesuit priest from Loyola, and he works with the gang members. He's come out in the newspapers, everything—he's all for helping the gang members live a better life. He married Anthony and Mary, and saw them through their ordeal. He married Denise and Tony, my son-in-law. So I thought Father Greg was going to bless us."

Tony adds his view: "Michael didn't even say that—he only said 'We're going.' And I'm following him in our car and all of a sudden my mind lit up and I thought, 'If at that signal he goes to the right, he's taking us to the church!' But I didn't tell her anything. She still didn't know anything—they'd handed her some flowers, all the family is around her and she still didn't know anything!"

"No, no, no, they were inside the church!" Carmen maintains, as they compete in excitement over the tale. "How could I know? And you didn't know either!"

"I saw—outside . . ." Tony responds.

"I didn't see him, I didn't see anything!" she insists.

"And I knew exactly what was happening!" Tony concludes.

"I just thought Father Greg was going to bless us," Carmen repeats. "So my son handed me a little bouquet of flowers and said, 'Mom, you and Pop are going to march in by yourselves. After all, we were not here thirty years ago.' And I walk into the church and there's Father Greg at the altar and my family on one side, and his family on the other side. I cried. I cried. And the whole ceremony was so touching. I was on cloud nine. And having my Anthony there, and my Mary—both of them getting up and talking about the support we gave them through their lives, through their marriage, how they loved us. Oh, gosh, I was on cloud nine." Tears once more fill her eyes.

"Not only that—afterwards we went to my son Michael's

house and he had a reception there with all my family, like I'd gotten married all over again, and I had gifts. And here they all planned it without us—I never knew a word that was spoken about anything."

"I'm loyal to my wife because my father is very loyal to his wife," Anthony says in recognition of his parents' example. "I see that every day. Pop may not seem very romantic, maybe he isn't someone who [overtly] shows his love. But when push comes to shove, he'll break down and you hear it in his voice, how much love he has for his wife."

Manuel, who spends weekdays at his dorm and weekends at home, is perhaps the best source for a parental status report. "I've seen them argue," he admits, "everybody will argue. But if people are married for thirty-four years, I think it's something beautiful. And especially to the point where they had three children, and then me after eleven years. I think they just wanted to keep the family going, they wanted to keep a strong family. I know they're very much in love with each other."

What are the indicators of this deep love? "They like to spend a lot of time together," Manuel responds, then he pauses. "I mean, I can't really say that I see it. I know sometimes my mom's all 'Yeah, your father won't take me here or there for Valentine's Day or whatever,' but I know he does. If she wants it, he'll go get it for her. Or he'll give her the money and say, 'You can go buy it.'

"Basically, the love they have is shown in the love they give us. It's like full circle," he says. "I know they're very strong together—they keep each other going, especially now because for the first time in thirty-four years they're the only people in that house."

Manuel most feels the brunt of his folks' empty nest. "I'm not there anymore," he goes on, "and I know it bothers them. But at the same time I know that *they* know the time came that I had to leave, to get out, to become my own person and go out into the world. And I know they feel very comfortable with the fact that they prepared me, Anthony, Michael, and Denise to go out into the world. My father always told me before I went to Loyola [high school] and before I went to UCLA, 'Remember that you're a De La Rosa, and you're representing all the De La Rosas. Always remember that.'"

### *Denise and Tony Salazar*

Denise and Tony are the picture of a modern dual-career couple, enjoying the pleasures of their success.

When they first met, Denise was living in Washington, D.C., and Tony in St. Louis—but it was in Mexico City where they first set eyes on each other. "We were both there at the same time for two different meetings for the same organization," Denise explains. "And they brought the two groups together and took us on a tour of the pyramids. We ended up sitting next to each other on the bus for the hour's ride. And we just started talking."

The couple shared a bench seat again on the way back, and then shopped together for an hour before saying adios. "I picked her up on the bus," Tony smiles. But nothing really happened until another chance meeting five months later.

Denise goes on: "We had a tie to the same organization. I worked at the National Council of La Raza, where he was a board member." She had to attend some education hearings in Miami, and Tony's board was meeting there at the same time. "So we ran into each other again," she recalls.

They talked intensely on the phone long-distance and just two weeks later decided to spend time together over a weekend, "to get to know each other better, and see if we really did like each other or what—if there was really something there," Denise notes. "We'd decided that if it didn't work out, no hard feelings. We could be friends."

They went into their partnership soberly, since they consider it a lifetime decision and Tony's first marriage had ended in divorce. He is ten years older than Denise, and his daughters, 18 and 13, live in Kansas City. "I asked a lot of questions," Denise says.

"Because even though I hadn't been married, I'd been in enough extended relationships to know I didn't want to waste time. And since we were living so far away from each other, it was better that we just found out right away. So I asked him a lot of questions about his previous marriage and his relationship with his daughters."

But his past didn't scare Denise off. "I always thought I'd want to get married," she says, "but it was never really like a reality to me. And then here's this man who has two children."

"And I didn't want to get married at all," Tony confesses. "I said I didn't want to do that again." So what changed his mind? "Well, that's a De La Rosa," Tony shrugs. "You change your mind pretty fast when you come up against one."

That first meeting established the kind of ongoing communication that the couple credits with keeping their marriage strong. "If something's really bothering me, or if I'm upset about something, he doesn't let me get away with not saying anything," Denise says. "He won't let me just walk in and close the door. I guess the same is true the other way around too. He doesn't have a tendency to walk away, but he just gets quiet." So how does she open him up? "I just keep asking him what's wrong: 'Tell it to me,'" she ventures. "Eventually he'll get to it. It just takes a while sometimes."

They've got a more tranquil marriage than Denise's folks. "My parents have their moments," Denise admits. "They'll argue a lot with each other. My mom really picks on my dad, I think. He's really patient now, too, to sort of put up with it. I try not to do that to Tony. I might be really opinionated one way and he might be another—but we don't fight about it, and we don't yell at each other.

"And he doesn't put me down and I don't put him down," she adds. "I had that in other relationships, where I felt put down and always having fights. When we got together that weekend and talked, he asked me what I wanted out of a relationship. At first I didn't know how to answer. All I said was, 'Well, I know what I *don't* want.' And I laid those things out: I don't want to be put down, and I don't want to fight or argue all the time. I don't want to be in my corner and you in your corner. So out of that I was able to start deciphering what I was really looking for, not that I was necessarily looking for it at the time. But it happened."

I ask Denise if she could think of an aspect of her background that prepared her for a happy marriage. "Bringing the family together during the holidays or birthdays," she responds. "Birthdays are a big thing in my family—I don't think they were in Tony's. That's how my parents made each of us feel special, even if it was just a special dinner on that day."

I pose the question to Tony. "I think something that my parents have is this respect for one another, especially in public," he says. His father, a retired railroad boxcar repairman, and his mother, a housewife, raised nine children born over a twenty-year period. Tony notes that marital, family, and community values were always intertwined. "You have respect for your community, you have respect for your church and the whole extended family," he says.

"It's amazing in our community, no matter how little that one has, you never throw anything away, you still pass it on to somebody else. I mean, she takes my old clothes and gives them to her mother. Her mother gives them to others. It's always wanting to help and pass it on to someone else in the neighborhood. I think the value of marriage and respect for the family kind of fits into that."

Tony's respect for family was evident in his method of engagement to Denise. Carmen recalls with admiration, "He wrote us a letter and introduced himself and told us all about himself."

Interjects her husband, "He sent us a book! He sent us his resume, and the resumes of his brothers and sisters. He asked for her hand. They both came over here and in front of us, he asked for her hand and gave her a ring."

"With our approval," Carmen nods. "He did it the right way. I never expected that." When Denise had told her mother of her determination to marry Tony, Carmen "didn't believe her. I said, 'Are you sure he's your one and only?' She said, 'This is my one and only.' I'd tease her, 'Is there a lawyer in the house? Is there a doctor in the house?' because she'd had two lawyer boyfriends and a doctor boyfriend."

But this is definitely it. The entire family was thrilled at the birth of Denise and Tony's daughter in February. Carmen has been yearning for a grandchild, to the point where Michael had once volunteered to adopt one if that would make her happy. Now Carmen's wish has come true.

## *Anthony and Mary*

To tell the story of Anthony and Mary is to describe a most remarkable bond of devotion and loyalty. Their relationship began at the University of California at Santa Barbara, where both were in a summer transition program for freshmen. In the first six weeks away from home "we latched on to each other," Anthony recalls. "We were each other's strength, yet we were each other's weakness. It was the best of times—we had some very great times. We met, and then she asked me for some advice, and then we had a class together. And we just got closer and closer and built a relationship. She was in politics, the Students' Legislative Council, and the next year she was chairwoman of the student group El Congresso. Then I kind of got into that too. She left to go to Associated Students, I took over and it just grew. Nothing told us to stop; nothing said, 'This can't happen.'"

His first impression was definitive. "When I first saw Mary, something told me I was going to marry her. This is 1981," Anthony relates. "She had a good sense of humor. I'd never [encountered] her sense of humor before—it was 'Where do you get that?' It was clean humor, it was very silly humor. I liked that. But the more I talked to her, the more we became friends, which grew to love."

## *Anthony's Accident*

*For thou shalt go to all that I shall send thee, and whatsoever I command thee thou shalt speak.*

*Be not afraid of their faces: for I am with thee to deliver thee. . . .*

*I have set thee over the nations and over the kingdoms, to root out and to pull down and to destroy, and to throw down, to build and to plant.*

—Jeremiah 1:7, 10, a source of strength for Anthony De La Rosa

Immediately after Anthony and Mary graduated from college, and during the period of their engagement to be married, the De La Rosas faced their greatest tragedy. Anthony, at the age of 22, was involved in a serious car accident, resulting in permanent disability.

Carmen is visibly emotional as she tells the story. "My mind goes blank. There are some things I don't want to think. And of course we were in a lot of pain, and I'll never get over that pain.

"Anthony and Mary were going to her home in Fresno, to see a car they were going to buy. It was the rainy season; it was a terrible year for rain. It was raining, and I got the phone call. I couldn't believe it and even if I heard it, I didn't want to believe it—but I knew it was real. And so we had to fly to San Luis Obispo, because that's where Anthony went into the hospital. Before we left, the doctor called and said, 'It's a matter of life or death—he's got to have an operation. He's got to have an operation, he's in critical condition, a head injury.'

"So what could we do? We had to put it in the doctor's hands. By the time we got there he was already operated on. We went on a plane, my baby [Manuel, 9 at the time], my husband, and I. Denise was in Seattle, Washington, studying for her master's. My son Michael was at UC Berkeley, and I didn't want to tell him but I had to tell him.

"So we all flew into San Luis Obispo. It was a very rainy night, very windy, very cold. You don't know where you're going; we didn't know anyone in the town, of course. And the doctor came out and told us that my son wasn't going to make it through the night and to prepare ourselves. I asked the male nurse who was taking care of him to call a priest for me, because I didn't know this town. And so he did and before I knew it there was a priest waiting to talk to me.

"It makes me cry now. And so the priest took me—once I saw him it was like I was looking at the Lord, that's all I know. I know what I saw, and I said, 'There's God in front of me.' And he spoke to us and he said, 'Let's go pray around his bed.' And we did. And he told me, 'The bishop from Monterey is going to come next weekend and I'll have him come over and pray over your son.'

"[That night in the hospital chapel] I prayed, 'You want my son, okay. I don't understand it—take him. I don't know why, but take him if you want.' I was so brokenhearted and praying and praying and praying. At one o'clock the doctor said, 'We're going to turn off the machines.'

"[The next morning] he called us in and he gave me a hug and he said, 'I want you to go home and rest. Your son's going to make it. I can't turn off that machine. There is too much life left in him.' He said, 'He's a healthy person. That's what's helping him—and God.'

"So then the priest found a home for us to stay with in San Luis Obispo. These people, they were so nice. We stayed a whole week. [The woman who was hosting us] washed my clothes, she made food—which I didn't want to eat. I quickly lost weight. They were very, very religious—I was so fortunate.

"And another family lent us their car to go back and forth to the hospital. And we're still friends to this day. . . .

"For so long we had to leave [Anthony in the hospital] in the hands of God. The priest went every day—also he called me and told me, 'Oh, Anthony moved an eye,' or 'Anthony moved a toe,' or 'Anthony moved his hand.' Something, you know? And we just grasped onto that. Every weekend we went back to San Luis Obispo, my little boy, my husband, and I. I was silent the whole way going, the whole way coming. I was in a trance.

"And so about a month later the doctor said, 'It's time to move Anthony to rehabilitation. Look at these certain places and decide where you want him to be.' In the meantime, my daughter-in-law—she wasn't my daughter-in-law yet—told me, 'Carmen, do I have nothing to say about this?' She'd just gotten engaged to my son in December, and the accident happened in February. And I said, 'Mary, the doctor said to tell you to go and live your life, because you're very young. And you're going to get tired of waiting for my son because you can't tell me when he's going to be rehabilitated. Or just how or if he *can* be rehabilitated.'

"And she started crying and she said, 'Why can't I keep him in Santa Barbara? There's a place here.' I said, 'Are you going to be able to take it? The load for yourself? Going to see my son every day and going to work?' She said, 'Yes.' So, my daughter and my other son got mad at me and said, 'Why did you tell her that you're going to move Anthony and that she should go and live her life?' I said, 'Because the doctor told me I had to tell her. You didn't think I was happy having to tell her that?'

"So I told Mary, 'You're welcome to come and live with us during Anthony's recuperation. You could get a job—you're qualified. If you really want to be by him, you could come and live with us.' And she did exactly that. She went to work for the board of supervisors at city hall—and she couldn't wait to come home from work every day. She and my 9-year-old baby, every day the three of us went to the hospital, and we decorated Anthony's room very cheerfully, like a family atmosphere. Pictures of Mary, pictures of his brothers and sister, signs, 'We'll be back.'

"When he was in San Luis Obispo—it was during the time of Lent that this happened—the priest had told me, 'Carmen, the Lord has plans for Anthony. The Lord has plans. You watch and see Easter Sunday.' All I can think was, 'I am the resurrection and the life.' That stood with me and stood with me in my mind, over and over again. And [I remember going to] the hospital and it was Anthony's first day up in a wheelchair. Of course he couldn't hold his head up, and people who went through the corridors just stared at him and I got so angry. I felt like fighting with them, you know? 'How would you like to be looked at in this condition?' You don't know until you go through something.

"And I took him to the windows of the hospital and I said, 'Look at the trees outside. It's Easter Sunday. Look at how green the trees are.' And he responded—he knew what I was saying. They tried to get him to eat but he couldn't eat yet. So then he [was transported by helicopter] to Daniel Freeman Hospital, the one we chose, and when we saw him he was so sick. Oh, God, my heart went out to him, he was so sick. So, gradually the Lord saw him through that part. Then we started to get him up, to eat—he was being fed through a tube. My daughter-in-law would sit by his bedside and they would communicate with each other."

Tony explains how. "I made this board, and he'd spell out a word. As he got better, still not being able to speak, they'd use that board like it was a typewriter. That's how fast it was. They'd be over there laughing and nobody knew what they were doing."

"Only they knew, only they knew," says Carmen, winking. "And he was very happy and she was very happy. And you know what they were doing? They were planning the wedding. They were planning the wedding for when he got better, that's what my daughter-in-law told me. She believed in him, and all through his recuperation, that they were going to get married, and that he was going to walk."

"And all the way through this, the nurses and doctors would say, 'He's never going to be able to walk,'" Tony remembers.

"And I kept on saying, 'He's going to make it,'" Carmen affirms.

"Every weekday they'd give us a report," Tony goes on, "and say that the family wasn't realistic. We said, 'He's going to make it, you wait and see.' And sure enough: They were amazed at him before, but before you knew it he was the number one boy. I mean, they'd have doctors come and see his progress. But that was *his* determination. According to them, he wasn't going to improve. He was going to be a vegetable."

"He was going to be a vegetable," Carmen repeats, "and when they found out that he wasn't, they said he was a miracle. All of a sudden it just came out—their words!—*he's a miracle.* He's not supposed to be doing what he's doing. We kept on telling them, 'You don't know my son. If he's here, he's here for a reason, and he's going to improve.'"

Tony and Carmen are sure there's a divine hand in this. Not only in Anthony's astounding survival but in the kindness of the DeAngelo family, who first took them in, and the generosity of Sissy Dunden, a woman who kept the bedside vigil when the De La Rosas had to leave Anthony during their workweek in Los Angeles. "She would go to him every day and pray," Carmen remembers, "and tell him, 'Your pop says you can do it!' She would whisper in my son's ear, 'You can do it, you can do it!'"

Subsequently, Mrs. Dunden contracted terminal cancer. The only place where the therapy she required was available was Los Angeles. She stayed with the De La Rosas for the duration of her treatments. Later, her husband suffered a bicycle accident. The only site equipped to perform the surgery he needed was in Long Beach. He, too, stayed at the De La Rosas' home. The bishop of Monterey, who coincidentally was scheduled to visit San Luis Obispo at the time Anthony required prayers, happened to have been born and raised in Boyle Heights—just two blocks away from the De La Rosas' address. "There's got to be somebody taking care of all this, to put it in perspective, right?" asks Tony.

But the story continues: "My son had said that he felt that he was in a very dark tunnel," Carmen relates. "And all of a sudden he could see the light at the end, and he told God, 'Don't take me away from Mary—not yet, not yet.' He told me those words. And God heard it. And I guess the Lord knew that Mary was going to be a very special person, because she could have spent her life looking for another boyfriend—and she waited for him. And one day

Anthony came out of the hospital and said, 'Mom, look!' He went from a wheelchair to a walker to a cane. When Anthony would be picked up for therapy, they'd say, 'You're not going to do more. He's going to walk with a cane.' He said, 'When I get married, I'm going to be walking [unassisted].'

Finally—after struggling through daily therapy—Anthony took Mary's hand in marriage on July 25, 1987. It was a day none will forget: "People were crying; they were overcome because my son walked down that aisle," Carmen says, tears flowing again at the memory. "They each wrote their vows and they were so beautiful, you couldn't help but cry. If you have a heart, you cry. But in her vows Mary said there was a reason for [the accident and recovery]. That God knew they needed each other. . . . They each wrote beautiful, touching vows."

"Like I said, he was our number one boy," beams Tony.

"She was strong, she has strength," Anthony says of his wife. "She was right there, she put the spine in me, she kept me afloat, she kept everything together. Our whole world turned upside down," he says, "and she set it right again. So I applied myself, we put our relationship back together, and we improved it. Mary has been patient, an inspiration. Every time I would make a bit of progress, I'd say, 'I got that from Mary' [or] 'Do it for Mary.' And that's how I continued my rehabilitation. We're very close."

The wedding became an extraordinary event. Anthony recalls his vow: "'Mary, you be my strength, and I'll be there for you. Keep understanding my needs, and I will do likewise.'"

"When Tony was done speaking," Mary remembers, "I couldn't talk—it was my turn but I couldn't talk. Because of what he'd said, and how determined he was to be understood by the whole audience, I just had a big lump in my throat. And another thing [that stood out about the day] was Father Greg Boyle, who married us. He said that we were celebrating being married, but he felt we'd already displayed the commitment that goes along with marriage. In other words [the ceremony] was just a formality."

Mary continues to help Anthony, interpreting the television, which is difficult for him to comprehend. Telephoning, clarifying. She is protective but not overbearing and is justifiably proud of her husband. They reach for each other and squeeze hands when the talk becomes emotional, a gesture of reassurance that clearly comes naturally to them.

"I guess I never thought about it," Mary answers when I ask about the source of her devotion. "I guess I displayed loyalty mostly because of the relationship Tony and I had. We were friends, and so it felt logical to be there 100 percent. And we often talk about this. If the situation were reversed, and I was the one head-injured, he would have been behind *me* 100 percent, without thinking twice. The sense of loyalty I get is probably from my parents. They always instilled in me that your family, your loved ones, are what you have in life to rely on."

So it was especially traumatic when, at age 13, Mary endured her parents' divorce. "They'd been married for twenty-two years," she relates. "When I think about my parents as individuals now, I can understand why they split up. They're two different people, and it's more understandable now. I did see a lot of arguments. To this day, they pretty much keep us out of what their problems were. They still won't tell us what led up to it. I've asked, and it's pretty much a closed issue. I mean, it happened, and they want to move on."

Her parents had married right out of high school, and her mom supported her father through Fresno State College. After the divorce, Mary's mother raised the four daughters on her own and two years ago entered a second marriage. Her father is also remarried, and Mary has a half-sister, 12, and a half-brother, 7 months old. "You always want your family together," Mary recalls of the sadness surrounding the divorce. "You see other families together, and you don't want anything different for yourself. You want that family behind you, too.

"My mom was always there for me," she notes. "For example, in junior high and high school I started being in band, doing a lot of activities like sports. I got on the honor roll a few times, and it was always one parent going to the events. It's not the same; you don't quite enjoy your accomplishments if only one parent is there to help you celebrate. It just felt like it wasn't complete."

At the time of the divorce, her older sisters were college age and "blamed themselves" for the collapse, feeling "they could have helped out more" to alleviate their parents' strain. But the heaviest burden fell on Mary and her younger sister. "It was a custody situation because we were not old enough yet to be out of the house," Mary recalls. "So my mom wanted us, and of course my dad did, too. We ended up being with my mom, and it was hard for us to understand—we always had hopes this would resolve itself. But that never happened. We lived in a great neighborhood, and we had friends there. But then we ended up moving out of the house because my mom couldn't afford it on her income.

"The other thing that was hard," Mary continues, "was that we'd visit with my father on weekends, and on Sunday night you had to say good-bye. That made no sense: 'You're my father, why do I have to say good-bye to you?' And holidays were very hard. 'Who are we going to spend time with on this day?' If it's Thanksgiving or it's Christmas: 'When are we going over to Dad's? When are we with Mom?' We were very resistant to that because Christmas and Thanksgiving and all that was a time of togetherness, and then you had to go to different places."

Notwithstanding the past, Mary has gained a sense of deep security through her complete acceptance into the De La Rosa family. And she's found unwavering love with Anthony De La Rosa. His youngest brother Manuel summarizes: "Anthony has a beautiful marriage, because Mary stuck by him through the whole recovery. It was the 'Stick by your man' thing, because she could have said, 'Forget it, you're never going to be the same.' But she didn't. Anthony gives such love back. It's a very beautiful, special marriage."

## Parenting

Strength, reliability, solidity—these are Tony and Carmen De La Rosa's strong suits as parents. The tasks they place above all others are to provide a home for their children and to live up to their own family ideal. "Always back up the kids!" admonishes Tony De La Rosa. "I'm here on this earth for only one thing," he says. It's to be a foundation for his family. "After my job is done," he adds, "throw the dirt over me."

His children easily recall the most important lessons of their upbringing: "A De La Rosa never gives up!" "Apply yourself!" "I'll be there." The phrases come up repeatedly. These lessons have been taught and learned in the very traditional environment of respect for elders, love of parents, and acceptance of chores, schedules, and discipline. All the rules of life have been reinforced by extended family, school, and church. Though some things vary—such as the safety of the neighborhood, the background of the people on the street—*the basics of behavior don't change*: You don't talk back. You try your best to please. You work hard in school and continue your education. You pray.

Here's some of what each De La Rosa has to say about growing up in their family.

### *Mom and Pop*

For Carmen De La Rosa, life with her children is a joy. Her primary goal has always been to "be there" for her children, to take pride in their every accomplishment, and to revel in their development. She was their preschool teacher, devising little games, buying art supplies, and fixing picnic lunches. When they got older, she spent her time helping the nuns at their parochial school, in the playground, classroom, lunchroom, and office. She was there for the children, but along with that, *she was there for herself.*

Carmen still bristles at a comment she heard when Michael

was five years old. "His teacher told me he was a mama's boy—and he was only in kinder[garten]!" she exclaims. "It angered me because what did *she* know about him being a mama's boy? Yes, he was attached to me because his brother and sister were in school before him. My children didn't grow up running around the street —they were in the home. And yes, they had a lot of kids over, and I never let them go over to anybody's house.

"So she thought I was doing wrong by keeping them home with me," Carmen says, "but the poor thing—rest her soul, she's gone now—but I wish I could see her now and tell her: 'He's a mama's boy? He went further to study than my other ones!' And as soon as he came out of college, he went on his own to live—he didn't want to be dependent on me. And he bought his own home and just about a day or so ago he told me, 'Mom, I'm going to remodel your home for you, don't worry about it.'"

Part of the reason Carmen kept her children close to home was to insulate them from external risks. "The crime, the gangs, the graffiti, the shootings—all of that is very frightening," she says. "None of my children were involved in gangs. I can tell you that they were here at home most weekends. Once in a while they'd go out, but I feared because of the other ones [in the streets], not because of them."

"And in our house we don't drink, we don't smoke," she affirms, "so they can't say, 'Wow, my parents helped us go on liquor, on drugs.' Yes, my sons and daughter take a drink socially, but they're not going to get crazy about it.

"A woman asked me about a month ago, 'Carmen, how did you do it? You have four children and they all got their education!'" She repeats her secret emphatically: "*My children were always in the home.*"

Tony pipes up, "We always had them busy doing something."

"We had them busy—in sports, always in sports," Carmen relates. "Their father was a coach, and he still is a coach and an umpire." Denise led the way with an interest in track. "And she was a cheerleader—and she was in student government in Catholic elementary school. My sons Anthony and Michael were presidents of their eighth-grade class. All three of my sons got high-achiever awards because they did so well in school," Carmen boasts with unabashed motherly pride.

She still resents the implication that somehow her involvement with her children and her helping out at the parish school brought unfair advantages. "Other parents would tell me, 'Oh, of course they got good grades, because you're always there helping—so how could they not get good grades?' And I told them, 'Do you think I could be a teacher's friend and pull an A or B on the report card? Do you think they're doing me a favor because I'm helping out?' I'm helping out because *I'm interested in my children*! That's why I'm there. They thought that I got paid—I didn't get paid for many, many years. Many years after, I decided to ask for a paying job, and even then I got low wages. I got four dollars an hour for six years as a paid secretary of my parish—four dollars an hour, because I was too embarrassed to ask for more money."

Tony, though a soft-spoken man, was the firm family disciplinarian. Just one look from Pop kept errant youngsters in line. "The parents are the foundation, and if they don't build the child right . . ." He pauses to consider his own example. "My father—sure he drank, but he never did anything wrong. [There was] respect there. So, like a rubber band, I would stretch so far, and then as a respect to my parents, I'd come back. Nowadays, there's not a lot of respect for a lot of the parents. You can walk down the street and see, you know?

"Then too, when we were raising our children I'd tell my wife, 'Your daughter is yours—the boys are mine. I'll take care of them,'" Tony explains. "'You discipline her, and yet I'll have the last word over all.' And we've been a partnership ever since.

"I have a very heavy voice, so when I gave my kids a command, they'd obey me," he goes on. "I actually only remember hitting my children one time." The children remember that "one time," too: Each brought it up independently in separate interviews. It made a lasting impression on all of them, since it happened about twenty years ago. Was it something life-threatening? A major family embarrassment? No, says Tony: "They were jumping across the bunk beds."

"We thought they were asleep, and we caught them in the act. They were all playing," Carmen recalls.

"And just to teach them not to do that, it was the only one time that I really spanked," Tony says. "And I would only spank one time, I mean—thwack!" He smacks his hand abruptly in demonstration. Usually, just the *threat* of a spanking would solve a problem.

"They knew he was strict," says Carmen, "and now that they've grown up they say they're glad they were brought up strict; they understand now. It helped them out through their life."

"All I had to do was, 'Hey, you're not supposed to do that! That's it, and I don't want to see that anymore!'" Tony recalls. "And they were so funny. We would go to church—you know kids at church are always squirming. But our kids would sit there like—"

"Like a statue," says Carmen.

"People would say, 'How do you keep your kids so quiet?'" Tony goes on.

"When we would get to church, I would tell them, 'We've come to pray,'" Carmen says.

"They would sit there," Tony explains, "and if they started squirming all I'd have to do is look at them, give them a stare. I taught them by example—I was always home and always took an interest in what they did, and maybe from that they got the respect for me. They knew that when I said something I meant it."

Respect: Tony says that it's the most important value he passed on to his children. "Respect for others—that's what you want your children to have as they go out into the world." And by extension, respect for the dignity and reputation of one's family: "Michael was saying that when they went to a party, they were representing the De La Rosa family. You're not just there by yourself. You're not just Michael De La Rosa. You are Michael De La Rosa *and family*. Whatever you do, you reflect back to the family. Now I see a lot of people don't care about their kids. They throw them outside. When *we* walked down the street my kids were right in front of me, or right beside me. I could put a hand out and they'd be there. There is no respect anymore."

A major contributor to the children's respect for their parents was the *daily routine.* "They were on a tight schedule," Carmen notes. "You took a nap, you took your bath so when your father came home you were nice and clean. The kids would run out the door, down the driveway to meet their father. We'd put them to bed at seven-thirty every evening."

So the respect Tony receives was engendered not only by his own behavior but by Carmen's *building up her husband in her children's eyes.* She didn't just waltz through the evening's tasks but always offered Pop's return as a reason for their preparation and an event to be anticipated and cherished. Carmen's own excitement about Tony's presence in the home as well as his response caused the children to look up to him.

And another lesson: The value of *structure* can't be overemphasized. When there's a schedule to follow, children balk less and enjoy a heightened sense of security. It's when they can always test—and get more—that the parent/child relationship unravels.

"I think that maybe now parents give their children too much," Tony offers. "In my day, a pair of socks at Christmas was great. Of course, we didn't have much. We appreciated what we had. Too many people think that the material things are more important."

Tony offers this recommendation to parents: "Show a child that 'whatever you do, I'll be there. And if you do wrong, then I'm going to correct you—*but I'll still be there.*'"

### *Denise and Tony*

Denise, as the eldest child, has always been eager to please. She holds a master's degree and works as a consultant in educational policy, so it's understandable that her clearest childhood memories are of her parents' encouragement in schoolwork. "Whenever we'd have research projects to do for school, my father, as busy as he was with work, would make sure that he would take us to the library, help us figure out the library system, do research and look for books. Really spend a lot of time with us. He'd help figure out how we should do our outline for a report, or what kinds of books would be helpful. And then my mom would actually help us with the writing—checking our spelling, and always asking, 'Does this make sense to you? Is this really what you want to say?'

"And I always remember my father helping me with my math, to the point where I had to count beans when I was in kindergarten and first grade. My father would sit there and try to be patient with me when I got very frustrated in figuring how to just add and subtract. That was one of my biggest nightmares at the time. And he'd always tell me not to give up—his saying was, 'A De La Rosa never gives up—so don't stop here, keep going!'"

Ironically, the discouraging words of a high school counselor were what incited her to apply to the University of California at Santa Barbara. Though she grew up expecting to attend college, she'd always assumed she "wasn't good enough" to start out at a four-year school. But after running high school track meets on the UC Santa Barbara campus, she began to reconsider her options. "It just looked like a neat place," she says. But there was a twenty-dollar application fee, and "the counselor at the time told me I shouldn't spend my twenty dollars because I wasn't going to get in, because I didn't have the grades.

"I was just furious!" Denise exclaims, "and I just got it in my head that nobody's going to tell me I can't do something. It goes back to my father saying 'a De La Rosa doesn't give up.' And I went to my geometry teacher, who was also my track coach, and told him what the counselor had told me, and he was very supportive. He said, 'No, you go ahead and apply.' And he went to the counselor, told her she shouldn't be discouraging students from applying to college. He helped me out with my application."

She also made contact with the university admissions office and began preparing by taking extra tests and working out the financial arrangements in advance. "So when I [was accepted], there was just no question that I would go," Denise explains.

No question, that is, for *her.* "My mom didn't want me to go away to school," Denise admits. "She didn't understand why I wouldn't apply to Cal State L.A. or somewhere close. At the time, I just wanted to go away, get out of home, and have some freedom, I guess. But my father was very supportive, and I think if it hadn't been for my father trying to convince my mom that it was okay, I probably wouldn't have gone to UC Santa Barbara. Now she says she's glad that I did it, that she's glad I pressed the issue. We used to have conversations about everything—the whole family—and that was one of the big ones, whether they were going to let me go away to college."

From her earliest years in school, Denise says, her parents' involvement in her education went far beyond that of other parents she knew. And with her mom "always at school," Denise seldom misbehaved. Even a minor incident in eighth grade sticks in her mind today. Apparently Denise had laughed at a cohort's antics and whispered a bit in class. The nun had to change her seat, a horrific event that a scared Denise confided immediately to her mom. But when Carmen asked the teacher for a report on her daughter's progress, the word was, "She's a joy."

Catholic schools, Denise asserts, were better able to engender respect for authority because of their emphasis on religion. "You were going to listen to the nuns," she says. "You weren't supposed to get into trouble, because what they said was God's word."

With the same firmness, Pop made sure his daughter knew the authority of his word, too. "One example that I always bring up, and she hates it," Tony chuckles, "happened when Denise was 14 or 15 and wanted to go to a Halloween party. 'I don't have a costume,' she said. I said, 'All right, I'll make you a costume. Put on your gray sweats.' So she put on her gray sweats and she had a hood and I put on a mustache and said, 'Now you're a mouse.' And all day long she was arguing with her mom, 'Oh, I want to be out till one o'clock in the morning!' "

"She was not 14 years old, she was about 16," Carmen corrects.

"Well, whatever," Tony continues. "My wife said, 'Oh no, no, you have to come in at twelve.' Denise said, 'No, no . . .' And as I told you before, Carmen had the daughter [to discipline] and I had the boys, and so I listened to this all afternoon. And finally that evening I said, 'Hey, stop your arguing. Your mom told you already that you come in at twelve.'

"'No!' she said again.

"Then I said, 'Okay, fine. Don't come in at twelve. You come in at eleven.' She said 'No!' I said, 'You don't come in any earlier or any later than ten o'clock!' And this was twenty-five minutes to nine. You know what time she came in at? Five minutes to ten. And she never again argued about curfew. Why? Because she knew I stuck to my word. Basically, you know, if your children understand that you don't bend when you say 'This is what we're going to do,' then the road gets opened up in front of you."

Echoing her parents' words, Denise says, "My father always believed in strict respect for your elders; it was always pounded into us. We called our uncles 'Tio,' our aunts 'Tia.' We never just called them by their first names; I still don't. Even to this day, parents of friends I went to school with are 'Mrs. Hernandez' or 'Mrs. Valquez.'"

Her husband, Tony Salazar, had a similar upbringing in Kansas City. He, too, attended Catholic schools and lived in a stable home. Respect was central to his childhood, and he also used titles and formal modes of address. He adds that "no foul language was allowed. My parents were very careful about it. They'd say, 'Did we send you to school to talk like that?' Not that they speak the greatest English, but they instilled that in their kids."

Tony adds that his parents—and his wife's parents—have a special appreciation for America. "As the forefathers of this country did, they came here to work hard, to raise a family, to earn a living, to better themselves and better their family members, as they have," Tony says. "But you ask them about their other values [and they'll tell you]: democracy, freedom—everything you read in the United States Constitution. It would be just like they're reciting it. My father fought in World War II. Her [Denise's] father was in the army in Korea. My brother went to Vietnam. You would swear they could have written the Constitution."

Good families make for a great country.

### *Anthony and Mary*

Like his sister Denise, Anthony De La Rosa tells of an upbringing that emphasized education, faith, respect for others, and the trademark De La Rosa determination. He speaks also of his mother's *protectiveness.* "She wouldn't want her kids to suffer," he says. "For example, if food fell on the floor and I picked it up, she'd take it out of my hand and eat it. And if she saw the food wasn't cooked enough, she'd throw it out. She's still like that," he says, smiling. "Today we went to lunch and we had *albondigas,* little meatballs. Well, she saw the meat was kind of pink and tender, and she kept picking at it, but she wouldn't let me eat it."

After Anthony's accident, Carmen and Tony were deeply pained at their inability to directly help their son. Whenever an opportunity to help did present itself, they quickly stepped in. When they learned that frequent physical therapy could speed up Anthony's recovery, Carmen was determined that he receive as much as possible. The hitch was that the family had to pay for the transportation costs. "I said I want him to go five days, and I'll pay for that," Carmen recalls. "And they wanted to charge me more than I was making a week. I was only making $120 a week. They were going to charge me $200 to transport him back and forth."

Anthony felt uncomfortable placing such a burden on his parents. "He said he didn't want to, but I convinced him," Carmen says. When she phoned the supervisor, and they heard the van was for the miraculous Anthony De La Rosa, they lowered the charge. "Anything for Tony," they responded. "So they called me at work and told me they'd take him for $120," Carmen recalls.

Anthony's parents taught him to be strong. "I applied myself," he says repeatedly, describing the agonizing process of recovery. It's a characteristic he's honed since childhood. "I've had a pattern of being a leader—in grammar school I was president, in college I was vice chairman of my study group. I just thrive on speaking—if you put me in front of fifty people and give me something to talk about, I'll be talking like I am now."

In fact, he volunteers his time at a rehabilitation institute in Santa Barbara, teaching survival skills to other head-injured people. He also helps teach a cooking class for such patients. "I have pride in myself," he says, "and I applied myself to the area of head-injury rehabilitation." His greatest challenge, however, may not be physical but rather emotional, as he attempts to meet the demands of earning a living. He has tried, unsuccessfully, to find a job. A position he held at the university was cut from the budget two years ago, and since then he's found that his disability has kept many avenues closed.

"It's an ignorance about disabled people," Anthony declares. "When someone thinks 'disabled,' he thinks of someone in a wheelchair; with 'hearing impaired,' the [inference] is that [the person] is deaf. I'm disabled, but I'm not in a wheelchair; I'm hearing impaired, but I'm not deaf. I've got to teach those people that. And it's hard to get there, but I'm working toward it. I can say that this is work God wants me to be in, and with patience, I'll succeed."

Once again, Anthony shows the determination and courage he acquired from his mother. He fortifies himself with reminders of her resilience. "She faced a lot of heartache," he says. "Her mom died when she was born, her brother got killed, her father died. She's got religious strength, she looks toward the Bible. As we grew up she showed her strength in different ways, but God is the ultimate administrator." He also praises her self-sacrifice. "Kids come first," he declares. "She'd rather go without than deny her kids. That's love."

Anthony's picture of his childhood is a group snapshot. "We were always together," he says. "We'd go together to the neighborhood market, Ray and Roy's." It's a view he'd like someday to replicate with Mary. He says they want five children: "Daniel Anthony, Anthony, Michael Anthony, Melissa, and Jenny."

"He's given it some thought, obviously," says Mary, smiling.

Mary and Anthony now live in Tempe, Arizona, where Mary has embarked on her master's degree at Arizona State University. As of this writing, Anthony has a temporary job working in the vault of a Wells Fargo Bank. "Thanks be to God," says his mother.

For him it's just a start. He has a lot of potential left to fulfill—and a De La Rosa never gives up.

### *Michael*

Michael is perhaps the most eloquent member of an eloquent family. He was able to contribute several insights on parenthood beyond the many already presented. "My parents have always been very focused with us, and they always knew what they wanted out of family life," Michael says. "They always ingrained in us what it meant to be a family and what love was, not necessarily telling us but demonstrating it. I think their idea of family was grafted onto us. They wanted to make sure that love was included, and everybody had—I hesitate to say a job, but a role. They've always been supportive and loving, always wanted us to be successful. I think that is partly why we are who we are—because there was always love and respect between the two of them.

"I just always thought everyone was like us," Michael says. It was a feeling of security, of comfort. It's certainly not the *Brady Bunch*, you know. I think that's kind of an extreme. . . . Certainly nothing is perfect, but since I was a child we always talked about whatever we were going to be or whatever we were going to do.

"There was no question we shouldn't do well in school; there was no question we weren't going to be whatever it was that we were going to be," Michael continues. "We were always looking ahead toward some goal or objective. We came home and did our homework before anything else got done. Everything was attached to a responsibility."

When he went away to college, Michael was surprised to discover that other families were not the same way. Just recently, he was asked to help a cousin type a student essay on her ambitions and was amazed to see that even a relative raised on the same block in Boyle Heights didn't have his drive. "She said it was never really discussed!" Michael exclaims. "They never said 'when you go to college,' or 'when you're this or that,' and I just thought it was strange, because from the [earliest] time I can remember we were always asked, 'What do you want to be?' My first memories include discussing college. This is certainly a distinct value, because although school is not for everybody, it's not an impossibility, and it shouldn't be extracted out of anyone's life. It seems like it's either absent or extracted from other people's lives. As are religion and having parents who are self-sacrificing."

Michael calls these "home values" and adds to them "discipline, responsibility—one person to another. I think to some extent everybody needs to make some kind of sacrifice. . . . If it's a value not to be selfish, you're not going to do anything to hurt your family members or to cause envy between siblings or between parents. Weeds will grow in an environment that allows them to. Jealousies *won't* grow in the family that doesn't allow them.

"There was no apparent favoritism [among siblings], at least not in my memory," Michael adds. "At Easter we all got a new Easter suit. At Christmas, I remember we always got new pajamas. For years my brother and I were dressed alike, which drove us crazy. It finally stopped once we protested, but there is picture after picture of us in the same outfit. There was no question—we were never going to be lacking for anything."

One of Michael's most vivid memories is of an "old Plymouth

Midnight Fury III, 1965, which was probably as big as this living room. It was a huge car, it was like a boat. I remember one vacation we [drove it] and it felt so big. We used to sit in the backseat and I could just see the top of my parents' heads." The automobile was part of the family from when he was 6 or 7 until he turned 21 or 22. "I'd always tell my father, 'That car needs to be taken out and shot like an old horse,' " Michael reminisces.

But how could the family abandon a car that still had some good miles left in it? Messages often heard were, "You use up your resources and never waste" and "You finish your chores."

"Finishing *whatever* it is," Michael and the other children were taught. "It builds your ego and [eliminates] 'loose ends,'" Michael says, "which aren't a good thing." When he was a child, he remembers, "nothing was ever undone. There was a start and finish to everything. Finish raking the leaves. Finish taking out the trash. Finish cleaning your room. You have to reach the end of whatever you've begun. Finish painting the house. Finish mowing the lawn."

At the De La Rosa home, those last two chores are carried out with another trait Michael has inherited—perfectionism. "The lawn is obviously something my father is very proud of," Michael concedes, "and the garden is something we've always worked hard on. Now there are motorized edgers, but at the time there was only a lawn mower, so my father's gas mower would mow the lawn but the edging had to be done by hand. So we were either out there with an ax doing it, or using the scissors to cut it."

Painting the house, too, was a matter of pride. "It had to be just so," Michael stresses. "I remember my father fondly recalling *his* father, who was a painter, and saying, 'Your grandfather never let the bristles get wet past there.' Just an inch of the brush would get wet. If you allow paint to go farther down on the bristles, you're not a good painter. I said, 'Well, I have to be a good painter!' So I'd try not to let the paint get farther down on the bristles than what he said. *Standards*—I think we have a lot of personal standards or family standards that are either unspoken or taught to us just through different activities we're involved in."

Michael makes an excellent point: Parents can ask more than the completion of a task; they can require that it be done well. The De La Rosas emphasize not just *finishing* responsibilities but *perfecting* them.

Like Denise, Michael tested his parent's curfew limitations. "Certainly my father would be displeased when we were not home on time," he says. "I can recall the next day, Saturday- or Sunday-morning breakfast, my parents would say nothing to me about what time I got home, and my little brother would say, 'What time did you get home last night?' I'd say, 'Shhh! Don't say anything!'

"It was good to know that my parents were always home waiting for us," Michael admits. "And they trusted us doing whatever it was we were doing. Now I appreciate that very much. My parents are very much an emotional pillar in my life. When anything is not going well, it's so soothing just to call up and say 'hello' and to hear their voice and know they're there."

After observing his parents all these years, he's able to offer some wise and useful recommendations for would-be parents. "You have to *want* to have a family," he says. "You have to want to nurture something, more than a garden. Discipline is not a negative word—it's a positive word. Sharing responsibilities as much as sharing fun things together. Knowing how to give the right doses of love can create the right atmosphere.

"Neglect is a big mistake," Michael offers. "Letting your child be without definition is a mistake. Give the child rules and regulations—nurture him to give him self-respect."

"Self-respect" *paired* with a small amount of indulgence—if the De La Rosas are any example. Michael recalls those "summer nights and the ice cream truck. 'Go get a dollar and tell him to wait!' So we'd all go out, and my parents would get ice cream too. It was a family thing. An allowance was not necessary because whenever we needed something we'd reach into my father's pocket."

The De La Rosa children also reached into their own pockets, since each one had a job. Michael's early resume includes four years as a counter attendant at McDonald's ("Every adolescent should do fast food"), janitorial work, office help, and baby-sitting. "I love kids," Michael declares. "I really do love kids. I enjoy them to a fault."

Willing service to others, particularly in straightening up their yard, is a De La Rosa specialty. Even now, Tony carts his mower to Michael's home and mows his lawn. "He says, 'Son, there's no reason why you need to go out and buy a lawnmower,'" Michael relates. "It's not like I can't afford it. My mother says, 'It keeps your father young. Just let him continue to come over to do your lawn.'

"I think that's what I mean about self-sacrifice," Michael suggests. "Anything they ask me to do as a favor, or I ask them to do, or my sister or vice versa—it's not a question of 'Well, no, I can't do that.' If I have the time, I'm going to do it. There's nothing we don't do for each other, and that is just the way it's always been for us."

He gives an example. "One of the jobs I've taken on, because I don't like my mom to work a lot, is I have holidays here at my house or my sister has them at her house," he says. "If my mom has to go anywhere, because she doesn't drive, I come and pick her up and take her. If my father needs something—if they have to borrow my car because their car's on the blink or whatever, they can borrow it. I buy them things 'just because.'

"I have this need to take care of them now, just like they've taken care of me. Obviously they're not in need of care, they're not frail or incapable, but I have this need to take care of them. My sister and I were discussing this, about the purchase of our next home—I said, 'The next time I buy a home I'm going to buy it with a guest house, and you do the same, so our parents can be close to us.'"

## *Manuel*

With eleven years separating him from next eldest brother Michael, Manuel has the best of both worlds: the parental attention of an only child and the family's overall doting on "the baby." Father Tony concedes, "When my last was little, well, I was always there for him. Mom was there and I was there, so he was maybe a little bit more spoiled. I was a little older, and of course when the other three would do something wrong, 'Hey!' And when this one came along, he'd drag my best sweater through the mud. It's different. I'm not a grandfather now, but I think that's what a grandfather must feel. Because even then people would say, 'Oh, is that your grandson?' I said, 'No, that's my son.'"

"My kids were already in school and Manuel was by himself," Carmen notes, "and he was like an only child, so we gave him everything." What? The kid was spoiled and yet he turned out okay? Which is better—to be strict or cut a child some slack?

There seems to be some debate about whether or not Manuel really *did* have it easier. "I see some things that my parents let them [the older siblings] do a little bit more than I did at this age," Manuel asserts. "They probably gave them a little more leeway." He knows that the rest of the family believes he was the pampered one. And he disputes it.

"The car was one thing," he maintains. "I thought I needed a car to go to high school, at least to commute. They said 'no, no, no.' I barely got my license my senior year, and my brothers and sister had had use of a car!

"My father might say that my mom never disciplined me, but I think I've been well disciplined," he continues. "I never turned to drugs or drinking or stuff like that. Mom told me when I was little, eating at the dinner table or at someone else's place, 'Children should be seen, not heard.'"

Manuel remembers that his parents were always looking for wholesome activities to keep him on the right path. "There were always other doorways, opportunities for us to keep occupied, like sports for example," he says. "Sports and education were probably the two biggest things." He reiterates the same essentials of growing up that were mentioned by Denise, Anthony, and Michael:

"We had to work for what we got. But my parents are always there for us—I can call them and say, 'Hey, I need to pay for this,' or 'I need some money,' and they'll give it to me."

Being younger, he views his parents in the context of a more complex world. "They are as parents should be," Manuel says, "and I think they're so successful because they don't have problems themselves. They're not divorced like some parents can be. My father doesn't drink, my mother doesn't drink. They're strong themselves, and in a strong, loving marriage. And they always stress Catholicism, in themselves as well. They're just trying to reflect it back on us."

Manuel had the benefit—and at times the drawback—of his siblings as additional guardians. His brother Michael even feels better prepared to be a parent himself because of the experience he gained helping to raise Manuel. "We knew what it meant to have a child because we had one in our home," Michael says of the arrival of his brother. "There wasn't a time when he wasn't being watched or didn't have a hand to catch him when he was ready to fall—he had *five* pairs of hands, and if one of us wasn't there, then one of the others of us was there.

"It was very important to make sure nothing happened to him," Michael tells me. "Manuel is still very spoiled, because we all watch out for him. He called us all together when he was going to make a decision about choosing a college, and at one point he got up and left the room because everybody was discussing him. And I thought, 'Poor kid, here he's only supposed to have two parents in this world, and he has five-plus,' with my in-laws taking part in the discussion too."

Anthony wants his own youthful missteps to be lessons for Manuel. "I saw the mistakes I made when I was growing up, being lazy," he says. "I saw my little brother in high school, being just the way I was. In college no one's going to hold your hand anymore, going to scold you. You've got to do it all. So I'd try to tell him, 'You have to give it a better effort!' And he'd shy away from me, he never really understood.

"He thinks he's an adult. He pretends like he knows the answer, and knows what to do as if he already has the experience," Anthony says. "But I hit on one statement that he responded to. I would say, 'Wow, you're 17 years old and you know everything.' And I kept repeating it to the point where he hit me on my arm, he actually wanted to get away from me because I was emotionally bearing down on him. Later I found out he was very intimidated and scared of me—one thing he said was, 'He scares me, he's just like Pop.'"

"Anthony was very rough on me," Manuel confirms. "He was going to give me an education. He kept telling me I didn't know much because I was 17, and he said he wanted to be hard on me now so things wouldn't be hard on me later." The lesson even influenced his choice of college. He'd applied to three University of California campuses, but "in the end, I decided not to go to Santa Barbara because Michael and Denise told me, 'You know he's going to be on your back.' And I didn't want to be in a dorm like this one day studying, hear a knock on the door, and see it was him." That feeling aside, Manuel speaks with respect and admiration for Anthony, and he views the slight emotional distance they're experiencing as only temporary.

Part of the bond among the siblings is their common high school experience. All four went to Catholic schools, the three boys choosing the single-sex Loyola High Preparatory School. Tony and Carmen allowed their children to make the choice, even though attending private schools increased their financial burden. "I think the biggest reason my father worked so hard was so we could get our education," Manuel says, "wherever we wanted to go. I remember my parents telling me, 'We don't want to pressure you.' My brothers told me the same thing, 'Don't go to Loyola because we went there—unless *you* want to go.'"

"I felt very privileged to go there because it's a really good academic school," Manuel says today. "I feel very prepared for college life or university. The Jesuit priests make sure students stay on the right track, that they're learning, not only in the classroom but outside the classroom within their own experiences."

He especially appreciates the spiritual dimension of the education at Loyola, which reinforced the values he lived at home. "They have retreats that you can go on," Manuel notes. "I realized there that I'll only go as far as I really want to, and I have to continue pushing myself. Not giving up."

However, despite all the indoctrination on the value of perseverance, Manuel found himself discouraged by the difficulty of his college course work at the beginning of this school year. It wasn't long before his parents stepped in to remind him of the De La Rosa motto. "The basic rule my father always taught me was, 'Never give up, never say die,'" Manuel says. "I was giving up first quarter with my economics, and my mom said, 'You underestimate yourself. Don't do that. You are capable—you are at UCLA for a reason.' I think I'm very privileged to come here, and now that I have that honor, I better make the best of it. I don't want to flush it down the toilet."

Manuel sees his father as "the rock of the family," steadying the kids and protecting his diligent mother from stress. He shares his father's concern. He omitted mentioning to her a jaunt into Westwood after a huge football victory, lest she'd get upset about potential riots. And in the disturbing aftermath of the January 1994 Los Angeles earthquake, which left him feeling nervous and insecure, he tried to calm her fears for his well-being by racing to his room to receive her instant phone calls after each tiny aftershock.

Like his siblings, Manuel loves his parents dearly and strives to please them. He describes as "the biggest blunder of my life" an incident from his schoolboy baseball career when he wanted desperately to do his pop proud. "It was the championship game four years ago," he recalls. "We were ahead two to one, [with a man] on second or third, two outs and two strikes. I remember thinking, 'I don't want the ball hit to me! I want somebody to catch it, to stop it and throw it to me. I'll catch it, and then jump up and celebrate.'

"So then the ball is hit to me—and the ball went through my legs! I remember kind of backhanding it, and at the last minute I thought, 'Oh, I should turn around,' and I did that—and that's when it slipped. I just remember looking back. My dad was one of the assistant coaches, and I thought, 'He's going to kick my butt now!'

"I walked back in, and the first coach said, 'Don't worry about it.' But that night, I cried myself to sleep. I was heartbroken. And my mom kind of blamed my dad, saying, 'Why is he like that? It's just a game.' My father didn't even say anything to me until he got me home. He just basically told me, 'You'll never do that again, so take that as a learning experience.' And I never did it again. And here I thought, 'Gee, he's going to really kill me,' and he didn't—he comforted me."

Manuel, affectionately nicknamed "Mano" by his mother, is still exploring his future options. At the moment he's leaning toward a career in marketing or business administration. He plans to stay in the Los Angeles area, maybe live in the family home his parents promised would someday be his. "You know, coming from East L.A., I feel grateful for my parents, because they've given me more opportunities than, unfortunately, most people have."

He sums up: "I'm not the type of person who's going to go back and say 'I'm better than the people who live there,' because I'm not. I'd rather go back and *help* these people, and give them opportunities, too. That's what I'd like to do; that's how I see it."

## Neighborhood and Cultural Influences

The people Manuel wants to "go back and help" are the residents of Boyle Heights, one of Los Angeles's earliest established neighborhoods. His commitment to service probably comes from his father, who has distinct childhood memories of the area, where "nobody had anything and everybody shared with everybody else."

Tony was born here in 1935, the second youngest of eight boys. His father, a printer, was a second-generation American, and his mother, a housewife, was born in Chihuahua, Mexico.

Tony's first employment, from the ages of eight to twelve, was as an extra in the movies, and his early brush with fame has become the "big joke in the family." His screen credits include *Anchors Aweigh* with Gene Kelly and Frank Sinatra, *The Red Pony* with Robert Mitchum and Myrna Loy; *Anna and the King of Siam* with Rex Harrison and Irene Dunne, and *Tycoon* with John Wayne.

During his childhood, the now notorious White Fence Gang "basically started with my older brothers," Tony recalls. "It was just a neighborhood gang, for friendship."

Tony was not personally active in any gang, but his next eldest brother, the only sibling to participate heavily, "got shot one time. Otherwise none of us ever went to jail or anything." His father was a heavy drinker, as was the gang-member brother who Tony says underwent a personality change when he was drunk. "He'd come kicking me around, pushing me around." This spurred Tony to start working out. "I started picking up weights and getting bigger. And he'd come home drunk, and he'd say, 'I'll beat you up even if I have to get a baseball bat.' That meant he didn't want to tangle with me anymore."

Tony calls himself "the black sheep" of the family because of his unusual and intense involvement with sports. "After I came out of high school I'd run the streets—jogging. And there was never anybody around." He'd run the several miles to his mother's house in the early years after his marriage, "just to keep in shape. It just felt good to me."

When Tony went to Roosevelt High School, two blocks from his home, "There were only three black students in the whole school," he recalls. "We had Japanese, Slavs, Greeks, Russians, Chinese—there was a mixture and you never had any gang activity. I came out of high school in '53. Sure, there were a few gang members, but you would have a fight with your fists. Nowadays you can't trust anybody. All they want to do is kill you. It looks like [things have gotten] so bad they'll take you for a nickel."

The neighborhood has deteriorated over the years in many ways, Carmen and Tony agree. They say they've noticed more crime. People are less friendly. And they feel that a large part of the decline is because those moving in tend to be renters rather than homeowners. "From here on that way to the corner—this small block—you have owners," Tony gestures. "And basically, we know most of these people. Back toward us, most people rent. And they are in and out of the house; they're not going to be here that long. And the culture is a little different. We were born here, whereas a lot of [those] people are coming from Mexico, Central America. We're the same nationality but the culture is kind of different."

Tony describes the renters in his area: "I think they've had trouble where they come from. You have revolutions in El Salvador, so they tend to lash out more. Be more protective. Where the other generations when they first came, nobody really had anything, and everybody was coming up at the same time. Now, we are born here, we think American, you know. They're born in Mexico and they have their own way of living. Where I may be wanting to clean my house up to a certain point, they may not want to clean their house all the time because they were farm people. It's a different culture; they were brought up differently."

"You hear the music, or they have Mexican flags, or they make some comment about they should go back," Carmen says. "We shouldn't feel [angry], because [they share] our nationality . . . but I was born here; this is my upbringing." Carmen admits to sometimes feeling awkward simply because she's behaving in an American way. "For instance, like our church, when we go to Mass we're a minority among our own people—you can almost count the people who go to an English-speaking mass."

Tony and Carmen's discomfort has driven them to attend church in Pasadena, but Carmen is dissatisfied with its lack of warmth. "In our church [in Boyle Heights]," she explains, "we hold hands when we pray the 'Our Father.' That's a closeness."

"I guess I've been close to my kids and I participated," Tony says of a major difference between the De La Rosas and the newcomers. "Whatever they chose to do, I was backing them up. And we see these people who don't seem to back up their children. Their kids are running around the streets. Maybe because they come from farm country, or you know, they're hustling all the time. They have to; they have to make money, and so they're not really taking care of their children. And that bothers us."

Tony Salazar makes some good points about the relationship between Mexican communalism and American capitalism: "America is very interesting," he says. "We believe in democracy, freedom, and equality—that we're all equal. And it fits with our [Mexican] communal kind of thing; the way we live as a family, an extended family. We all raise ourselves up *together*, or [not at all].

"But the economy here isn't like that," he states. "The American economy is very individualistic. You're out there for yourself. To me there's a dichotomy between America's economy and its philosophical views," which supposedly support the family. "Once we break out of the communal mold, then it's harder and it puts a strain on the family."

Michael, for one, believes that sensitivity to ethnic origins has increased. "I think we want to know if our neighbor or person across town is more like us or different," he says. "That is going to have a lot to do with what type of relationship we're going to have with that person."

Adds Manuel, "I think in some sense, it could be good, because if you're in a big cultural mix-up, you can gain an understanding about others—how they are and why they are—and you can gain an understanding of yourself."

## *Crime: "The Worst Experience of My Life"*

The neighborhood changes have greatly affected the younger generation as well. They, too, cite increases in trash, graffiti, and crime. Last year Manuel suffered "probably the worst experience of my life" when he was mugged at a local McDonald's: "I remember just seeing these guys come by the table, putting the gun on the table," he says. It was a surrealistic moment. "When it finally occurred to me, I'm like, 'Oh, God!' And the guy said 'Give me your ring' [Manuel's Loyola class ring], so I put it on the table. 'Give me the chain!'" the robber demanded, meaning the special crucifix his brother Michael had given him for his confirmation. "I took off the chain," Manuel continues. "He said, 'Give me any money you got.' I gave him like ten bucks. He said 'Stay cool 'cuz we have a blade.' So they walked out and I said 'Guys, let's get out of here.' I was with three friends from high school, and they took me home.

"And I was crying, I was just so scared and terrified," Manuel relates. "I ran in and told my parents, and my father said, 'Well, we could go to the police.'" Manuel decided against it, in part because he feared that such a report could cause problems for one of his friends who was employed by McDonald's. He was also reluctant for other reasons: "Just the experiences I've had with police—they're really rough on [guys] my age," he says.

"They pulled me over one time," he recalls. "They go, 'Why aren't you in school?' I said, 'I'm on vacation.' And they said, 'Yeah, right." One of them said, 'Where do you go to high school?' I told him, 'Loyola High School.' And he said, 'Where's that?' And I said, 'It's over on Venice Boulevard between Normandy and Vermont.' And I said, 'Look, here's my ID.' And I said, 'If you want to go call the school, go ahead and call the school.'" After a few tense moments, the policeman relented, with, "'Okay, don't cause any trouble.'

"I felt like if I went to the police [over the mugging], they would really interrogate me and my friends, so we decided not to," Manuel explains. "But I wanted to see Father Greg. . . . He has a little office near where we live where he offers jobs to gang members. And my mom called him up, and he said 'Come on in.' I told him what happened, he talked to me, and I went to confession with him. And I felt a lot better after that. I felt like I got this monkey off my back. I think if I hadn't done that I really would have freaked out, just gone crazy or something. I don't really know, but it was just the scariest moment of my life.

"I remember that weekend I was going to go out to a club with my friends," Manuel recalls, "and my mom said 'No.' My father said, 'Let him, so he can get everything off his back.' I told my mom, 'Look, I don't want to be afraid of walking down the street whenever I'm out and thinking, "Oh, my God, somebody's going to do something." I've got to get out, just face reality. But honestly now, I look around, and if I see anybody suspicious I look and see what's going on.'"

There's a happy ending to the story. A priest who'd led a school retreat Manuel attended heard about the mishap. "Over the summer he called me up and told me, 'I have this package for you.' I went back to Loyola to get it. And it was a brand-new ring."

### *"Spanglish"*

Language is another fundamental aspect of life in East L.A. that has changed. Tony and Carmen never spoke to their children in Spanish because they themselves were chastised for it when they were in school. Carmen says her goal for her offspring was to "protect them [by teaching them] English, because whatever they read—their applications, their studies, their school—was not going to be Spanish. They had to know how to spell, how to read."

Adds Tony, "As a young kid growing up in Los Angeles, you didn't hear anybody speaking Spanish—you spoke English. Not because you wanted to forget your background, but because those were the rules. You were forbidden to speak your language out in public.

"So that was good, but to my father I would speak Spanish," he continues. "A lot of times he corrected me and he got angry at me for not being able to pronounce a word, but I could speak it. I could write it." His own children did not begin learning Spanish until high school. "My son, Michael, my son, Manuel, they're learning every word [so they'll] write correctly—the accents, everything, where it goes," he says with pride.

Eldest child Denise also took Spanish for the first time in high school. "It's stuff you're very familiar with," she notes. "I used to hear Spanish a lot when I was young, and I can understand most of it. I just can't really carry on a deep conversation. My husband Tony's mom only speaks Spanish, and I understand everything she says, but even her kids answer her in English."

Tony Salazar capsulizes, "Latino baby boomers don't speak Spanish because of the bad experiences our parents had. There was no value in their teaching us Spanish."

Denise remembers spending lunchtimes as a child with her great-uncle, Guardino, who lived in her mom's family home down the street. "We'd always take off—'Mom, be right back! Going to Tio's house!'—because he'd always have something for lunch," she says, smiling. When with him, she spoke in "'Spanglish'—tripping on ourselves, just all of a sudden saying something in Spanish and then we'd go back to English."

Bilingual education in the public schools has been a hot-button issue in California since its introduction almost two decades ago. Denise, who is an educational policy consultant well versed in such topics, explains: "Everybody agrees that you have to learn English to be successful, and everybody realizes that English is the *de facto* language of this country," she says. "Within the educational system, the intent is to teach the children English. There are different methods to do this, and the method of teaching the native language first so that they can keep up with their subject matter is very valid, I think. I've been to many schools in this state where they've utilized that method, and within four or five years the child is well into the English language. They haven't fallen behind. They go on to college. They do well and they're not stigmatized. [And as an added plus] they have the asset of being bilingual."

Denise says that the current trend is toward so-called immersion programs, which are geared toward a transition from the native language into English.

### *Religion*

As much as language and shared heritage are a defining aspect of Latino culture, so is the community parish. "If you go around the east side," Tony Salazar says, "you see every church has their own little fiesta. It's a focal point, so it's social, it's spiritual, it's common ground." He and Denise had just attended a local Boyle Heights event. "It's about as big as my yard here, or that parking lot across the street, and they have it twice a year," he reports.

Tony adds that "loving thy neighbor is what religion is all about," and because more than 75 percent of Mexican Americans are Catholic, the church is a major source of unity and strength for Latinos. Certainly that's true for the De La Rosas. From the welcoming statue of the Virgin Mary on their front lawn, to the ongoing volunteer work both Tony and Carmen have contributed to their parish, to the moving stories of comfort and support the family received in the most trying of times, their unwavering trust in the Almighty stands foremost.

"[The Church] was always a constant in our lives," Michael confirms. "Every Sunday morning we'd get up and go to nine o'clock mass, as well as to whatever social activity went on after mass. We knew everybody who was at church." He looks back on it as a positive experience, important in shaping his respect for authority. "I remember my sister would go out, and if she got home late we were still expected to go to Mass. She'd say, 'Wait for me!' and my father would go ahead. Sometimes we'd get to church just a little bit late, and he'd say, 'You have to stay for the next mass.' And we'd complain, 'Oh no, we don't have to stay for the next mass, we were only five minutes late!'"

Over the years, Michael has had moments of distance from his faith. "Certainly people sway from church," he admits. "There've been times in my life that I've gone to church many times a week, and there've been times when I've not gone for several months. I think your faith can't grow if you don't question it. My parents—if they've ever questioned their faith, they've never stopped going to church."

Denise has had her own ups and downs with respect to religious affiliation. She recalls the diligent church attendance of her childhood and has a special memory of how the family observed Good Friday. "We had to read or do something quiet," she relates. "We couldn't have the TV on; we couldn't have music; we couldn't play outside. We'd have to just stay still and be quiet. It seemed like such a long day because then we'd have to go to church. Yes, religion was a big, big part of growing up, as well as with all my cousins, my aunts, my uncles, and my grandmother. It was, 'Always go to church.'"

She believes the most powerful religious influence was her parents' own devotion. "When we'd go to church, my father would sing. My mom and dad have Bible readings and prayer classes at their house," she explains. Denise drifted away somewhat during college, but Anthony's accident "pulled me back, closer to church and God and religion." While living in Washington, D.C., she attended "some churches . . . and I felt very much a part of the community—I felt I got something out of Mass." Then, "We moved to Alexandria, Virginia, for a year. And the church we'd go to was an African American parish, and I also felt very much a part of the community there and very spiritually uplifted every time I went to church."

The Virginia church was Baptist, with a gospel choir that Tony Salazar recalls was "like watching a show. It was just beautiful."

Since returning to Southern California, however, Denise and Tony have attended Mass irregularly, though both continue to integrate their relationship with God into their lives. "She has her own way of praying," Tony says of his wife. "I have a book in my desk, and every morning I read from my daily prayer book." It keeps him from being too "aggressive" in his business, he asserts. "Otherwise I just plow through my day."

Manuel describes his religious path: "I guess it started off by going to Catholic elementary school, because we had our classes, our first communion," he says. "I know Anthony, Denise, and Michael got confirmed by eighth grade." By the time Manuel reached that age, however, confirmation age had been changed to 16. "At that point my parents said, 'Do you want to do this? Do you want to get confirmed?' And I said, "Yeah, I want to do it.'

"They didn't ever have to tell us, 'You better go to church, you have to, you're going to do this no matter what,'" he says. "They gave us the opportunity, the choice to say, 'If you want to, great. If you don't want to, then when you're ready.'" Manuel didn't even consider saying no. "I know my mom is very strong with it, to the point where it would probably really hurt her if I didn't do it. But by the time we were old enough, we realized 'This is what we want. We've gone through it, we're used to it, we're going to stick with it.' That's the way I felt."

Though he attends his parents' church, he prefers to go alone. "I need my own spiritual time to reflect," he says. "I don't know too many people around here [UCLA] who are Catholic. So I go to Mass, and I listen and I pray. I just basically ask God to help me get through everything, and I know it's not going to be easy. If it were easy then life wouldn't be [much] fun—maybe not fun, but like a roller coaster, with ups and downs. You have to have variation, or else it's not interesting or challenging, I guess."

## *Media*

Though they live only a few miles from the famous "Hollywood" sign, and moviemaking provided Tony his first employment, the De La Rosas report that film, television, and print media play a minimal role in their lives. Up until eighth grade, the children were permitted to watch TV only after homework and before their bedtime of 7:30 P.M. Typically, their viewing included such shows as *I Love Lucy,* and movies like *Ben-Hur* and *The Ten Commandments*.

Individual family members tend to get their political news from television and newspapers, though Tony De La Rosa says his first interest in the paper is "the sports page. Then I'll read whatever else, because I'm hearing over and over, 'This person has done this.' Everybody has problems."

"Media focuses always on the negative," Manuel says. "It gives you the impression that everything, the whole world and this country, has something bad about it. You're constantly bombarded by it. We can't deny that there are negative things going on in our country, but there *are* positive things."

Carmen adds, "I look at TV during the day. I look for a movie or something pleasant to take my mind off of things. I do read a lot of articles in the paper. Yes, I know there is the negative, but I'm not working, so I read to see what's going on about this or that. I never followed politics before, but I got interested in what's going on."

There was a consensus that the media are manipulative and can slant facts for sensation. Graphic coverage of damage from the Los Angeles earthquake, according to Manuel, turned his moderate reaction into one of intense fear. "I'd always tell Mom, 'I don't want to see it.' We'd get into arguments over that," he says. "But she always wanted to put it on. Mom likes to watch the news, and my father says she worries because she watches too much news."

## Making It Work: Lessons from the De La Rosa Family

"A De La Rosa never gives up." That's the message that carries across every aspect of this cohesive family's life, a theme that each family member applies broadly and intensely.

Tony and Carmen exemplify it with their insistence that "*a parent is always there* backing up your child." The senior De La Rosas "never give up" directing their attention to the children, whether by showing up for sports events or enforcing behavior with strict but loving standards.

Denise and Tony Salazar didn't give up on their *relationship*, even though they were geographically distant and had issues to sort through. Neither did Denise give up when told in high school that it was useless to apply to her preferred college, the University of California at Santa Barbara. They're also unwilling to give up on their heritage. Each is dedicated, Denise through her educational policy consulting and Tony through his real estate development business, to furthering the interests of the people who share that heritage.

"A De La Rosa never gives up" applies most forcefully to Anthony and Mary, who made their love and devotion thrive through arduous months and years of rehabilitation from his near-fatal head injury. Anthony still refuses to give up on his desire to be a leader, to speak publicly about rehabilitation of the disabled, and to show the way to recovery for others. He never ceases feeling gratitude to his wife, and she has undiminished admiration for him.

Michael, articulate in his insights on current issues as well as his family, might be most notable for not giving up on Los Angeles, a city beleaguered by tragedies ranging from earthquakes to riots. Despite the problems Los Angeles faces, Michael sees only its potential. He hopes to return some of the kindness that he has received in life—to his parents, his teachers, and his civic employers.

Manuel, still in college, is most focused at this stage on "never giving up" on himself. He is living the family's emphasis on education, the belief that each should continue to learn and strive in his own way. And although he recently experienced a mugging that shattered his sense of well-being, he immediately sought to regain his confidence by traveling the streets alone.

The De La Rosas' durable faith has seen them through every parent's worst nightmare, the severe injury of a child. The De La Rosas will never "give up" on their connection to God. This is not unusual. In my informal survey, which asked almost one thousand people to identify "the most important ingredient in maintaining a healthy family," religion was the number one answer. Thirty-eight percent of respondents listed religion, faith, or God in their open-ended reply to the values question.

Here is a summary of the lessons offered by the successful De La Rosa family.

- *Emphasize the positive goals of your partner.* By helping your mate feel fulfilled, you strengthen your marriage's foundation. Tony not only accepted Carmen's staying home with the children but welcomed it.
- *Faith cements marriages.* It gives a broader perspective that motivates spouses toward higher standards of behavior. Carmen considers attending mass with Tony each Sunday to be the anchor of their relationship.
- *In choosing a spouse, use your head, not just your heart.* Denise and Tony Salazar deliberately set aside a weekend to soberly examine the pros and cons of their relationship.
- *Learn from your parents' marriage.* Denise Salazar observed her mother's argumentative style and vowed not to replicate it. Many couples repeat their parents' mistakes in relationships without even noticing.
- *Make insults taboo.* Denise demands an ironclad rule in her marriage: No put-downs. It keeps tempers in check.
- *Be attentive and especially respectful of your mate in public.* Tony Salazar was always impressed with the way his

parents respected each other in public, and the lesson carries into his marriage with Denise.

- *Elevate holidays and birthdays.* It's worth the effort; Denise credits this simple ritual with giving each family member a sense of worth.
- *Cheerlead the children.* A parent teaches values by *example* and *repetition.* The senior De La Rosas never stopped teaching their several mottoes, "A De La Rosa never gives up," "Apply yourself," and "I'll be there."
- *Don't be afraid to restrict your child to a controllable environment.* There is nothing wrong with protecting your children from outside menaces and focusing the children's attention on the home. Carmen still bristles at the memory of Michael's kindergarten teacher calling her son a "mama's boy" because she made home the center of his activities.
- *Children need standards.* Dad could quiet the squirming children in church with a searing stare.
- *Respect for the family is essential, and one way to teach it is at the daily send-off.* "You're representing our family as you go to school today!" is an important vote of trust a parent can pass to the child.
- *A set and somewhat inflexible schedule of activities gives children a sense of order, security, and stable expectations.* The De La Rosa children's bedtime of seven-thirty gave them a framework. It retained parental authority.
- *Anticipate the other parent's arrival.* As the children prepared for bed with their nightly routine, Carmen increased their excitement about their father's return, creating and reinforcing the children's respect for their dad.
- *Engender love for education by reading to your children and working through their homework with them.* It's tempting to say that homework is just for the child, but then you're

missing a chance to show your own interest in education as well as to bond with your child.

- *Stick to your word.* You might try Tony's trick with 16-year-old Denise's curfew challenge: With each protest, tighten the reins a little more.
- Ask *long-term questions of your children.* "What do you want to be?" "What colleges do you like?" "When you grow up . . . ?" These should start at the earliest ages to plant a certainty about college and career success.
- *Emphasize completion.* As Michael says, "Finishing is a good thing. It builds your ego."
- *Point out privilege.* When your children receive special services or goods, remind them how lucky, honored, or blessed they are.
- *Punctuality, especially on the part of parents, teaches reliability as well as respect for others.* The senior De La Rosas often arrive early for a dinner party. And when they were young, the children were penalized for arriving at church even a few minutes late.
- *Sports have intrinsic benefits, such as teaching fair play, teamwork, physical development, and tenacity.* They also help to mold character and provide a structure for the child's leisure time. They're also gratifying for coaches, as Tony De La Rosa learned.
- *Cultivate patriotism.* Recent denigration of our unique American culture has caused a loss of patriotism that further erodes our work ethic and shared values. The De La Rosas see their American upbringing as offering a special overlay for their Mexican heritage.
- *Take pride in your home.* Tony De La Rosa maintains a perfectly groomed front lawn. It may seem unimportant, but since he sees it every day, it provides personal satisfaction and sends a message of pride in ownership to the whole community.

- *Build a special relationship with a local hero.* Father Greg Boyle is someone all of the De La Rosas respect for his role in their lives, as well as for the contributions he makes to Loyola High School, parishioners, and struggling youth.

# 3

# The Wallace Family of Indianapolis

*May there always be work for your hands to do.*
*May your purse always hold a coin or two.*
*May the sun shine on your window pane.*
*May a rainbow be certain to follow each rain.*

—Irish blessing displayed in the Wallace home

KATHY WALLACE IS A SINGLE MOTHER OF FIVE children. Her home is on the near eastside of Indianapolis, Indiana.

Kathy and I had met briefly in 1992 during my visit to Holy Cross Elementary School when I was Vice President. She was there with other parents of children who were attending the school under the Educational Choice Charitable Trust program. The program, which provides private-school tuition vouchers to low-income families, was founded in the early 1990s by a civic-minded Indianapolis businessman named Pat Rooney. A strong believer in school choice, Rooney is as convinced as I am that competition is the only answer to restoring quality to elementary and secondary education. He's backed up this program with extraordinary amounts of his own money, and a number of Indiana individuals and companies have also contributed.

## In Transit

As I drive to Kathy's home to meet with her and her children, I can't help but think about the so-called Murphy Brown speech. I look forward to talking about Kathy's reaction to the speech, but I can't plan that part of our conversation. It has to come up naturally. I don't want her to feel she has to hedge her answers.

I arrive at the Wallaces' at the scheduled time of 2:00 P.M. As I ring the doorbell, I notice the scattered basketballs and baseball bats that signal the presence of a busy young family.

Kathy welcomes me and introduces the children who are home at the moment, Gabe and Sarah. Kathy is a very pleasant, articulate midwestern mom. She's earnest and answers questions clearly and emphatically. As we take our seats at her round wooden dining-room table, she begins telling me the remarkable story of her life. She's suffered, yet triumphed. She's seen some of the uglier aspects of life, yet has retained her optimism and sunny disposition. Kathy is definitely in charge of this household, and her children are clearly loyal to her.

## Introductions

Kathy grew up in eastside Indianapolis. In 1975, at age 19, she married Mike Wallace, four years her senior. They immediately began a family and for several years resided only a few houses from Kathy's childhood home. Later they bought and renovated their own home on the same block. While Mike was completing college, he and Kathy both worked in various part-

and full-time jobs. The marriage endured the usual difficulties, but ended abruptly after ten years when Kathy, four months pregnant with their fifth child, discovered that her husband had been having an affair with a longtime family acquaintance who'd been a teacher to one of their daughters.

Kathy has since raised the children—Sarah, 19, Gabe, 17, Donovan, 13, Katy, 12, and Molly, 10—alone. Mike sees them weekly and contributes $500 per month to their support; Kathy earns $27,500 a year working full-time for Eastside Community Investments, a publicly funded neighborhood-rehabilitation project, where she trains volunteers to help homeowners improve their surroundings.

---

"Don't forget where you came from" is a phrase I hear from everybody in the Wallace family. It connotes a certain modesty, a humility about their heritage and about this neighborhood called Holy Cross–Westminster (for the two churches in the area, one Catholic, the other Presbyterian). The motto ties Kathy to this block, where, within eleven houses, she's lived her entire life and feels comfortable and secure. She entrusts the education of her children to the religious staff of Holy Cross School, the same institution she and her three siblings attended. Neighbors and friends constitute an extended family that gives her support and friendship.

As I chat with Kathy, a gripping story emerges of a closely knit family united around Mom. The two dominant themes are the effects of their *financial struggle* and the impact of *divorce* on their daily lives. Kathy, I soon learn, has endured much sadness and tragedy. Despite this, she exudes happiness, primarily because of her love for, and total commitment to, her children.

## Marriage

"I remember my wedding day completely—I remember crying and crying," says Kathy, recalling her misgivings about marrying Mike Wallace. Undermined by infidelity, lack of trust, and poor communication, the relationship didn't survive. Yet both Mike and Kathy still cling to the ideal of marriage, even after a difficult, emotional divorce.

The couple started out young and naive. In a separate telephone interview, Mike says he chose Kathy because "she was [available] and she said yes. All the wrong reasons. I was alone in Indianapolis. I think at the time I thought that was what I should be doing, that I should be settling down and getting married. At the tender age of 23—and, of course, she was 19. Neither one of us had jobs when we got married. I was still in school finishing up my degree."

"I don't regret being married," Kathy says. "There were some things about being married that were great. At the end of the day, because we had a lot of little ones, it was so great to get the kids into bed and just sit down and eat popcorn or something and talk with an adult. I treasured that. It was just wonderful to say, 'So this was the day for me—what did you do today?'"

Mike and Kathy performed the usual juggling of family responsibilities familiar to young couples. "I got a job doing patient billing at a medical center," Kathy recounts. "I had to work four-thirty in the morning until eleven o'clock. It was convenient after I had Sarah, because Mike took her to the baby-sitter in the morning and then I was home by noon, so I got to be with her awhile while Mike was in school." When Sarah was seven months old, Kathy became the office manager for a retreat lodge, where she worked for four years. "We'd already bought this house and were working on it," she recalls. "I had Gabe and stayed home with him about six months; then, after returning to work, I got pregnant with Donovan and child-care arrangements became too complicated, so I decided to stay home."

Mike, Kathy says, "was pretty chronically underemployed in terms of his ability and training, but not very ambitious and, again, I took on my role of 'Kathy the Great.' I did different things on the side to boost our income, including day care sometimes. I saved, I did whatever it took." She describes their relationship as functional. She rose to the challenges as they came along.

Mike believes his stalled career played a role in their eventual divorce. "I was distant, I was depressed. My job prospects weren't getting any better," he remembers. "Here I have a bachelor's degree and all I can get is a six-dollar-an-hour job and I've got three children at that point, then four children, and every time I looked around she's getting pregnant. We're living in a house that we have to renovate so there's plaster dust all the time, and we work until midnight putting up drywall, and I have to get up at six o'clock in the morning and go to work. I was a mechanic, it was physical labor. It wasn't what I was brought up to be. I was educated at college prep, I was an English major, I was working my tail off for this family and for the marriage, too. And there just wasn't enough of me left over to give to her, and vice versa."

Kathy has her own view of what went wrong. "Mike was not a very happy person," she says. "He didn't take much responsibility personally for himself. You know how kids say 'It's not my fault'? You know, 'I broke the window and it's not my fault; I didn't throw the ball there on purpose.' Nothing was his fault, and I sensed that about him before we were married. And that really is what finished our marriage. He had an affair and 'it wasn't his fault.' I remember him clearly saying that to me. Well, who *is* responsible? If it's not your fault, whose is it?"

Kathy now sees that she'd always been the one to accept responsibility. In fact, taking on too much, she feels, has been her "fatal flaw." She and her three older siblings were forced to learn that prematurely. Both of her parents were alcoholics. Her mother died of cancer when Kathy was 15. Her father, 61 at the time and retired from structural iron work due to injury, was devastated and needed care for the remaining ten years of his life. He'd always been an unusual figure, she says—he'd been bringing in money for years as a bookie until arrested by the FBI, accused with sixty-two others of "running a dive." Eventually, his was the only case dismissed.

Her sister, Maureen, two years older, took over as head of the family, but "when I got out of high school, I decided I had to be the champion or something," Kathy recalls. "Certainly the jobs I took [such as houseparent for a runaway shelter at age 20] and the people I involved myself with [established a pattern of] not very healthy roles where I was the adult and they were the child."

This, she says, characterized her relationship with Mike. And he agrees. "She was a caretaker; that's what happens to the children of alcoholics, they take care of everybody except they don't take care of themselves," he says. "And it's very hard to love a caregiver, because they have no needs. I wanted to take care of her, and there wasn't anything she wanted that I could give her. It was too one-sided.

"If you ask me why we were divorced, I'll say 'because she was never home,'" Mike explains. "She was attending meetings at the church. She was the president of every committee at the church that possibly could meet, and they met four or five nights a week. And I didn't like it, and I *told* her I didn't like it. And when she wasn't at meetings she was talking on the phone. And she's still like that today."

The catalyst for the breakup, though, was Mike's infidelity. But the affair alone would not have necessarily meant the end of the union for Kathy. "That's what *started* the collapse," she explains. "But it was his *response* that finished it: 'I had an affair, it's all your fault.'"

Kathy has a vivid memory of the night Mike revealed that he was involved with another woman.

"It was the day after Christmas and I was doing child care, a million kids because there was no school. I was making a big institutional-sized pot of macaroni and cheese, and typically, Mike called me from work in the daytime. He said, 'Hi, what are you doing?' And I said, 'Well, I'm just draining macaroni right now. Is this important? Can I call you back?' He said, 'Yeah, this is important. I don't want you to hate me.' So I looked into the phone and said, 'Well, this is pretty weird.' He said, 'I don't want you to think I've done this because I hate you but I'm in love with someone else. I guess you probably want me to leave.' I said, 'I guess you want me to tell you what to do, and I can't believe that you would choose this and try to put it on me so I would be the bad guy.' So he said, 'You don't care.' I said, 'No, I care a lot.'

"I made it through the rest of the day, I don't know how. At the time, Mike was selling some kind of investment insurance, and he was supposed to have appointments at night. He came home and we had a normal dinner, that's how bizarre it was. He said to me that he wasn't going to his insurance appointment, but that he had something he had to do. And I said, 'Right.'

"I remember that Katy was sick and I took Katy and Donovan upstairs and put them in the bathtub. I was kneeling on the floor and Mike came upstairs and said, 'I guess you're right. I do have some decisions to make but I have to talk that through with someone else.' As he left [the house], I turned, and Katy, who was sixteen months old, grabbed my razor that I shave my legs with and cut her fingers to the bone. Sarah was there and became hysterical. So, very controlled, I said, 'Very calmly call Pat [a male family friend next door]. And don't scream.'

"Pat came over and helped me get the fingers dry, and we thought we could handle it without stitches. We bandaged each one of Katy's fingers and Pat looked up at me and said, 'Kathy, where's Mike?' I broke down, and he said, 'You stay right here.' He came back a little while later with boxes and said, 'Let's box up his stuff.' I said, 'Oh, Pat, I can't do that. I've been married ten years. He's not getting out of it this easily. He at least owes me an explanation.'

"At about three o'clock in the morning, Mike came home,

and he'd been drinking. It wasn't typical of him; he wasn't a drinker. It had never occurred to me [to ask] who the woman was because I knew from that first moment it was much deeper—I knew I shouldn't focus on the affair, because if I did, then I wouldn't be able to let go of it, and if I was going to be married, I'd have to get past that. But when Pat had gone, he'd pursued an inkling he'd had—and found our car parked in front of Sarah's teacher's."

Kathy indicated to Mike that she'd accept him back *if* he stopped the relationship immediately and joined her in counseling. They attended just two sessions. The first hour was spent on Mike's perspective, concluding with an appointment for a second meeting. Before that first meeting ended though, Kathy announced a need to confront her husband's lover. Soon after, she went to the woman's front door.

"She wouldn't answer the door, so I realized he was still seeing her, that he had told her that I was coming," Kathy recalls. "I was really, really angry. I pounded and pounded on the door and she finally answered, and she said, 'Hi, do you want a Pepsi or something?' I just looked at her like she'd lost her mind. I said, 'No, I don't think it's really appropriate that I drink a Pepsi with you.'

"She said, 'I know you're pretty mad about the Mike thing. I'm just really screwed up sexually, Kathy. I really think you're a neat person.' I said, 'You've known me for eight years and that's all you can say about me—that I'm a neat person? You have the morals of a Styrofoam cup.'"

Kathy challenged Mike when she returned home: "He said to me, 'I don't want to be married anymore. This is really just a lot of trouble,'" Kathy recalls. But he wanted to wait to leave until the birth of their fifth child. "I said, no, I can't do that. Why live in that kind of pretense, Michael? We both go to Holy Cross Church, and you'll sit with me—or [the lover] will sit with us—or how will that work?' He said, 'We could be just like it was before. Just not tell anybody.' I said, 'If you want to leave then you do that, and then you gain people's sympathy honestly—but not with the pretense of your staying with me.' So we went to the counselor the next day and he said, 'Too much trouble, too much hassle. I don't want to do this.'"

It was back and forth for two weeks of his indecision, she recalls. "Every other day he'd say, 'I love you,' 'I hate you,' 'I want to be married to you,' 'I don't want to be married to you,' until I just couldn't do it anymore. I finally said, 'You need to get back over and clear your stuff out of here.'

"We had an agreement that he'd tell Sarah and Gabe his intentions. But he waited until Gabe fell asleep; I was really mad. Sarah had excellent instincts, and she willed herself to stay awake. And he left, he snuck out—you know, he slid out the door. It was snowing, I remember, and Sarah followed him to the front door, and she said, 'Mom, he told me he would never, never leave me, and look at him just walking down the street.' And she walked outside and called, 'Dad, who will take care of us?' And he said, 'Your mom.' And she said, 'Who will take care of mom?' And he said, 'God will.'"

Kathy remembers the next few months as a "daze." She lost all the weight she'd gained in her pregnancy to that point, and, fearful for the health of the child, decided to put aside thoughts of the separation until after the baby's birth. "I knew in my heart that Mike would never file for divorce; that he'd just continue not making a decision about it, so when Molly was six weeks old, I went to see a lawyer, mostly just to get information. The information I got pretty much said there was no reason to wait. So I filed for divorce that day.

"Mike was really, really angry, and to this day will say that he didn't choose the divorce, that I chose. I was in therapy for a year and a half. I would talk for about fifty-five minutes nonstop, and the therapist would always say something kind to me, and finally one day he said, 'You know, Kathy, we're going to do this a little differently. It's going to be my turn for a while. This problem didn't just start yesterday, this started a long time ago.' And so as he confronted me with some things that maybe I didn't know, maybe I did know. I learned a whole lot about myself and about other relationships I had. Not male-female relationships, but relationships in general—and most of them were based on the fact that I am strong, and people who are weak love me.

"So I've learned a lot about myself, and I have skills that I had no idea I had that I wouldn't have ever used had I stayed married to that person. Certainly, he had gifts too. He's still really angry at me about the whole thing.

"He stopped seeing [his lover] the summer after he left. Intermittently, when he didn't have a girlfriend, he'd come back here and say, 'What happened to us? Why are we divorced?' It was real clear that it had nothing to do with me; it was because he was desperate. So I'd just say, 'Not interested.' If I would have ever said, 'Please do come back,' it would have scared him to death."

From Mike's perspective, his affair was "just a symptom." He recalls his unwillingness to give up his lover as a condition of counseling. "I'd already made my decision that I was leaving. Essentially, there was no point in going to the marriage counselor. The affair was my way out. I wanted out. I was dissatisfied with the marriage.

"It was a big mess. She was one of the teachers of my kids at school. We sang in the choir together. She ended up losing her job as a teacher and leaving town, like rode out of town in tar and feathers. I screwed up *her* life at the same time [as causing the divorce]."

And yet Mike says emphatically, "The divorce was one of the best things that ever happened to me. Probably made me a much better person." How? "The pain. Made me more human. Before, I was pretty much a jerk. I hate to even admit it right this moment but I was insensitive."

Kathy looks back on her divorce as "a horrible thing. That's not the life I had figured out for myself," she says. Perhaps the most trying consequence of the divorce has been the relentless financial hardship. Its ongoing anguish led to another phase in her relationship with Mike—one culminating in violence. In Kathy's own voice:

"Last July I realized I'll never have money. That as my kids got older they got more expensive. Mike was in another relationship and looking at a $120,000 house on the north side. He was telling me this story that he was going to do this and that to it, and I just burst into tears and said, 'I don't have money for the gas bill, and you're buying a house! The roof is leaking in the bedroom, and you're buying a $120,000 house!' So I asked him, 'How would you feel about rehabbing the back half of the attic and living up there?'

"The next day he called me at work and said, 'Are you serious about that?' I said, 'I don't know what else to do. I can go and get a job at night, but then I'll be away from the kids that much more. This is desperation.' So we talked it through, drew up some plans on how it could be done, and he moved in this past September.

"We had a pretty clear agreement going in: 'This is not about sex, this is not about being married to you or being connected to you—this is about money.' From his viewpoint, it would give him a chance to be around the kids too, a chance he hadn't had in years, because an every-other-weekend dad is not a dad."

The children had varied reactions. Kathy reports that Sarah, 18 then, "cried for two days." Gabe, 15, was shocked that their financial need was dire enough to require this. Donovan worried about clashes over furnishings; Katy had mixed feelings, saying, "This is pretend because it's like Dad is here, but he's not." Molly simply clung to her mother.

The arrangement lasted seven months. Says Kathy matter-of-factly, "He left because I had to file battery charges against him. He beat me up."

It happened on a school holiday when she'd brought two of her children with her to work. Mike, who had never been violent before, appeared at her office "with a really angry face," Kathy recalls. She put him off until later; at home after dinner on that warm April evening she followed him out the front door, assuming they'd speak away from the children on the porch. He walked to his minivan parked at the curb, however, and Kathy followed.

"I got in it and he whipped around out of his seat and said, 'You had an affair when we were married!' He started cussing at me and just screaming and he said, 'This is a letter I found upstairs in your jewelry box!' And he's like, up in my face, and I said, 'What letter are you talking about?' It was a letter that I'd gotten from a friend of mine in the summer of '87, when Molly was two. A friend of mine who died from AIDS, a good friend but not an intimate friend—that was about the last time I heard from him. I have no idea what was in it [that would cause Mike to become upset], but it was making Mike ballistic.

"He's screaming 'You're a slut!' and I said, 'No I'm not,' and he said, 'Yes you are! You're a whore and I'm going to tell everyone that's who you are! I'm going to tell your kids! All these years everybody has blamed me because we're not married and really it was your fault! It was all your fault!'

"And I said, 'It was not my fault. Mike, why are you upstairs looking through my stuff?' He whipped out of his seat and jumped on top of me and started beating my head into the door of the car. He was on top of me and he had his hand on the handle of the door, so I couldn't get out. I had a pretty severe case of TMJ [temporomandibular joint disorder, a problem with the jaw], and he had hold of my jaw so hard that I thought he was going to break it. I was like crying to myself, pleading that he wouldn't break my jaw, and he was saying, 'Admit it! Admit it!' And I would not admit to something I did not do. He said, 'I'll make you admit it—I'll kill you!'

"I was able to get his hand off the door, and I ran into the house, into the bathroom. My lip was bleeding and Gabe ran up and followed me, screaming, 'He hit you! He hit you!' And Gabe grabbed a baseball bat. Donovan started crying; Molly was upstairs in the bathtub, she was crying. Sarah had just pulled up in her car, and she came in and asked what was going on, and Gabe said, 'Dad hit Mom!' Sarah starts screaming; Mike comes back in the door and said, "Your mother deserved to be hit—your mother is a whore, your mother is a slut, your mother had an affair when we were married!' And Sarah said, 'So what? What if she did? How long ago was it? Who cares?'

"I'm just thinking to myself—'Kathy, this doesn't make any sense. Don't try to process it—he hit you. All you need to process is that he hit you.' So Sarah said, 'Just leave,' and Mike said, 'This is my house and I won't leave.' And it never occurred to me to call the police. I went upstairs with Molly and Donovan. Gabe sat at the top of the steps guarding me, and Mike sat at the bottom of the steps, and didn't leave until six o'clock in the morning.

"When he left I got our bags together. I took the kids to work with me, and I went to the prosecutor's office and got a restraining order to get him away from me. I looked horrible; I had a black eye. I went to work and put sunglasses on. I had to deliver food to an open house, and when I got there it was gloomy weather and, of course, I looked ridiculous. People kept teasing me and saying, 'Are you hung over? Or did somebody hit you?' And then I would take my glasses off. I see myself as lots of things, and I've seen myself as lots of things, but I've never seen myself as a battered woman, ever."

Kathy says it took seven days for the restraining order to be served on Mike, during which time she and the children stayed with friends. Arrangements were made for Mike to remove his belongings the following week.

Says Kathy: "When I came home from work that Friday he'd taken everything he'd ever brought into this house—and I don't mean just since September but ever. He took the pots and pans, the dishes, the dining-room table. He took the couches, he took the TV. There was nothing here.

"So that night I kept saying to the kids, 'It's okay—we didn't lose our lives. It's just stuff.' And I'm in the kitchen sobbing, telling them that it's stuff, and they shouldn't be upset—and here I am falling apart. So this has been a real hard year, all the way around."

Mike explains the violent episode: "Yeah, I hit her. I was angry, and a lot of that was anger that I had shut aside, and hadn't dealt with because the way I left the first time [via the affair] made me so guilty that I didn't get a chance to get all that anger out. Ten years of anger. I guess that goes back to expressing your feelings sooner. It's like if I'm angry there's going to be some repercussions. . . . In the long run it's 'pay me now or pay me later,' as far as that goes." He says he's currently working through his remaining issues privately.

He has now become engaged to a woman with six children of her own. "I'm looking forward to this," he says. "I'm in love, but with socioeconomic, background-oriented, values-oriented aspects. We talk, we're friends, we can be honest with each other, and we share a lot of common traits that I didn't particularly share with Kathy."

## Parenting

Kathy Wallace is no Murphy Brown. She never intended to raise her children alone. She never had the luxury of hiring a nanny to care for her child while she pursued a fast-track career. Kathy expected to play the traditional role, to raise her children and create a home for a husband of whom she was proud. "That's why it takes two people to make a child," she says, "because a kid needs both parents."

Not a novel idea. A 1992 poll found that "90 percent of all Americans—*and four out of five single mothers*—believe the best family setting for children is a two-parent household headed by a father and a mother." In a *U.S. News & World Report* survey, 71 percent of respondents said it is "very important" for "every child to have his or her father living at home."

Yet many children never see their fathers. It's not like the Wallace family, where the children know the father and periodically see him. Of the children born out of wedlock—30 percent nationwide and 70 percent of black children—many will probably never know who their father is. Thus, one-half of the family vanishes. It is not only the absence of the father but the loss of the brothers, sisters, parents, aunts, and uncles of the father who might someday be helpful to the child.

Divorced families are unusual in an Irish Catholic neighborhood, so the Wallace children found their status difficult to understand. "When Mike and I divorced," Kathy says, "Gabe was 5, Donovan was 2, Katy was 1, and I was pregnant with Molly," Kathy remembers. "So the little ones don't remember him [living there married to their mother]. The two older kids remember that it was just awful—no bullets fired or that kind of thing, but just one sad day, Dad wasn't there.

"I remember sitting on the porch with Sarah," Kathy continues. "She kept saying, 'Tell me why he really left! There's another reason but you're not telling me what it is.' And I said, 'Your dad didn't want to be a grown-up, he didn't want to take care of us, and

I'll tell you that when you're twelve and when you're fifteen and when you're twenty.'

"The kids went with Daddy on the weekends. That was normal for them because that's all they ever knew."

The requirement of discipline, Kathy says, puts her in the position of being the rule enforcer, the "heavy," while Mike's time with the kids tends to be more fun. "There is a part of me that resents it that when they come back from vacation with him, they've had no limits. I have those instances of resentment about being a bad guy. I can think of three times since I've been divorced that I just sobbed myself to sleep being overwhelmed. Mostly, I just try not to think about it at that level, because it's really overwhelming."

Kathy's transition from "involved wife in a traditional family" to "single mother of five" was only possible, she says, because from childhood she was part of the Holy Cross community. It's the source of the values she teaches her children and the point around which her life revolves. Without the security of that friendship network, she'd feel isolated and ungrounded. "That's my family," Kathy says simply. "Those people know me. Those people did not make a right or wrong judgment about me when I got divorced. I do know people who belong to other Catholic churches where they stopped going to church after they divorced because they felt so alienated. That's not been my experience. I was as welcome there when I got divorced as I was when I got married. And those people have supported me through all these years of that transition."

Kathy feels enormously blessed by this "support system" of neighborhood and parish. Her work supervisors give assistance as well, allowing Kathy the necessary flexibility when illness or other unexpected family needs arise. Next-door neighbors Pat and Val have been known to shuffle their schedules, or even leave work early, to help out with the kids. "I do have people I trust if I need them," Kathy says gratefully.

Another of the keys to her success is a determinedly optimistic outlook. Kathy automatically swings to the upside of any situation, without hesitation. When her ex-husband cleared out most of her home, she reassured the kids with "It's just stuff." And she sees the divorce as a vehicle for her emotional growth. She didn't want divorce. It was painful. However, now she seems to be hitting her stride.

I can't think of a better illustration of Kathy's optimism than the following incident. It's the story of a thoughtful neighbor who generously gave Kathy two hundred dollars for Christmas, knowing how cherished that gift would be, and Kathy's equally benevolent attitude toward its loss.

"It was the night of the school play at Holy Cross," she recalls. "I was crawling around the floor in the gym taking pictures, and that's when the money fell out of my pocket. I noticed it missing, so I told Sister Barbara to announce it. But no one turned it in. I was devastated—finally I had two hundred dollars in my hand that wasn't needed for the gas bill. Gabe and Donovan were really, really upset, and I tried to keep myself in check and not get overly upset. I said, 'We didn't lose our lives. I mean, it was two hundred dollars, but Christmas is still going to be Christmas, it doesn't change that. Maybe whoever took it couldn't have Christmas without it. Maybe they did go out and buy their kids something decent for Christmas.

"Gabe said to me, 'How can you believe in God when these kind of things happen?' I don't have any other answer except that I do. I mean, I didn't want to think the thief was our next-door neighbor."

Community, optimism—again and again, these themes resonate. And in listening to Kathy describe her fundamental messages to her kids, I'd say another of her survival principles is *education.* Even with severely limited means, Kathy is committed to ensuring her children a value-based education.

"We live in a neighborhood where I'd bet 44 percent of the population doesn't graduate from high school. I'm certain that's relatively close," she insists. "There are two kinds of people who live in this neighborhood. There are people who live and work here because they don't know there is anything further east of Sherman Drive, and there are people who live here because they've chosen to be here. If my kids want to stay here, I want them to choose to stay here, and not just be here because they have no other choice. Education is a way out. Education gives you all kinds of options. And if they choose to stay here, they stay with the option of leaving."

As I noted earlier, Kathy and I originally met at a gathering of parents whose children received funding from the Educational Choice Charitable Trust. She'd found out about the scholarships from an alert Holy Cross priest who realized that several of his parishioners would qualify. The stipends are based on income, and Kathy has received the grant for three years. This year, with her youngest three enrolled, Kathy pays twenty-four dollars per week. The remainder is paid by the program. The contribution of eight dollars per child is not that much, but the investment is an important indicator of parental commitment.

From that investment, Kathy gains both academic standards and the comfort of her community's parenting *in absentia*. "Katy's class probably has twenty-two or twenty-three kids who've been together since kindergarten," Kathy noted. "It's true of all my kids. Their teachers know them and they know me. They call me, they see me at the grocery store, they see me on the playground. It's much different from Gabe, who's in public school this year. When you call in [and report him sick] you have to use his identification number. It's just really different from calling in and saying, 'This is Kathy. Katy is sick.'

"What I'm paying for is a real high expectation of their behavior. That it's not acceptable that kids fight and call each other names; it's not acceptable that they do nothing. It *is* expected that they excel."

That comment really hits home with me. I believe that teaching children what is right and wrong is essential. Today, the tendency is to blur the difference and contend that children shouldn't be punished or have shame brought upon them. I disagree. Both elements are indispensable to the development of children. How else are they going to learn right from wrong? The only effective response to bad behavior is condemnation from moral authority.

Kathy further motivates her children by setting her own standards of completion. Offering an example of her approach, she says, "I'll tell them: You joined softball. You didn't like the first practice but you can't quit.' That's what I said to Katy and Molly. And they stayed with it and they loved it. But the first practice they were both saying to me, I hate this, I'm not going back tomorrow." Like the De La Rosas, whom we've already met in this book, the Wallaces are big on "finishing." Which is as it should be. Once you undertake a project, you shouldn't quit.

Kathy also maintains an unspoken confidence in her children, and it's pretty clear that they sense it. "They are really fine people and they have lots to offer," she explains. "They have lots to contribute to whatever they choose. They're very insightful and very bright and very good. Whatever they choose to put their energy into will be a good thing. People will learn from them."

## The Wallace Children

### *Sarah*

Sarah, 19, is now the same age Kathy was when she married Mike Wallace. But she is miles away from the serious tasks of marriage and parenthood. She's studying at Ivy Tech, the college where her dad now teaches heating and air-conditioning, mainly because tuition is free for the children of faculty. She's undecided about a career path, admitting, "I change my mind all the time. Right now it's between paralegal, interior decorator, and X-ray technician. I want a nice house and a nice car," she says. "That's all I want. That's all I ask."

Sarah has a nighttime job at JC Penney, where she works for five dollars an hour plus commission selling clothes. She might even take a second job during the off-hours at Cub Food, a store that's open twenty-four hours a day.

Sarah recognizes that raising five children has been difficult for her mother. The two most trying aspects? "Probably the financial part of it, and that Mom can't be everywhere at one time," she says. "She can't help me out and be helping the little kids out, too. And I understand the financial part, because I have bills of my own and I'm stressed about my credit cards." Sarah learned at a young age about the tremendous responsibilities that come with raising a family.

Sarah was 10 at the time of the divorce, so she's gone through the most with her mom. "I realized when Sarah started into puberty that what I said mattered," Kathy notes. "She was asking me a question, and I realized that *I was the one*, that I had better be really clear about how I was answering her about life in general, because it was on me; she didn't ask her dad questions."

Kathy worries about the impact her failed marriage has had on Sarah. "The behavior that I modeled for Sarah and Gabe when they were young was not healthy behavior," she concedes. "I was a miracle worker—'Mom can do everything . . . Dad's not happy so it's Mom's fault.' They never said that but they knew that I took that on. And for the last ten years I've tried to undo that with Sarah. Maybe because she's the oldest, maybe because she represents my ego more than the other kids do, I don't know. But I've tried real hard to work with her to say, 'You cannot take responsibility for somebody else's happiness. It's on them. All you can deal with is your own. You can love someone but you can't change other people.' I did the 'girl thing' when we got married—I said, 'I think he'll get better when we're married. I think he'll be nicer, or be more social or I think he'll change.' I didn't say that out loud but I know that's what I believed. And so that's what I try to say to

Sarah: 'What you see is what you get. This is who this guy is. Love him for the rest of your life, though you may not change anything.'"

Kathy gives Sarah frank advice about relationships. "She's made some pretty bad choices in boyfriends, and I've explained to her that probably no one she brings home will be good enough, period. In terms of her own self-esteem and her own happiness, you have to have a bottom line with people. You have to know yourself well enough to know 'what it is that I will put up with. Is it when somebody lies to me, or when someone is disrespectful to me? Is it when they hit me?' Everyone has a bottom line, and you have to be willing to put your hand up when people cross the line."

I ask where she draws it. "I think the bottom line is disrespect and being controlling. Sarah had a boyfriend in high school who was always really angry at her if she went out with her friends, which is insane when you're 15 years old. What I try to say to her is, 'Try to find somebody who is comfortable with themselves, and then there's no argument.' You get comfortable with yourself, and they get comfortable with themselves, and then there's no game. What I try to say to Sarah is, 'You have good instincts; go with your instincts.'"

Sarah acknowledges that her "attitude toward guys is different" as a result of her parents' divorce. "I wouldn't depend on somebody," she says. "I think it's going to be hard for me to get married, because I don't trust anybody anyway. I guess I've just learned a lot from my mom and dad, because I don't want to just get married and get divorced."

What does Sarah think are good criteria for selecting a mate? "I think I have to have something for myself first. I need to have my own job and my own career, so I don't depend on my husband. [Then] even if it didn't work out, I'd still have something. But I'm not really worried about guys right now. I'm just trying to go to school and work."

Sarah admits that even in her short dating career she's had experiences similar to her mother's. Her "mistake," she says, was "trust. They weren't faithful. It's going to be a long time and very hard for me to trust somebody. But I don't regret any of it because I learned a lot."

She's also learned about the importance of family, and despite the freedom her driver's license offers, she's choosing to heed her mother's plea to stick around the house. "That's another important thing—staying together," Sarah adds, though she still says she hopes to leave the state after college. "I haven't realized that until now. I was gone a lot when I was younger; I always wanted to go be with my friends. Now I realize how much I love my little sisters. My mom tells me how they talk about me all of the time, so I've been home a lot. I guess I feel the same way about my brothers, too, but I feel that my sisters look up to me because they're girls."

Sarah wants to give back some of the support her mom has provided over the years. She'd like to find a career she enjoys that will enable her to "take care of my mom." Taking care of Kathy is something each Wallace child considers important. "I think my mom has done a good job," says Sarah. "We have a better home life than some people with two parents." The comparison shows she's aware that the Wallace kids are beating the odds. They're achieving happiness despite the divorce, but Sarah has no illusions about the magnitude of the struggle.

Her admiration for her mother is reciprocated in full measure. Kathy beams when she tells me that Sarah's graduation from high school was a high point of her life after the divorce. "I cried for a month before and a month after," she says, "because I'd never been able to see that far out. Eleven years ago, I would never have thought I'd see that happen. Not that I was going to die or something, but life was hard, and I couldn't see to when she'd be 18.

"And I beat the odds. She's 19. I'm not a grandmom. There are a whole lot of odds against a daughter with a lot of siblings, growing up without a dad. Her graduation was a big celebration moment."

### *Gabe*

Gabe Wallace is 16. He's an Indianapolis Pacers basketball fan who likes Reggie Miller and Rick Smits, and thinks Hakeem Olajuwon is the best player in the business. He's not talkative and doesn't volunteer a lot of information unless prompted by questions. Like many teenagers, he rarely offers more than a sentence fragment.

Gabe is fairly competent on the computer his dad bought for the family, though he's annoyed that his dad recently removed the printer. A typical Saturday finds the teen sleeping till midday, watching some afternoon TV, and then heading down to the park for his usual "three or four hours" of basketball.

He recently began attending Arsenal Technical High School, a public school, after nine years at the parochial school. Says his mom, "It was like taking him to day care for the first time. I mean, he was absolutely overwhelmed on that first day—by the *number* of people, first of all. I've never sent my kids to IPS [Indianapolis Public Schools] before [as opposed to private parochial schools, which entail a cost], and I hate the idea of money being a value indicator. . . . But at IPS they're not concerned about environment, they're concerned about maintaining numbers. [When] that is the important thing, they [don't] necessarily focus on making sure the kids have homework or that the classrooms aren't too full. They just route them through like cattle."

Gabe says, "The kids are real rowdy and it's kind of hard to learn because of the anarchy." What about the teachers? I ask. "There's not much they can do normally," he responds. "It's like a messed-up school. I mean, it's a good teaching school but they just can't keep things under control most of the time. It's not a violent school—maybe sometimes, but I don't think they'd beat up the teacher." He hasn't seen any guns on campus.

It's interesting that even this young man, who is not academically oriented, bemoans the lack of discipline at school. Essentially, he's saying that unless there's order, kids can't learn. And from my travels, I know that what's going on in the Indianapolis public schools is going on in too many others. Lack of authority within the institutions themselves has diminished the amount of knowledge kids are able to absorb.

Kathy's disdain for the "herds" at public schools undoubtedly reminds the children of her strong belief in education. Even so, lighting a fire under her youngsters is a task she confronts every day. At present, Gabe aspires to folllow his dad's career in heating and air-conditioning, though he admits, "I'm not inspired or nothing. I don't have any goals right now. I'm only 16. When I get in college, I'll think about it."

Gabe sees his dad every other weekend and enjoys playing golf with him. He's not worried about the divorce's reverberations. He doesn't think being brought up by a single mom has had any negative impact on him or his siblings, and he says his family is no different from those with both parents at home. He denies that the divorce has influenced his view of marriage, shrugging, "It just didn't work out." Meanwhile, he doesn't like to talk with his dad about the family split. Subject closed. "I love him," Gabe concludes. "I don't like what he did. He divorced my mom but I still love him."

Gabe was unhappy when his dad moved into the attic "because I thought of *myself* as being the dad, because I took care of things sometimes. And then he came back and he took that away from me. I had liked it the way it was." Gabe's self-appointed role seems to be that of guardian of stability.

He doesn't foresee much change in his own future, that's for sure. He expects his mom to give him their house on Arsenal Street when he turns 18, and he plans to reside there permanently. "I like this neighborhood since I've been here so long," he comments. "Everything I've got is in this neighborhood, so I don't want to leave." Kathy humors her son's wish for her to relinquish the house to him, remarking with a knowing nod, "Yeah, Gabe says that.

"I love Gabe. He's very hands-on. He's 'yeah, yeah' about daily schoolwork," she says, waving her hands dismissively. "But the big projects—he loves that kind of thing. Technical school would be very good for him in that way," says Kathy.

To "get that diploma" is a top value hammered into him by his mother, Gabe reports. "Keep clothes on your back and food on your table," he summarizes. "Get an education because that's important." Good lessons. Good values.

Gabe is a solid kid who engages in the usual teenage activities and has even assumed some adult responsibilities. But along the way, he provided his mother with her "worst moment" as a single parent. The night and aftermath of Gabe's arrest is something Kathy recalls in chilling detail.

"He'd gone to an eighth-grade party on a Friday night," she remembers. "He was supposed to get a ride home with his friend's mother. Instead, two kids from the neighborhood said, 'Do you want a ride home?' He got in the car with them. They got pulled over for a traffic violation. They had a gun in the car.

"Everybody was sent to jail. By one o'clock in the morning, I'd called everyone I knew to try and find him—from ten minutes to eleven on out. I got a phone call from the juvenile center saying, 'We have him and you can't get him.' Not only were they giving real sketchy details about why he was arrested but they were telling me I couldn't get him until Monday. That was my worst time. And all weekend I couldn't get ahold of Mike; he was out of town. I was walking around the house practicing how I was going to tell Mike that this happened."

When Mike did arrive, Kathy says he treated the situation matter-of-factly, but she was near hysteria. "The court case continued for four and a half months," Kathy recalls, still emotional. "Gabe was on home arrest all that time. If you're on home arrest, they put something on your telephone like a monitoring system and if you get—I don't know—ninety feet away from the house, the alarm goes off. I had to give them a schedule—'Gabe leaves for school at five minutes to eight o'clock; he gets home at five minutes after three o'clock.' One time, Gabe locked his keys in the house and he had to break a window to get in, because I was so afraid they'd come and arrest him. They'd made it clear to me that if the alarm goes off and you're not where you're supposed to be, they would arrest him."

It was another worry added to Kathy's already burdensome load. Her son was in the classic "wrong place at the wrong time," and the entire family, most of all Kathy, suffered for it. The police handled the matter in a serious and efficient way. Better an innocent teenager is scared than kids learn they can get away with flouting the law. I'd guess Gabe will be a lot more careful about people with whom he associates, even for a quick ride home.

In this, Gabe reminds us of an important lesson: *associations matter.* Sure, he was just entering a car for a ride home, but hanging around the wrong crowd can have enormous repercussions. Kids—*and* adults—may be determined not to follow bad examples. But *anyone's* resolve can weaken the more he or she is exposed to a group where bad behavior is the norm.

The "just say no to drugs" idea is great. It lets at-risk kids know they can make choices apart from their friends. In the same way, children should be encouraged to just say no to certain kinds of friendships. It may take heroic efforts to oppose the only friendship network nearby, and not many kids may be able to do it. But a campaign in homes and schools to *talk* about it and reinforce the importance of high standards would only help the situation. While it is wrong to be too judgmental, it's even worse to refuse to make a judgment about anything. If we do *not* judge, if we don't evaluate, then no action is better or worse than another. And surely that is not a mind-set we want to instill in the next generation.

As it turned out, Gabe's case was dismissed. "We had a big party," Kathy recalls. "It had affected our whole life. And I said to the kids, 'You know, there are some records in a family that are not meant to be broken. Gabe had the most stitches in our house growing up, and nobody needs to break that record. Nobody needs to break this record either."

Kathy, Gabe says, "does a great job" as a mother, and one reason is that she's seldom out of touch with the location and activities of each of her children, especially the mobile teenagers. "Not that I sneak around or that I have to know everything that they do," Kathy notes, "but when Gabe says 'I'm going to Ryan's,' I know they're either playing cards or listening to music or playing basketball. I know that if he's at Chris's house they're eating, because Chris's mom is an excellent cook."

Gabe sees this as another example of his family "caring about each other." They "try to" eat dinner together every night about six, when they talk about "the schedule." Dinner allows the family to live that caretaking theme. "We help her," Gabe says. "My mom only has one job and has to support five kids. She does a lot of work and we try to help her out." Indeed, they do.

### *Donovan*

Donovan Wallace is 13 and in eighth grade at Holy Cross School. He's looking forward to Broad Ripple High School next year. Donovan's dreams are not academic or even of making his future in Indiana. He dreams of Florida where there's "nice weather and beaches. Out here, there's corn and streets and just nothing else to do," he complains.

We talk about sports—he's up on the players and the teams, but that's no surprise. He thinks sports professionals are overpaid. I commented that a $2 million player ought to be good. "I'd play for ten dollars," Donovan replied. "Why would you get paid to play something that you like?" In fact, Donovan even enjoyed the sore muscles he earned at summer camp this year in a strenuous endeavor called "Ironman."

Donovan is comfortable with his home but dissatisfied with it all the same. "It's not the best place I'd like to be. I mean, it's a nice neighborhood but it's just too cold, especially in the winter."

As the conversation continues, Donovan reveals the discomfort of growing up in the city. "There's a lot of violence," he admits. "Like I walk down the street and all of sudden this [man in a] car whips around the corner, asking me if I've seen this little guy in this orange shirt walking around. It sounds like he's angry and just wants to kill him or something."

He says it's especially risky outdoors after 9:00 P.M. near his home, and marvels that in his friends' new neighborhood on the north side, "You can walk outside at ten o'clock and there's nothing to be afraid of." At every hour, Donovan feels it's unsafe on the street where he lives. "I won't go to the store," he says. "Somebody might beat me up—because I'm wearing the same shirt they are or I'm wearing a color they don't like." His self-defense tactic? "Run! Tons of times I've had to run."

Donovan wants to be his own boss. In fact, he wishes he could just skip high school and get into the job market. No college decision yet, though: He's considering Ball State but will probably attend Ivy Tech because, he surmises, "Dad won't pay for anything."

There's been a big change in Donovan's school performance this year. Last year he got five Fs. This year he got Bs and Cs. Why? "I never paid attention in class," he confesses. "I just goofed around all day." The source of his improvement was a conference between his mom and the teacher, which resulted in a contract that Donovan signed and honored. "I wrote a contract saying if I didn't do better I wouldn't get as many privileges as the other kids did," he explains. "And my mom made the difference too. She helped me with my work most of the time."

Here, once again, Kathy's commitment to her children's education comes through. The commitment extends far beyond occasional meetings with teachers. She has taught Donovan to set goals, helps him reach them, and rewards his achievement.

Donovan's main career goal is to make money and be successful. "I want to give some to my mom and my brothers and sisters and some to charity." Though this altruism may appear a bit stretched coming from a 13-year-old, he's sincere in saying it. The virtue of charity for the Wallace children is real, and it is continually reinforced at home and church.

He's got it all figured out. He wants to be a family man, ideally marrying at age 25–30 a woman who is "loving, funny, kind at heart—and with no previous husband." His friend's mom has "lots of sets of husbands," which is a scene he doesn't want any part of. Donovan wants two or three children, "boys, girls—they're all kids," he says cheerfully. He likes babies, who are "just perfect. They cry, they eat, they sleep." But watch out for those toddlers—"They run around, slip and fall, whine, and kind of get on my nerves. But I can get used to that."

Donovan shares his mother's priorities—especially education, which he says will make you a "better person." When it comes to disciplining children, Donovan answers, "I'd never say to smack a child. That would give them the idea they could hurt somebody. Talk to them in a firm voice. Very firm." He always responds to a strong reprimand. But when asked about how to reach kids for whom harsh words don't work, he's stumped.

When asked, Donovan speaks freely of the other advice he'd give parents. "The first thing I'd say would be don't cuss around your kids," he says. Donovan has one friend who hears so much swearing at home that "his first word was a cuss word." Donovan tries to be a positive influence, modeling clean language and pointing out how much he objects to crudeness. Most 13-year-old boys love shocking adults. But Donovan doesn't. This is contrary to Hollywood's portrayal of a public that readily accepts profanity.

A second wise recommendation from Donovan is, "Don't let children watch too much TV." He allows that he used to watch too much "when I was littler" and says it had a negative effect. "I sat in front of the TV all day, even in the summer," he reflects. He finally broke free via a new bicycle, which allowed him access to the larger world, and now watches television only occasionally.

Again the lesson from our families is that television should be taken in small doses. And the criticism doesn't always focus on sex and violence. Donovan, for example, uses his own vernacular, but his essential point is: Look at the opportunity cost. You could be doing something else more broadening. Of course there is too much sex and violence on television. But a greater problem is simply too much TV.

The average American spends twenty-eight passive hours per week in a near-sleep state in front of ever larger and more engulfing screens. "The FCC estimated that 'children's unsupervised viewing ranges from 40 to 222 minutes each day,'" write Barbara Hattemer and H. Robert Showers in their 1993 book *[Don't] Touch That Dial*. "'In certain age groups the amount of unsupervised viewing may average as much as six hours a day or more.' This makes parental supervision a source of frustration for all parents and a task beyond the capability of the 9.4 million single parents."*

Another point that we often overlook is that a person staring at the tube is *not* interacting with others, building a marriage, tending to the emotional needs of children, or supporting friends. To the contrary, television is a destroyer of intimacy and a distancer from children. One way to accommodate the existence of television in our society and yet help families bond is the idea of circling worthwhile programs on the TV schedule that comes with Sunday's newspaper. Let each family member choose one. Try posting your selections and stick to the plan.

Here's another of Donovan's sage warnings for parents: "Don't spoil your kids. Don't give them too many things." He goes on: "I mean, give them the things they need and maybe a few things they want, but not everything they want." Remember, Donovan's mother watches every penny and recently took out a mortgage on the home that originally cost her $2,000 so she could repair its leaking roof. You'd think a boy in those circumstances would love to be able to get anything he wanted. Instead he believes parents should hold back.

Finally, Donovan believes in acceptance. "Don't *judge* who your

*Barbara Hattemer and H. Robert Showers, *[Don't] Touch That Dial* (Lafayette, La.: Huntington House Publishers, 1993), 23.

children's friends are. I mean, when you're just being formed in your mom's stomach, they can't picture who you are or pick the perfect baby. It's like that," he says. "You can't pick who your kids' friends are. Because they would be miserable."

But what if a parent sees that the friends are a bad influence? "They could say, 'Stay away from those people,'" Donovan says, "and that's pretty much all they can do. They can't stop you from seeing those kids really." True. But parents can and should keep tabs on their children's friendships. After all, Gabe's arrest was due to his hanging around with the wrong crowd.

### *Katy*

Katelin Wallace, universally called "Katy," is entering the seventh grade at Holy Cross School. On my second interview with the Wallace family, I join the family in celebrating her twelfth birthday. I watch her open two presents: a Cranberries CD from neighbors and longtime friends Pat and Val, and a video of the movie *Maverick*. Katy loves the last scene, where Maverick leaves the four cards on the table, draws one, but never looks at it. Of course, the one card turns out to be the ace of spades for a royal flush. Katy likes that cool confidence. She's even got a bit of it herself.

We enjoy Kathy's homemade cake with two kinds of ice cream, and Katy shows off the new bike her dad has given her. When I ask her to describe her personality, Katy responds easily: "Smart, artistic, creative, intelligent, beautiful." She's also athletic; volleyball is her best game, and she looks forward this year to learning how to "set" and continuing to spike the ball. She holds her own in a three-way conversation with Gabe about basketball, not too shy to make her opinion known. ("I knew that the Rockets would beat the Magic," she said, referring to Houston's four-game sweep over Orlando for the 1995 NBA title.)

Talking with Katy gives one a good feel for her mom's success as a parent. Katy is a happy child who says she's good "89 percent of the time." While her favorite subject in school is math, she says she wants a career writing "just stories." She looks forward to marriage at her ideal age of "about 27 or 28," which gives her enough time to accomplish the goals of "finishing high school and college and getting a job." College has always been in her plan, she says, "so I could be smart and be prepared when I have kids." She'd like to have three: two boys and a girl, with a husband who's "smart, takes responsibility for his actions, and is intelligent." "Takes responsibility for his actions" clearly shows Mom's influence.

She echoes the Wallace watchwords. Asked the "most important thing your mother has taught you," she answers without pause, "Don't forget where you come from." Then she adds, "Our home. Don't forget about where we came from. This is the only place."

I notice an interesting difference in the way Katy and her mom mean this family phrase. Rather than the humility Kathy implies with that line, Katy sees it as a reassurance of security. For Kathy, remembering "where you came from" means not judging others, recognizing her own modest roots, and therefore viewing everyone with equal respect. For Katy, however, "remembering where you came from" means staying emotionally tied to the embrace of the family.

Katy is quick to include "not judging others" in her list of most repeated admonitions. While hoping for higher education, she stresses that she's "not trying to judge people or anything but they [educated people] will have a better chance than most."

A third lesson Katy says Mom emphasizes is "common sense," defined as: "When people ask me to do something and I don't think it's good, then I won't do it." An example of the kind of actions she'd resist is "throwing rocks at a car. I won't do it." She notices that other kids at school misbehave and thinks the best way for a parent to discipline an unruly child is to "ground them." Her mom does it to her, Katy says, and it works: "I know I'm not supposed to do it again."

With the consistency of the same house, a stable community,

and a reliable routine, Katy says she hasn't suffered from growing up in a single-parent home. She was 2 when her parents split up but says she's "still mad" at her dad for leaving. Katy concedes that it's probably preferable for a family to have both parents home, but "I like it better with just the one."

After all, Katy thinks her mom's doing "a great job" raising her. She can't come up with a thing Kathy could do better and considers it the children's job to "look after our mom." Katy defines the family as "loving, caring—and not *all* the time sharing, but . . ." The advice she'd give parents is to simply "love your kids as much as you love yourself. Everybody should love their kids." Katy smiles self-consciously. She knows how loved she is.

## *Molly*

Molly, now 10, wasn't born when Kathy and Mike Wallace separated. Like her closest two siblings, she has no recollection of ever living in a two-parent home. That means no wrenching memories of a family torn in two directions. She's relatively unscarred, but far from untouched by the divorce. She sees her dad on a schedule of every other weekend and occasionally accompanies him on out-of-state visits to her aunt and uncle in Texas or her grandmother in Missouri.

She's the youngest and the most shy of the group. Heading her list of favorite activities is "spending time with my mom" baking cookies or cake, or helping her with work "like if she had to unpack some envelopes, and sometimes when she works [rehabbing] at a house, I would go work with her."

Molly has the cuteness most 10-year-old girls exude. She's happy at Holy Cross School, where she's entering fifth grade. She has special fondness for the teachers. "They're nice to you, and like if you fall or something they give you a Band-Aid. If you're sick they call your mom to come and pick you up." She likes baseball (her position is third base), swimming, and art, and in school enjoyed creating a journal so much that she aspires to be a writer. On her own, she writes "stuff about what I've been doing in school, and stuff I've been doing at home." Then again, she might become an artist, following up on a love of watercolors.

As typical as all this sounds, Molly says she's from an "unusual" family. The usual kind, she says, has both "a husband and a wife, not just a wife or not just a husband." In her mind, the usual kind is home together in the evening, "not just to eat dinner, but to have talks and stuff." The key difference is "being separated. I get to spend most of my time with my mom" (with the phrase "get to" showing her preference). And "usual" families have more money as well.

Molly says she lives in a "peaceful" home—it's the fighting she's seen at another homes on the street that makes her want to move to a different neighborhood. Not necessarily to another city—she can't think of anyplace better—but there on Arsenal Avenue "I don't really like it because it's a bad neighborhood." Molly's job in the family, she says, is to "watch over my mom. Like if she doesn't come home early then I like call her and ask what's wrong and she'll say she has a meeting or something." Aside from mother duty, Molly doesn't have any regular household chores, she reports, though "sometimes I do the cleaning and sometimes everybody else does."

Of course, Molly *can* mention a few things that frustrate her mother. Her foibles: "A room that's messy then she tells us to clean it and we clean it and then it gets dirty again and then we have to clean it over and over again." Then there's the popular bath hassle: "If she tells me to take a bath I never do it, and then I tell her I'll take one in the morning—and I never do. And I take one that night, and then whenever she tells me to take a bath in the morning I say, 'I took a bath last night!' And it gets confused."

But Molly knows when Mom really means business. Her one piece of advice to other children is "listen to your parents." Children who don't, she says, should be subject to "getting in trouble," which means in her case that Mom "just yells at us and then when you do it right, then she would yell at another thing and we would do it right, until we get all of them right."

Molly's advice to parents is more sobering: "Not to beat on your children, not to just care about your work—but to take care of your kids." This interview takes place a couple of months after Kathy was abused by her former husband. It's clearly something prominent in the children's mind. Molly has spoken to her mom and Sarah about the incident. "They said that Dad is sorry and that he didn't really mean to do it, but I didn't listen." In other words, Molly thinks he *did* mean it.

Even when she's talking about her future, the issue comes up. She hopes to marry, between the ages of 18 and 21, "somebody a little bit older than me. Somebody who has a good job and doesn't sleep at home and be lazy. Somebody who doesn't beat on people." She continues, "A very caring husband who doesn't just care for you but if you have kids, they care for the kids."

The main goal for families, Molly says, should be "to have a home. Just to have somebody that cares for you. Somebody that you love."

Kathy has high hopes for her children. "If I could have my way," she says, "they'd all go through college, and they'd all be able to live on campus someplace so that they had that little experience away from me that was kind of controlled." Her greatest fear is that "they'll feel stuck. That they won't see the possibilities for themselves. That they won't push themselves to try something new."

She's obviously done something right but declares, "I don't have any secrets. I got up out of bed every day, and every day I said to myself, 'I have a prior commitment to my kids and nothing will take that place.' I have people who say to me, 'You're stupid. You'll just die when your kids leave.' I *will* be one of those parents who has that anxiety when their kids leave home. But I don't want them to feel like they were second.

"The decisions that I've made, even in regard to myself, have been based on what is the best thing for all of us, not necessarily what is the most convenient thing for me. That's the first thing you give up when you decide to have children, or I think at least it's supposed to be. You give up a part of yourself that says I want things *my* way. When you have kids, it starts being about them."

Kathy's had a tough time being Supermom. "When the water heater blows up, I guess you learn how to install them," she sighs. "Life is hard sometimes but, you know, it's mine, my life, and I wouldn't trade what I have for anything." She really loves her children. They *are* her life.

"I do [love them], I do," Kathy replies. "They're the best thing I ever did."

### *Culture and Other Influences*

By this point it's easy to list the major external influences on the Wallace family: media, church, and community.

They're not heavy media consumers. Not much TV ("a few hours a night," says Donovan; Gabe has his Sunday small-screen zone-out; other than that, the kids say they watch "a little"). None of them goes for MTV.

Kathy is careful about television. "In the evenings if I'm here, I say 'This is not appropriate' if something is on that I think is inappropriate. If it's on the edge of being appropriate, I watch it with them. I don't like bloody movies, I don't like gore, so I have a real low tolerance for anybody wanting to watch that sort of thing."

She doesn't consume much television herself, Kathy says, because "when I watch TV I fall asleep," but overall she thinks its influence on children is "horrible. The commercials—forget [the regular programming]—just the *commercials* teach kids that if they buy something they'll be happy. I think part of growing up is knowing you have everything inside of you. God made the capacity to be happy right here," she says, gesturing at herself. "So to have blond hair or buy a certain kind of jeans—you shouldn't reach outside yourself to look for that kind of stuff. It's real confusing for adolescents who already feel ugly and fat."

And what about the other messages on TV? Kathy's reaction to my Murphy Brown comments is candid. "I'm dead serious—I work with people who are married who had really strong reactions to [the speech]," she began. "They thought it was just horrible." Why? "Because single parents are real and women make all kinds of choices. I personally have been stereotyped as lots of different things; at work I'm stereotyped as a white woman with a lot of kids, and that's okay. If those people don't know me, then the stereotype is what they would think."

I ask Kathy if my comments came across as overly harsh toward single mothers. "Yeah, they did," she answered. "You didn't know me and so you weren't talking about me.

"I'll be honest with you," she continues, "the other part of my response to that whole thing is, if I were 35 and not married and I decided I wanted to have a baby, I probably wouldn't choose to have a baby by myself. I think kids need both the influence of their mother and father. There's a difference in *choosing* to have children and finding yourself caught up in it. I made a conscious decision to file for divorce. I didn't have to do that. I probably would have still been separated ten years later."

Kathy points out that her co-workers' responses had little to do with my actual words. "Your comments were about men being like a side note to parenthood. *Their* response was about how we should all look up to Murphy Brown because she's like a national hero," Kathy says.

"Everybody loves to read those stories about the woman on welfare who went on to get her Ph.D.," she continues. "That's not *real.* Yes, that happens, those stories are pleasant. But single parents, Dan, they don't have million-dollar jobs. They don't have fun when they stay home with their kids. So, I don't like or watch *Murphy Brown* for that reason. Because it has nothing to do with my life."

It's impossible to talk to Kathy about raising her kids without her financial struggle entering the picture. She makes $27,500 a year at her job, and yet it's not enough, restricting the family in terms of what they wear, where they go to school, how they spend their time, and what they eat. A trip to McDonald's is a rare treat, with every penny counted out. For recreation the family plays cards around the dining-room table.

Kathy thinks the television show *Grace Under Fire* is more accurate than *Murphy Brown*. "She's a single parent," Kathy explains. "Her ex-husband is an alcoholic. He sometimes shows up to take the kids and sometimes he doesn't. That's reality in America. I don't think most women are choosing to have a baby and not be married. I just don't believe that.

"People will say to me, 'Oh, don't you think that your kids need to be around a man?' And I'll tell you I used to really worry about that when they were little. I was really concerned—I thought maybe I should go to Big Brothers and make sure. But they *have* a dad. Maybe he wasn't who I wanted him to be, but he's their dad."

Aside from television, the other influential medium for Kathy has been print. Two books in particular have made their mark. Kathy found great comfort in *The Road Less Traveled* by M. Scott Peck, M.D. "I read that book when Sarah was molested and she and I both went to counseling. The therapist gave me that to read at the time. And then I read it again when I got divorced. It was pretty important."

Other books? Kathy thinks. "Well, *Trinity* by Leon Uris. I know it's a fiction book but I think it tells a lot about the history of Ireland. When my mom died I was at an age that I didn't want to hear what she was saying. But I wish I'd asked her a thousand more questions about who she was. I'm 100 percent Irish. My parents came from two very different kinds of families. Both emigrated to this country. And I think reading that book and reading about Irish culture has explained to me about who my parents were in ways I could never have known. Probably asking them I wouldn't have gotten that information. But reading that kind of stuff has told me a lot about why they had such funny quirks about such odd things. Why some things were so important to them.

"For my dad, it was owning property. And now I understand—they couldn't own anything back in the old country. The Protestants owned it all. The Catholics couldn't own land. That was the most important thing in the world to my dad. For my mom, it was to eat. My mom was very tiny. She was like four foot eleven and ninety-five pounds maybe. But it was to eat, because they were so hungry in the old country. So for them it was to fix a big feast and to eat it. That was the most important thing in my family. Those are my favorite books. I always return to reading them."

Music is another part of Kathy's life, both listening to it ("Any kind. Rock 'n' roll, classical is okay, not my favorite") and making it. "A group of people I grew up with get together once a month. We have a basement band. It's not a serious thing." Kathy sings and admits the ensemble sounds pretty good. "We play rock 'n' roll. Not so much Elvis but Rolling Stones, Van Morrison, even Tom Petty and more recent stuff. Whatever anyone suggests that we sing. People just sing and laugh and have a great time. That's one of the things I do to relax." Even the kids tag along sometimes and hate to miss it when they can't. "That's my funnest thing," Kathy says, smiling.

For recreation she also loves to sew and to continue making improvements to her home. She enjoys the hands-on construction that's a part of her job training volunteers to work with homeowners. "I never would have seen myself doing that kind of thing," she muses, "fixing roofs and building porches. I sometimes think my kids have an unrealistic idea about what moms can do for that reason. My boys will say, 'Mom can do anything.'"

Maintaining foundations is a good summary of Kathy's connection to her neighborhood. She'd be hard-pressed to separate that connection's integral parts—the homes in her neighborhood where she grew up, the focus of her workdays at Eastside Community Investments, Holy Cross Church and School, and friendships.

Her Catholic faith has been especially pivotal in shaping her social calendar, her values, and her children.

"My church is very important to me," Kathy states. "The Catholic Church in general—I just pretend like it doesn't exist. It probably sounds very narrow, but the Catholic Church has taken a turn back. After Vatican II the Church decided they were losing members drastically and it was all because of the impositions the Church made on people to repent, and the guilt thing . . . [They loosened things up but now they're concerned with the trends they're seeing.] So priests are more conservative. The instruction that is given to kids is much more black and white than it has been." Though she feels the church is sometimes "too conservative," she places Holy Cross at the center of her life. She attends mass regularly and wants her children to do likewise, though she admits that doesn't always happen.

"I don't have a big expectation that they always go," Kathy notes. "They're members of that community as well, and they know their absence or presence there has an impact on other people. People wonder how they are. Gabe and Sarah both chose not to be confirmed in the Catholic Church. They didn't feel they were ready to make that commitment, and that was okay."

The most influential people in her life were local heroes, Kathy says. "Jim Byrne. He was the priest at Holy Cross when I was a teenager. He also was a tremendous community leader in this neighborhood back in the seventies. And he just retired on July 1. He taught me how to build a community, and what family was. And to be real honest with you, I don't know who I would be if it hadn't have been for him. My mother had already died, my dad was not present in our life after my mom died. Jim Byrne affirmed in me that I could do whatever I wanted to do. I was the president of the parish council for Holy Cross when I was 19. He affirmed in me that you don't have to be 90 to do this. You have the potential.

"And he always reminded me when I was screaming at my sister, and when she was screaming at me, that we were the two best things that could happen to each other. That we had each other.

And we needed to get beyond 'She's got my pants on.' She's your sister. This is all you've got."

Kathy's other hero is also part of the neighborhood landscape. "John Day," she says without hesitation. "He's the [Democratic] state representative here and he lives six blocks over. Poor boy made good. Grew up in a large family like my kids. Dad left early on. He's just real. He's not my idea of a flashy politician and actually he was not reelected this last year, which nearly killed him. He's a coach at Holy Cross, has coached for twenty years. He still wears the same clothes that he wore twenty years ago. He has four daughters. He's the least pretentious person that I know. He's about thirteen or fourteen years older than I am and I guess he reminds me of who I am too. I guess if I'm not sure about what I'm doing and I talk to him, he helps me keep that balance. That's real important to me too."

Kathy works right down Arsenal Avenue, a two-minute walk from her door. "This is home," she concludes. "I know my neighbors. I know the people who work on—and own the house across—the street. I think my kids have a good perception about life, based on the diversity of people in this neighborhood. They're exposed to some things I don't like. I wish they didn't know that there was a drive-by shooting two weeks ago. Two blocks from here."

No fatalities, but "a woman's arm was shattered," Kathy reports. "The woman is an active part of our neighborhood association. She's been working with the vice squad to deal with the crack house nearby. So that is troubling. I don't ever want my kids to have to understand that kind of thing. I wish that they didn't see people who couldn't take care of themselves. But that is reality too, you know, and I just assume that when they're adults they won't be shocked by that sort of thing."

Kathy's story is inspirational, and her children the best indicator of her success. What would she wish for now? "That everything doesn't have to be a battle," she responds. "I guess that's my goal. That everything doesn't have to be such a struggle. That paying the bills at the end of the month doesn't turn out to be so awful—that I could pay the bills every month and that when a kid comes home and says, 'My shoe ripped,' I can say, 'We'll go out and buy shoes,' instead of 'Your shoes aren't on the budget until next month.'"

For her kids, the goal is a sense of home. "I just hope that they do find a way to find some extended family for themselves, you know? A place where they're accepted. And that might be someplace . . . I'm not guessing where—as long as it's somewhere, I think that's good."

## Making It Work: Lessons from the Wallace Family

Kathy Wallace's messages to her children grow out of her desire to provide them with a sense of security and place that can carry them through an upbringing with only one parent constantly on the scene. As a single parent, Kathy relies on her church community to provide extended family, and it works well. The Wallace children are firmly rooted in their neighborhood. "Remember where you came from" is a reassuring call home to the values of their mother and the comfort of Arsenal Avenue. Their parents' marriage may have dissolved, but their home has remained a safe and comforting place.

Kathy's *optimistic attitude* toward marriage and family has been a critical factor. Though Kathy experienced divorce, she did not foresee or want it, and she has done her best—valiantly—to let her children carry the ideal of marriage and look toward a normal family life. All of them are continually benefiting from her powerful example of hard work, enthusiasm, and personal strength.

Kathy is proud of her children and sets high standards for them. "Never judge others but always judge yourself" is a lesson that is regularly reinforced. So, too, is her strong belief in *education* as a ticket to greater security in life. The underlying message is: With an education, you have control of your future. Kathy is up front in saying that education will give her children the ability to choose whether to remain in the neighborhood or to move on if that is their wish.

Son Donovan is a eloquent spokesman for three further values that keep the Wallace family strong: Watch your language, minimize television, and don't spoil the children.

Finally, Kathy's dedication to her children is the driving force in her life. "[E]very day I say to myself, 'I have a prior commitment to my kids and nothing will take that place,'" she summarizes. The commitment is mutual: All of the Wallace kids voice their desire to "take care of Mom." Here's a summary of the techniques that help the Wallace family beat the odds.

- *Appreciate the good, even in the midst of a difficult situation.* Despite the pain of divorce, Kathy considers her children her most worthwhile accomplishment.
- *In a problematic marriage—or even a good one going through a tough moment—look first to your own part in any problem.* No disagreement is 100 percent the fault of merely one partner.
- *Strive to find something positive to bring out of a negative event.* Kathy did this by viewing the divorce as a chance to make changes in her approach to life.
- *Parents: Try to stay together for the sake of the children.* Not in anger or martyrdom—but view your children's happiness as the motivator to really address your problems in order to turn them around. In the case of this family, staying together became impossible. Yet Kathy Wallace still says a strong marriage is a worthwhile goal.
- *Whether living in one or more homes, children do better with consistent discipline.* Parents need to unify rules and back each other up. Kathy resents being the "bad guy" to her kids when her children return from time spent with their dad—"Mr. Fun."

- *Active membership in a community can carry you through life's challenges.* Those with a religious basis are less fragile because they adhere to standards greater than any individual members. Kathy's association with Holy Cross sustained her through the divorce and the trials of motherhood.
- *Cultivate and discuss optimism.* Kathy lost a two-hundred-dollar gift but tried to envision a poorer family using the money for a better Christmas. Emphasizing the positive—that things will turn out fine—helps children gain a sense of well-being.
- *Choose a school—public or private—by investigating its academic and behavioral standards.* And then be a "squeaky wheel" so that expectations for children are defined clearly and evaluated regularly and fairly. Kathy went as far as obtaining privately funded scholarships to allow her children to receive such an education at Holy Cross.
- *Don't tolerate foul language.* It lowers the quality of communication and the character of those who use it.
- *Get to know your children's teachers and the school administrators and staff.* Your children will gain motivation and their teachers will feel more at ease to call you if you make the effort. "This is Kathy, Katy's sick" was the typical approach at Holy Cross. Kathy cherished that, especially compared to Gabe's large public school, where he was a number rather than a name.
- *Reinforce the principle that all change is internally motivated:* "The only person you can change is yourself." This is the essence of Kathy's advice to Sarah in choosing a boyfriend.
- *Know your "bottom lines" in relationships.* In advising Sarah, Kathy says she should pull back when there's disrespect.
- *Kids fear change; strive for consistency.* Gabe sees his role as guardian of stability. He wants to stay in the house where he grew up.

- *The choice of friends matters.* Gabe's ride home from a party with the wrong crowd caused great anguish. If he'd chosen other friends, his family might have been spared the ordeal.
- *Explicit agreements can be motivators for children.* Donovan picked up his sagging grades with a contract drawn up in concert with his mom and teachers. His mom's continued vigilance kept him on track.
- *Limit television.* The Wallace children say they don't watch much TV, and Kathy tries to monitor them when they do.

# 4
# The Burns Family of Hawaii

*"One is never more on trial than*
*in the moment of excessive good fortune."*

—Lewis Wallace [A quotation that Annie Burns finds true.]*

## In Transit

It takes about ten hours of travel time from Indianapolis to Hawaii, but the long trip is always worth it. Especially when the weather turns cold in the Midwest.

In Honolulu I'm met by the Burns family around 10:00 P.M. Hawaii time. I retrieve my luggage and then we're off to their home to spend the night. I'd met Rob and Annie Burns in Los Angeles in September at the home of Diane and Michael Medved. It happened to be the Jewish New Year, Rosh Hashanah, so there were several Jewish families gathered for the celebration. The Burnses, their niece, and I were the only Christians present—which made us feel privileged rather than awkward. It was a pleasant, tradition-rich evening.

Before sitting down to that dinner in September, I spoke at length with the Burnses. Rob Burns is an entrepreneur. With skill and a small amount of seed money, he built up Local Motion, a

*Quotation by Lewis Wallace, found in *500 Things Your Sunday School Teacher Tried to Tell You*, written and compiled by Arlen Price (Nashville, Tenn.: Star Song Publishing Group, 1992), 118. This is one of the books Annie keeps by her bedside.

chain of surf shops with a nationally known logo, which he eventually sold at a multimillion-dollar profit. From childhood backgrounds that included divorce and monetary struggle, he and Annie built a solid marriage and economic success that now makes most material indulgences possible.

Though they're obviously financially secure, the Burnses are quite unpretentious. On this drive to their house in December, I sit in the backseat while Annie takes the wheel and Rob navigates. We begin talking about Hawaii. Rob gives me a quick history lesson, from the overthrow of the queen by sugar barons in 1893 to the recent influx of Japanese money that has had both good and bad consequences for the islands.

Rob, a native of the state, says its people are culturally conservative. Family, faith, and neighborhoods are priorities in their lives. Their politics, however, are more liberal than you'd expect. Rob traces this liberal mind-set to the islands' history of being exploited, first by the mainland sugarcane moguls and now, they believe, by some Japanese. Thus, a strong strain of good old-fashioned populism is part of the Hawaiian makeup.

As I arrive at the Burnses' home shortly before midnight, daughter Jennifer is waiting at the door. So is Annie's mother, Phyllis Murray, who lives with them most of the time. I get big hugs from Phyllis and young Jennifer, which makes me feel like a member of the extended family. Jennifer is especially active this evening, and I'm treated to a gymnastic performance—cartwheels at midnight, room to room, literally bouncing off the walls. It's a great show by a young lady with superb balance and coordination.

After some brief conversation, it's time to get a little sleep. The Burnses' home is having some plumbing difficulties, so I stay at Phyllis's newly constructed home on the windward side of the island. With a five-hour time difference between Hawaii and Indiana, I'm totally awake and out of bed at 4:30 the next morning and begin making phone calls to the mainland.

A couple of hours later, I go downstairs and find Phyllis, the family's early riser, on the back patio. The sunrise and sunset are spectacular in Hawaii. People travel there for the climate, which is almost always perfect. If it rains in one place, just travel a few miles and you'll find the sun.

For breakfast, Phyllis fixes all of us a very mainland dish of fried eggs, bacon, orange juice, and bread. Her coffee is particularly tasty. After the meal, we all take a short walk to the beautiful beach.

## Introductions

Rob Burns met Annie Gunther when she was a junior at Kailua High School. They married a year after her graduation from George Washington University in Washington, D.C., in 1980. Faced with infertility, the couple adopted two daughters, Natalie, 11, and Jennifer, 9. Natalie's education is a major focus of Annie's time and concern, as the fifth-grader works to overcome learning problems of dyslexia and attention deficit disorder.

Since selling his company in 1991, Rob has embarked on several real estate ventures, including the transformation of a classic downtown mansion in Hilo from a low-life haven into a stylish bed-and-breakfast inn. He and Annie also conceptualized and produced—forgoing all profit—the bestselling debut album of the successful music group Hawaiian Style. Though Rob spent most of his life as a political liberal, he says, his experiences as an entrepreneur have caused him to take a somewhat different view of things.

The Hawaiian setting that forms the backdrop for the Burnses' story often comes into prominence as they talk about the daily tasks of marriage, parenthood, and earning a living. Rob and Annie are devoted parents and raise many issues and emotions associated with their daughters, particularly regarding their *adoption* and *learning disabilities*. The Burnses' *extended family*, particularly the presence of Annie's mom Phyllis, also plays an important role in their lives.

Perhaps the most consuming passion for Rob has been creating and building a flourishing business, a venture that depended heavily on careful forethought and determination.

The last of my overall impressions is that the Burnses seem to be an especially thoughtful and philosophical family, well aware of—and articulate about—outside influences. They listen to Rush Limbaugh, for example, and find him informative and challenging. A deep spiritual orientation underpins every action, expressed in a continuously growing *Christian faith* that stabilizes the family through its difficult times. Though Rob and Annie are partners in every aspect of their lives—the business as well as the home—it's clear each has specialized. On issues of parenthood and marriage, Annie's voice is stronger; when their livelihood is the topic, Rob is in charge.

## Marriage

When Annie first met Rob, her mother disapproved of this young man who apparently had no ambition or direction in life.

Their courtship was an on-and-off thing at first, "headed for the falls anyway," Annie says, "because we were both each other's first love, and everybody was saying, 'Oh, you can't just be together, you have to date other people.' So we'd do that. We'd break up all the time to date other people, and we'd just end up hurting each other so bad. And we always got back together."

They even lived together for a couple of years, keeping mum about it to Annie's mother, who, in a new second marriage to an air force general, had followed her husband to Vietnam. "I kept up this ruse for a few years," Annie confesses. "She would have died if she'd thought I was living with him."

On a family reunion one summer in Virginia, where her mother had relocated, Annie experienced a religious awakening. It was the last thing she'd expected or felt open to; previously, she'd even avoided a religiously involved sister to escape her proselytizing. After a summer of church involvement, she returned to Rob feeling guilty about their premarital living arrangement.

"Our relationship was on the rocks before I left," Annie admits, "but when I got off the plane I said, 'I can't sleep with you anymore because I've become a Christian.'" She assumed Rob would "immediately become a Christian and then we'd get married and live happily ever after," she says. "But it didn't happen. He was just kind of blown away by the whole thing." The relationship slowly fizzled, and "though I still loved him," Annie says, "I moved out."

She spent a short time waitressing, attending college, and spending aimless days at the beach until she decided to join her mother in Virginia. Meanwhile, Rob opened his first Local Motion store and did well selling his surfboards, T-shirts, and logo-clad casual wear. The two corresponded intermittently, and during her three years as a dance and elementary education major at George Washington University she considered herself "broken up from Rob."

But when Rob traveled to an Atlantic City trade show, he stopped by to see Annie, and their love was rekindled. "I knew deep in my heart I really loved him," Annie sighs, "and I was still hoping that God would turn him into a Christian so we could be together. I didn't think it would work if he wasn't, because I wanted to share my faith with my mate." By the time he returned to Hawaii, Rob cared enough for her that he "told all his friends that his girlfriend was in the mainland going to college." Frequent love letters further cemented their bond.

Annie was forced to return to Hawaii when her father lost a four-year bout with cancer. After the funeral, "Rob said, 'You have one more year of school. When you're done with that, come back to Hawaii and we'll get married.'" Her love overshadowed her hesitation about his lack of religious commitment, partly because it coincided with a time "I still believed, but I wasn't living real close to my convictions," Annie relates. "They were pretty shaky," she clarifies. "It was my period of what you would call 'backsliding'—because when I came back to Hawaii, I moved in with Rob.'"

Shortly, however, "certain guilt feelings" and "a hunger to be back with the Lord like I had been" inspired her to begin attending church again. And to her surprise, Rob accompanied her. The pastor of their church, Randy Phillips, and his wife, Holly, "were gentle with us," Annie recalls, until eventually, Rob accepted Christ as his personal savior.

At that point, he was 28 and Annie was 25. "We told the pastor we wanted to get married," she continues. "He said, 'You have to go through six months of premarriage counseling.' And we said, 'Well, we can't really do that because we're already living together. We need to get married right away.' So he made an exception for us because he knew our history and how long we'd been together. Because we were close to him, he said we could counsel after we got married. About four months later [in April 1981] we got married here in Hawaii with just our two friends. My mom wanted to have a big family wedding in Virginia, so we got married again in June at my mother's house, with bridesmaids and family members and so forth."

Rob tells his side of the story: "When Annie came back from college, it was time to make a decision," he recalls. "'Either let's get married or let's break up.' Although we had broken up while she was away at college, I felt like eventually we were going to get back together. If someone were to say, 'Honestly, Rob, do you think you'll marry her?' I would have probably said 'Yeah.' Because we got along together, and we loved each other, and although we fought once in a while, I've never felt better with anybody else."

He was also motivated by his own sense of morals. "I loved Annie, and I felt like we were going to get married, and I knew it was the right thing to do. Her mom once told her—and I had to agree that if I were a father I'd say the same thing—'Why buy the cow when you can drink the milk for free?' It just didn't seem right. My heart said I shouldn't be fooling around with somebody and not marry her."

"Rob's an interesting person," Annie muses. "Every goal that he's set for himself, he's accomplished when he said he would. He always said to himself, 'I'm going to get married when I'm 28' . . . Another of his goals was to retire at 40 and he did. Interesting things like that."

One of the remarkable things about Rob Burns is his ambition. His parents didn't encourage him to achieve. He never excelled in school, and he didn't have a mentor or counselor to show him the way. But early on, he laid out his life on a schedule, planning what he wanted to do and sticking to that plan. The result was a greater sense of control over his destiny than if he'd simply focused on the short term.

Rob and Annie's marriage has endured its challenges, and one of them concerned the goal Annie had always had for herself—to be a mother. "I wanted to have kids since I was a little child," she admits. "I played with dolls, almost strangely so, until I was twelve; I just loved my dolls and wanted to be a mother. College was just a thing on the side. Of course, that's a bad thing to say in some circles."

She cites the instance where a college commencement address by then–First Lady Barbara Bush sparked protests—because she'd dropped out of her degree program in order to get married. It's an incident I've always considered particularly unfair and demeaning to women who put family first. "In any event," Annie says unapologetically, "those were *my* goals. Rob and I were married for a year before we discovered that we couldn't have our own children naturally.

"Even though women's lib had come into full throttle in the seventies, I felt like I was in between," she explains. "I was a little bit too old for the full-throttle women's lib, and I was a little bit too young for the *Ozzie and Harriet* thing. But if I had to choose between the two, I wanted to be a housewife. *I wanted to be a wife and a mother.*"

## *Infertility*

Annie describes the sadness of her situation: "After a year, I hadn't gotten pregnant, so we had to start the fertility work-ups. They start with the man because the male is a lot simpler" to test, she says. It was a test that Rob failed. "We think they botched a hernia operation on him when he was little," she ventures, "some sort of natural vasectomy."

Annie was dejected. "I remember I cried a lot, every day for about a month," she recalls pensively. "And prayed and cried, and you know, a certain amount of anger toward God, but mostly just 'what now' kind of thoughts. If we went anywhere where people had children, I just would cry. I'd have to go in the back room and cry, and I remember that if anybody had a new baby at Bible study, I'd just be looking at that baby. I just wanted one so bad, and I wanted to be pregnant. I remember praying. I said, 'God, you've got to do something about my crying. You have to help me deal with this. I can't go the rest of my life crying because I can't have a baby.'

"And I feel that he really answered that prayer because at that point—I quit crying," she remembers. "I still longed for a baby, but I wasn't crying all the time." Then the couple had to face their future. "I've always wanted to be pregnant and to nurse a baby, and so we thought about artificial insemination," Annie says. "I even went so far as to talk to a doctor about that, but I didn't feel peaceful about it, and Rob *really* didn't. I don't know if men ever really do get over having someone else's sperm put into their wives, even if it's a medical procedure. I wonder if they feel like 'It's half hers, but it's not half mine.'" With that door closed to them, the Burnses turned to another option: "And then if you adopt, it's equal."

But even the arrival of their desperately desired child had its marital consequences. Shortly after they adopted their eldest daughter, Natalie, twelve years ago, "I started having one of those identity crises," Annie explains, "where I asked 'What am I?' I'm just a housewife and I don't do anything. I've got this baby. I don't earn a living. He earned all the money, and I felt that since I didn't earn money, I didn't have worth."

### *Meeting Each Other's Needs*

Over the years, each has learned how to meet the psychological needs of the other. The first lesson derived from Annie's boredom. "It was that women's lib cliché, where I didn't feel fulfilled," she says. "I didn't even have a lot of confidence in what I was doing as a mother. And Rob was being kind of chauvinistic. I wanted him to say, 'What a great help you are! What a good wife I have!' and 'I'm glad that you gave up all your studies for me!' I didn't feel validated. I still worked part-time at Rob's stores, because for one thing, I felt like I should. And for another thing, I wanted to. I wanted to be able to have something that was mine, that was a career of sorts, although I didn't get paid for it. So we used to have a lot of fights and power struggles.

"That was the thing: He didn't think I worked as hard as he did because he was at the office twelve hours a day and I would be home all that time. 'Well, what did you do today, then?' He was off earning a living, and giving me all this stuff. 'Why aren't you happy? I give you everything you want!' 'Well, I don't want your money,'" was Annie's response, "'I want your *emotions*. I want you to *talk* to me when you come home. Take away the Volvo, but just give me some time with you. Give me some respect.'

"By the time the second baby came, I began to feel better as a mother," Annie goes on. "I began to feel, 'Well, if you have two kids you can stay at home and it's all right. You don't have to go out to work,' and I felt content being at home. For the most part, I've gotten over thinking that I'm less of a person, that I have less worth because I'm not out saving the world and doing something really important. But that had to come from *me*."

And Rob seems to have come around. "I think he values me a lot more now than he ever did before," Annie comments. "Maybe I've brainwashed him, telling him how hard I work or something. Or maybe he just has come to love me despite the fact that I'm not perfect. To him, I'd be more perfect if I were more like my mother, because she never stops working, and I have a tendency to be lazy."

But she claims the most important lessons she's learned have come from Rob. Annie calls this example a pivotal event: "When I got married to Rob and I began to work at Local Motion, *he fired me because I was a bad employee!*" she exclaims. "And it was an eye-opener because here I was—I thought I was above some of the work he was telling me to do. Now, he wouldn't ask anybody to do anything he wouldn't be willing to do himself. That was just part of who he was—but I didn't know that.

"When Rob hired me for Local Motion, he told me to sweep the parking lot in the morning. And I said to myself, 'I'm not going to sweep the parking lot—I mean, I'm the owner's wife!' I felt like, 'Well, get one of the employees to sweep the parking lot and do the garbage.' I didn't want to do those jobs. I wanted to do the displays and help customers.

"After a couple of days, he told me he didn't want me working there anymore; he didn't like my attitude! It was like a slap in the face to me. He taught me the value of hard work, my husband did, what it meant to work hard and to work long. I learned that from him. So I continued working there, but of course I started to do the garbage and all that. And I didn't complain.

"Another thing I learned from him was that there's always something to do," she adds. "Like I used to get to the point in the business—if nobody was coming into the store, and I had already straightened the racks and done everything I could possibly think of—in my opinion there was nothing more to do. I mean, I was bored.

"And he'd say, 'There's always something to do.' And I'd say, 'But what? I don't see it!' And then he taught me that indeed, there *is* always something to do. If you wiped the rack, go wipe it again. You could *always* find something to do. He taught me that lesson, and at this point I think I could tell an employee that.

"We did go through some tough times," Annie repeats, "and in fact our seventh year of marriage was really bad, we fought a lot. We used to say the D word every once in a while in a fight—the divorce word. But a lot of people from church, Christian books, and pastors counseled us that you just don't use that word, ever. You don't even consider it an option. You just take it out of your vocabulary."

Annie keeps a journal of thoughts and useful quotations and finds that prayerful evaluation of her motives and tactics often reveals the flaws in her own behavior. In particular, she recalls an early problem in her marriage: Rob didn't call her when he traveled.

"We had this big ongoing fight," Annie confesses. "By that time I had two kids and he used to travel a lot for the business. He'd go away to all these trade shows, and it was a lot of work for him. But by the same token, he'd get to talk to people and be 'out there,' and I'd be home with the kids.

"The thing that used to drive me absolutely crazy was that he'd act like a single person when he was away as far as responsibilities of calling home. He *wouldn't call!* He wouldn't let us know where he was staying. He wouldn't call to say, 'I've arrived safely.' He wouldn't call to say, 'How are you?' And it was like a bone of contention in our marriage.

"He tried to put up all these different defenses," she continues, "of 'Well, the time difference,' and 'Well, you know I was busy.' Those were all true, but he could have done it. And it came right down to the fact that it's like spoiled behavior. 'You want to do what you want to do—not because of all these reasons, but because you want to do it and you don't want anybody telling you what to do.'

"And he said, 'Well, yeah, you're right. That *is* what it's all about. If I don't want to call, I don't want to call.' When he was raised, his mom never required him to call or say where he was. Whereas when *I* grew up, if you were five minutes late for dinner, you got in trouble. I talked to him until I was blue in the face about it, and he even agreed that it was the wrong thing to do. But it didn't make him call me; he'd still go on trips and not call me and then I'd get all wild. Finally, if he did call, maybe a week or maybe three or four days into the trip—I'd be so mad I'd be yelling at him. When he finally called, he wished he hadn't."

Annie grew frantic as she watched the problem weaken their relationship. "I'd cry and I'd pray—and that's when I felt God was telling me, 'Look, what he did was wrong, but what *you* did was wrong, too.' Screaming and yelling at him is wrong behavior. I was trying to complain about my *husband's* behavior to God, and I felt like I just kept getting hit with my own." A particular Bible passage, Psalms 37:1–8, jumped out at her: "Fret not yourself because of evildoers. . . . Trust in the Lord and do good; Dwell in the land and cultivate faithfulness. Delight yourself in the Lord, trust also in Him and He will do it. . . . Rest in the Lord and wait patiently for Him. . . . Cease from anger, and forsake wrath; Fret not yourself, it leads only to evildoing."

"I began to pray, 'Okay, God, you be my substance then,'" she says. "'I'm going to rely on you. You convince him to call me, but if he doesn't call me—make it so I'm not upset about it. I don't want to be getting this way. I don't want to be unrighteous about this.' I wanted my marriage to be saved too," she says, "so then I think He made a miracle. It got to where I didn't care if Rob called or not. Rob would go away, and if he didn't call, I wasn't all flipping out. I just came to accept it; I accepted something I couldn't change, because I had tried, by nagging and by every means you could imagine.

"And the interesting thing was"—she lights up—"Rob began to call when he went away on trips! I couldn't have cared if he called or not—but he *did* call! That was a big hurdle we had to get over, and it was kind of a miraculous thing."

"Sometimes talking about a problem can lead to a big argument," Annie notes. "We're still trying to figure that out. We just get so mad, and if we can't get past the anger, we'll go to somebody else. Like a third person we can counsel with." The couple has consulted a therapist twice to work out issues short term, and also counseled with their preacher.

"I would just pray about it," Rob says of divisive issues that came up. "I got to the point where I could let whatever the problem was slide off my back so I could think clearly. Also, I listen to her side of the story, rather than 'yeah, but, you know.' And submit to her, and her needs."

A recent example of how Rob has come to be sensitive to Annie's feelings involves the extravagant party he threw for her fortieth birthday last November. "I'd been feeling depressed about it for about a year," Annie says, "and as my birthday approached, I told Rob not to make a big deal of it." As the event drew closer, Rob admitted to having planned a small get-together, and on that Saturday, Annie did enjoy the festivities in her honor at their home.

Close friends and family had a leisurely meal, then spent some time relaxing around the pool. But then Rob told her to hold on a moment—and one by one, out strode friends from Annie's childhood, some she hadn't seen for as long as thirteen years. She was particularly floored to see friends Rob had imported from Oregon, North Carolina—even Germany. Not only did he arrange the whole surprise, but he paid for their airfare and put them up in their home for a two-week-long celebration of Annie's "Hawaii Four-0." The honoree reports that her negativity over the major birthday quickly evaporated, like the rain in their valley home.

## Parenthood

After my interview with Rob and Annie on Rosh Hashanah, Annie wrote a long and eloquent thank-you note to Diane Medved for her hospitality. Diane was so moved that she asked Annie if its contents could be shared. Written in round script on the pages of a yellow legal pad, it says so much about who Annie is and about the universal uncertainties and hopes of every parent:

> I've been meaning to write and share a few of my feelings about the interview with Vice President Quayle and to thank you again for the dinner—for including us in that special celebration.
>
> I have such a hard time accomplishing anything, really. You know, I think, growing up, I was probably a classic case of an underachiever, and I spend much of my adult life trying to overcome that. . . . Can an underachiever raise children who can achieve? What power, anyway, do parents actually have? Sometimes I feel like I try so hard and fall so, so short because there are just so many darn variables in this game. I mean, I hope my kids turn out OK in spite of me.
>
> When Dan Quayle asked us what we wanted for our children, I think our answer was probably rather unoriginal and uninspiring. I mean, Rob and I are rather simple, uncomplicated people. I may be a deep thinker, but that doesn't necessarily translate into anything tangible (except maybe tears

and a few letters to the editor!) And I guess, for whatever reason, our expectations for our children are not very high? I don't know. I'm such a worrier—I just want them to be "happy" (I hate that word!) and content and not alcoholics or drug addicts. I want them to know that absolute truth exists. I want them to know the God of their (my?) ancestors. I want them to respect authority, be hard workers, persistent, KIND to others.

The rest of the picture—how well educated they may become, what careers they may choose—I just can't worry about. Rob would like to see his children be entrepreneurs but he would be fine with them being UPS truck drivers. I have a kind of wait-and-see attitude, and a "Lord-just-get-us-through-this-day" type attitude. I don't know how much being the youngest of five has to do with the type of person I am, but I'll tell you—this parenting thing is so, so difficult for me. Half the time I don't feel grown up enough to do this, and I feel I do a poor job. I mean I never learned to push—myself or anyone else. . . .

And Diane, my children, especially Natalie [with dyslexia and attention deficit disorder], are extremely challenging. Natalie seems fine on the outside—polite and friendly and together—but I really fear for her. She has a lot of anger and frustration on the inside. Feelings that I can only pray for . . . She has always had a hard time bonding with us, really feeling and being able to even receive our love for her. You do a lot of hugging and kissing in your family, can you imagine how it feels to be constantly pushed away by one of your kids? Not being able to penetrate her armor of confused feelings? Who knows where this came from for Natalie—it must be related to the adoption, yet I know that much is probably her genetic makeup and possibly even the stuff that happens in utero when your birth mother doesn't want you. Very complicated stuff that seems to be coming to the forefront now that she's entering adolescence and beginning to pull away from us.

I see a rough road ahead. I worry about making it through myself! Am I up to this? I know I'm not; God will just have to strap me in to this harness for this rock climb! We may have money, but life is very hard for me. It's so ludicrous to think that money can insulate one from pain, as I know many people think. I know it does give one more options as far as paying for private schools, tutors and therapists, but still, there sure are no guarantees!

Well! I didn't mean to write a book here! But I wanted to talk. . . .

*Love, Annie*

## *Adoption*

Annie's beautiful words describing her hopes—and fears—for her daughters reflect the passion with which she approaches motherhood. Clearly, this is a woman who cherishes her children, which makes it all the more satisfying that her and Rob's adoption efforts were successful.

For the Burnses, it started at a dinner party at the home of friends in 1983. Rob, just 30, had found success with his first Local Motion store and was in the process of moving to larger quarters. Annie, 27, was an employee in the store. They consider it a strange coincidence that right when they'd decided to adopt, friends hosting them for dinner one night "just happened to know an adoption lawyer," Annie relates. "I called her the next day and we filled out some papers."

They were surprised to hear from the attorney just two weeks later. "It was the possibility of a baby with a certain kind of birth defect," Annie says. "She explained what the problems would be, and we didn't think with our age and experience we could handle a first baby with that birth defect." In another two weeks, however, the Burnses' life changed forever.

"I was doing a window display, and I got a call from the lawyer," Annie remembers. "She said, 'Would you be interested in adopting a non-Caucasian baby?' We'd checked that box on our application, saying we'd take any sex, any race—so I said, 'Yes, we would.' I thought she was just asking a general question. And she said, 'Oh, well, good—can you pick her up today at three o'clock?' This was about ten o'clock in the morning! At that point I was kind of stuttering and thinking, 'Rob isn't at the store.' I had to call him at the offices. And so I said, 'Well, can I call you back in ten minutes?'"

The attorney explained that the infant, Japanese-Filipino and one month old, had been in foster care after a previously planned adoption fell through. "When I called Rob, he was just as surprised and puzzled," Annie says. "We didn't know what to do—it was so soon! We'd heard that it would take *years* to get a baby. Here it was a month later, and we were going to have a baby right that very day. We thought, 'What if we don't get another one? What if the attorney thinks we don't want one because we already passed up that earlier birth-defect baby?'

"So I called her back and said yes. She goes, 'Well, you don't *have* to take her. You can go down and look at her and decide if you want her or not.' And that just seemed really weird to go down and look at her like a piece of merchandise and decide. What would make us say no—we don't like the way she looks? So we pretty much decided we'd take her."

Annie continues the story: "So that day at three o'clock we went to a little house where she was being cared for and just picked her up and took her home. And we didn't have anything to care for a baby, because we didn't have any advance notice. We didn't have a crib, or diapers, or food or anything, and actually, it was a strange day. They call it 'Black Wednesday' because the whole island was on a power outage. So you couldn't even go to the store and buy baby formula and diapers. When we picked her up, she came with maybe a six-pack of formula and the lady had a few jammies and diapers for her.

"So then I got on the phone and I called all my girlfriends, and they got together some stuff for us—clothes and a portable crib and that kind of thing. And that's how we got Natalie. After about three years, Natalie started talking about wanting to have a baby brother or sister, and of course, we'd always wanted to have more than one child. Natalie was really talking about it a lot, and she told us she was praying for it. So we said, 'Well, if the Lord wants us to have another one, we'll be able to get another one.' So we went back, but the same lawyer had become a judge and moved to Maui. Her sister had taken over the practice, so we applied with her." They passed up two babies, one because of the proposed terms of adoption.

"Natalie was what they called a 'closed adoption.' Her birth parents weren't married. They didn't want contact and all that, so we didn't meet them; they didn't meet us. We didn't know who they were. But this other one we passed up after Natalie, the girl wanted certain amounts of money. She not only wanted her rent paid—not to say I wouldn't do something like that, but at the time it didn't seem right. It seemed like we were paying her to give us a baby. Not that we were cheap, but actually—we *couldn't* afford the price. Now, it would seem low, because now it's standard to pay ten thousand dollars, but back then [1987] it was too much for us.

"So then the lawyer called again with Jennifer's story. Her birth mother was in the service over here in Hawaii and had become pregnant from a one-night stand. She'd already had three abortions, and she didn't want to have another abortion. She wanted to give birth to this baby, which I'm grateful for. She was pregnant with Jennifer when they called us; she had maybe four more months to go."

As I listen, I sense that Annie feels she was blessed. How fortunate it was that Jennifer's birth mother chose to *have* her baby. With abortion so accessible and so many single mothers keeping their babies, few infants are available to families like the Burnses who not only desperately *want* a child but have the resources and ability to give that child a life full of opportunities.

Natalie is aware that given other circumstances, she might not have been born. "I got here first, and I'm so glad it was in the past back then—not now. Because more babies are getting killed," she says. "I wish I could see my—what are they called?—birth parents. But I just heard recently that this boy was returned to his parents. He was crying, that poor little boy," she says with compassion. "I wonder if I would do that. If I *had* to, I'd probably go there and then run away and come right back," she decides.

The Burnses yearned to be parents, and they eagerly accepted daughters of different races. "We knew the race of Jennifer at the time she was offered," Anne says. "The father was black and the mother white." For Annie and Rob, entering into a mixed-race parenting situation wasn't as awkward as it might have been, given that they'd grown up in a milieu where whites are a minority. "Living in Hawaii, there are so many different races," Annie explains. "Plus, I was raised to believe that there's absolutely no difference in people. It's just the color of the skin."

Like Natalie's, Jennifer's was a closed adoption, although the birth mother "did request that we send her pictures every year," Annie notes. "And we did, up until last year, when we lost touch. Actually, I got to communicate with her by letter. I had a post-office box, and she wrote me a letter and I saved it. She was real glad to have us adopt her baby. And I thanked her a lot for what she did. How can you thank someone for that? You can try, but . . ." Annie's voice trails off as she becomes emotional.

### *Discipline*

Rob and Annie have researched the subject and considered carefully their approach to disciplining their daughters. Still, because of the girls' adoption they have more than the usual fears about following through on their findings. When a child talks back or disobeys, Rob says he'll first talk to her. Next, "I just tell her, 'Hey, go in your room if you do that again.' Or sometimes, if they keep doing it, I'm going to say, 'Look, I'm tired of sending you to your room. You're going to get a spanking next time.' And I mean three hard ones. And that does it."

Annie, admittedly more lenient, responds, "You know how I feel about spanking," she says, showing her concern. "They tell you 'don't spank them' anymore. Give them a time-out. You tell them, 'All right, you sit in that chair for five minutes and take a time-out.' And they'll go over there and they'll cry and they'll just sit there and that punishment will be effective for them. But then you have a kid like Jennifer, who you tell to go to the time-out chair, and she will not sit in it. You have to physically hold her in the chair, and that would be *your* punishment as well. So it got to the point where the spanking was a backup."

Rob nods. "It works. You say that, and her eyes open big."

Annie spends a lot of time ruminating about how best to raise her children, to the point of losing sleep. But Rob says when it comes time to laying down the law, she's a wimp. "She'll worry all night about their education, but when it comes time to do something in the morning, she won't say no, or keep them in line," he explains. "Of course, I'll go to sleep, no problem, but when I get up in the morning: 'You got to do your homework, because, you know, you've got to do it!' I think that's one of the things that we have differences with when we argue—how to motivate. I mean, you've got to expect things from your kids too.

"One thing Annie told me, and I really think it works well," Rob adds, "is when you ask them to do a chore or whatever, it's good if you participate a little bit, because then you're teaching them to help people as well as teaching them to be responsible for their actions."

Annie says she's not a very good enforcer. "I don't get them to do as much as he does, because I don't have as much confidence in my ability to implement what I tell them to do," she says. "I think to myself, 'Now if I'm going to ask them to do this, am I going to be able to *get* them to do it?' And if I decide in that split second that I'm not going to be able to get them to obey me, or I don't want to have to deal with them putting up a fuss and a stink, I just won't ask them to do it. And I think that that's wrong. It's just a cop-out."

"You don't want to take the consequences," Rob summarizes.

The question of how best to motivate remains unanswered for Annie and Rob, because they suspect there's a limit to their influence. "A lot of it is upbringing, but I think more than we ever imagined is inside [the individual himself]." Annie turns to Rob. "I mean, who was motivating *you*? Nobody! Your parents weren't there pushing you on." Rob's mother managed to work two jobs and was seldom home when Rob was growing up. She was separated from his father, who quit a career as a civilian naval engineer a month before his pension was due—to make a statement that he was overpaid all those years—and has since lived in his van, a free spirit.

"She has a good point," Rob acknowledges. "My parents motivated me by 'I didn't want to be like them.'"

### *"There's Nothing Worse Than a Rich Brat"*

And indeed, the self-made millionaire has turned out vastly different from his parents. With wealth, however, comes a raft of child-rearing issues. Annie and Rob agree that a primary lesson they want to teach their children is the value of a dollar. And how to save it. "We knew people who had real successful companies," Annie remarks, "but their companies didn't last more than a year or so because they took high salaries, bought BMWs, and lived the high life. Rob knows how to live the frugal life. Even when the business was making a lot of money, all of it went back into the company to make it run.

"Neither of us was raised with money," she says, "but here all of a sudden we have money to give our children whatever they would want, whatever we could want. What reason do we have to say no? Why *not* buy? I can afford it. If you can't afford it, you have a reason to say no. What are *we* supposed to say? We want to make sure we raise them like they weren't rich. We want them to appreciate the value of what they have."

"Natalie is much more willing and eager to work to earn something because she—I won't say idolizes me, but she does like the things I do," Rob observes. "And I don't spoil them. Nine out of ten times if they ask me for something, I give them nothing. I wouldn't mind giving a little more, but I feel like I'm trying to make a point to them, which I don't think Annie is giving them. Just a few months ago, Annie started to say no, [and their comeback was] 'It's just a *little toy*!' Yeah, it's just a little toy, but it's not the amount of money. Just say no for the sake of them being able to hear the answer 'no.'"

"We need to instill a work ethic and responsibility," Rob declares. "And another thing: Because you're rich, people assume your kids are going to be brats. For example, my sister thinks my kids are brats." Rob has two older sisters. "There's nothing worse than a rich brat. And I tell her, Donna, these kids are not brats. They're not the most perfect, humble kids, but they're far from being what you think they are. And you'd see if you just spent more time with them."

Chores are one tool the Burnses use to teach their children responsibility. They think their daughters should complete them as normal obligations without remuneration, "But by the same token," Annie adds, "there should be some chores above and beyond the call of duty that they could get paid for. Rob and I are negotiating as to what those 'above and beyond' chores should be.

"But one of my character flaws is my inconsistency," she confesses. "So I'll start off and they'll have their chores and they'll do them. Then all of a sudden, I'm busy and they're not doing their chores—and I don't even *remember* their chores!" She shakes her head. "I'm not strict enough, and I'm not rigid enough, or should I say regimented. But I bristle against that. I realize it's important, but I don't want to do the same thing everyday in the same way. But when you have kids, you need to."

Annie says the broader goal is to teach the girls to delay gratification. They've tried to give allowances and encourage saving, but Jennifer "just wants to spend it" and Natalie's learning disability has interfered with this area as well.

### *Natalie's Challenges*

Dealing with Natalie's learning challenges has consumed much of Annie's time, and most of her worry. The 11-year-old suffers from dyslexia, a brain disorder Annie describes as "deficiency of phonemic awareness," where sounds and letters are received jumbled and correct deciphering is difficult (often letters and words are backward or reversed). She also battles attention deficit disorder, another "brain wiring" problem in which behavior is inappropriate and concentration is impaired. An estimated 10 to 15 percent of the population has some sort of learning disability.

"It's been really difficult to justify giving Natalie an allowance because a hundred dollars to her is the same as five dollars," Annie says. "She just hasn't got that concept yet of 'more than,' 'before,' 'after,' 'yesterday,' 'today'—all those concepts are muddled in her thinking. So I've been waiting for her to get to the point where she realizes what money is, what it's worth, that five dollars is more than two dollars. This year, she's just now really beginning to get that. So I'm going to start her on an allowance now. But even *that's* frustrating; she's so irresponsible and disorganized that you can give it to her, and she likes to carry it around, and the next thing you know, she doesn't have it."

Natalie is a beautiful girl with straight black hair that she pulls back into a ponytail. Her skin matches the warm chocolate tone of her sister's. She's very tall and lean, coming close to her mom's height already, and moves with the grace of a natural athlete. Dressed in a polo shirt and shorts, she projects the Hawaiian attitude of casual friendliness. I asked her to tell me "Who is Natalie Burns?" and she describes herself as "a very kind person who cares for other people and considers other people's things. She's a Christian. And she likes to surf, just like the whole family. And she has good taste, the same taste as her dad." What she means by that, she explains, is that she and Rob would select the same color to paint a room, they both like plants, and they're both athletic.

Natalie tells me that currently she wants to be a firefighter, "because it seems interesting to pull out hoses and put out fires." She can't recall previous aspirations, except "maybe a photographer for surfing."

Natalie follows in her adored dad's footprints—on top of a surfboard. She's a good surfer, enjoys softball, biking, and in-line skating, is taking tennis, but really excels in golf. "She's never had a lesson but she can golf," her mom says proudly. "She can sometimes hit the ball a hundred yards."

But Natalie's talent poses a dilemma for her parents: Do you let her spend after-school time on sports and then flunk out of school, or are academic basics like tutoring first priority? It's just one of the ongoing issues the Burnses face with their special daughter. The sports choice is relatively minor, but many other decisions have taken a far greater toll.

Annie was unaware that her daughter had learning problems until Natalie was about 4 years old and in preschool. "I had noticed before that she didn't seem to learn a lot of things at home," she remembers. "She never really liked books all that much, even from a really young age. And when I started putting the magnetic letters up and trying to teach her things, like her alphabet song and what-not, she wasn't learning them. But I didn't know what 'learning disabled' meant."

Once in school, however, Natalie was tested, and Annie was told that though the child had an average IQ, she displayed "soft signs" of a learning disability. "We got all excited about it," Annie recalls. "We wanted to make sure we did whatever it was that you were supposed to do for this situation. They told us about a school in Hawaii called Assets, for kids with learning disabilities, that we might want to look into it for the fall, when Natalie would enter kindergarten." They applied, and even sent her to a summer session there, but they were crestfallen to hear that Natalie was not accepted for fall enrollment because she was "too far behind." There were few alternatives. They tried a second school serving a wide spectrum of problems, but they soon realized that Natalie didn't fit in with the group, which consisted largely of children with emotional handicaps.

Their next stop was a regular private school, but there Natalie fell hopelessly behind. At age 7, children can be definitively diagnosed, and the severity of Natalie's dyslexia was confirmed. This ruled out the mainstream school, and Assets was still unwilling to accept her, so Natalie had no choice but to return to her previous special education school. "Fifty percent of the children were behavior problems and emotional problems," Annie explains. "Natalie had not really been a behavior problem at school, but after three years there, she was beginning to [imitate] the children who *were* behavior problems. You know the whole phenomenon: The school doesn't realize they're doing it, but they think of a kid in a certain light and then that kid lives up to it."

Natalie had already begun receiving intensive tutoring in phonics, and continued with that when she switched to a private Christian school. Though old enough for fifth grade, "She went in third grade," Annie sighs, "and even with tutoring every single day, she couldn't keep up." Natalie then switched to a Catholic school for the learning disabled, remaining in the third grade "because she knows that her skills are so bad she didn't want to be in a classroom situation where she was going to fail and fail and have the other kids notice the gap," Annie says.

But then puberty arrived. "She shot up like a weed," Natalie's mom says. "Third grade was not the place for her. They moved her up in many subjects to fourth grade, but Annie says, "She's on her own time clock; she's outside the norm. Consequently, I'd use the expression that she's been one of these kids who has 'fallen through the cracks.' It's kind of sad."

"We're doing all we can think of," Annie volunteers. "And if we think of something new, we usually try it. I took her to a doctor in New York on Long Island a couple of years ago. He'd been on the *Oprah* show and *Phil Donahue* show. He'd written books about dyslexia. And [he advocated] a regimen of vitamins and certain stimulants. I tried his program for a year, but I didn't notice any great improvement. So I called him up and I said, 'I don't see any progress that I can attribute to anything more than another year having gone by in her life.' He said, 'Well, you need to try her on this other medication instead.' So we did, and it affected her really adversely. It was a stimulant, and it just made her so unhappy and so hyper and so angry and on edge. It was speed. Look how people get when they're on speed! That's how she was, so we took her off of that.

"I haven't had her on any medication since. It's been probably two or three months now," Annie says hopefully. "It's just been her, the school, and the tutor and she's doing a lot better not being on medication at all. At this point, I'm going to try one more thing. I'm going to take her to a doctor in New Orleans, a psycholinguist, an education specialist, who is going to test her and see if she can get a more accurate reading on Natalie's IQ. Up to now, she's scored so low on IQ tests, lower than she functions. If this lady can more accurately access Natalie's abilities, then I think I might be able to get her back into the other school here in Hawaii, which is Assets.

"And if that doesn't work," Annie says wearily, "Rob and I are considering moving, at least for a year. Somewhere else in the country that will have a school that can help her. I feel like since we have the money, if we don't do it, I'll always wonder: 'What if we'd done that?'

"Luckily, Jennifer doesn't have learning disabilities," Annie adds. "She can probably go to any school and fit in. But I do worry a little bit sometimes that so much of our energy goes out toward our older daughter. They say that the one who doesn't get attention will later on have problems because of all the focus on the child who needed it. So we have to be aware of that, and try to give Jennifer as much attention as Natalie."

After this interview took place, Natalie was accepted to study at Assets school. She's now in a fifth/sixth-grade class, enjoying it, fitting in, and showing great improvement. Meanwhile, Annie continues to study her daughter's problems extensively, has joined the Dyslexia Society, and attends conferences and seminars. Natalie has also caught up socially. After years of a hostile attitude, "She's just opened up now," her mother exults. "We had to work and work, and love and love, and pray and pray," Annie begins, "and now—"

"Now she looks you in the eye," concludes her proud dad.

When I ask Natalie to describe what it's like to have dyslexia, she looks at me straight on. "It's like if you're to tell a boy to take off his glasses and read—[in other words, it's] kind of impossible," she says. "Well, you can read, but it's just like reading something in a different language. Over the past month, I've gotten real good."

How? "I have a teacher who has dyslexia," she replies. "She teaches me 'Slingerland.' It's a word process. She finds ways to sound out the word easier."

I ask for an illustration, and Natalie dissects the word *children* into component sounds that she remembers through key associations. Annie adds that the "Slingerland method" has helped Natalie learn to write; her tutor used the "Orton-Gillingham method" to teach her to read. Natalie smiles, laughs, and jokes, and is simply a pleasure to be with. Though her academic challenges continue, her progress is a real tribute to the dedication and perseverance of her parents.

### *Jennifer*

If you want to know 9-year-old Jennifer Burns, don't try to interview her. I did, and I found how an adult's questions bring on "one of those moods." She answers with off-the-wall responses, especially appropriate since that's where she's bouncing. Like a spider, she crawls across the tops of the sofa backs, onto the easy chair, across the coffee table, and around the edges of the room, clearly wanting to do anything but sit still for questions. Here's an example: I ask what makes her family run smoothly, and she replies, "Going to sleep. Doing gymnastics."

"We also go for bike rides. And we take care of our puppy," she says, referring to Jessie, a year-old Jack Russell terrier. Jennifer's in her third year at Our Redeemer Lutheran School, where she is "learning everything about Jesus."

I try to zero in on values from many angles—her advice to parents, how her mom and dad run the family, what she does for the family—and she's off on tangents. For example, her advice to parents is "I'd tell them give me ten thousand dollars."

Asked to describe her mom, she says, "She's very kind and gentle. She's a good mother. And I never hit her or bite her. I only bite my uncle." Okay, I'll let that one pass. . . . And what does your mom like to do? "She likes to watch the news, which is very, very boring." I don't give up. When I ask her what she likes to do, she talks at great length about the colors of each of the Power Rangers. Why? "Because they get into costumes and some of the boys are handsome."

To get to know Jennifer Burns, you have to turn off the tape recorder and spend some time with the family. There is some continuity between her distracted behavior in an interview and the

◀ The De La Rosas—Tony, Carmen, and their middle son, Michael—in their immaculately groomed front yard, where visitors are welcomed by a statue of the Virgin Mary, testimony to the importance of the family's Catholic faith. *(Photo by Diane Medved)*

► Carmen De La Rosa's proudest achievement is her children, whose photos are displayed with their high school graduation tassels in a living-room gallery. *Clockwise:* Denise, Anthony, Michael, and Manuel, who is younger than the rest by eleven years. *(Photo by Diane Medved)*

▲ In 1958, Tony De La Rosa bought his bride, Carmen, this two-bedroom house in East L.A., just a block from her family's homestead. Son-in-law Tony Salazar, daughter Denise, and sons Michael and Manuel are all frequent visitors back home. *(Photo by Dan Quayle)*

► Denise and Tony Salazar, who met while working for the Latino organization La Raza, were the first to thrill her parents with grandchildren. Baby daughter Marina was born in February 1996. *(Photo by Diane Medved)*

The high point of the De La Rosas' lives was seeing their son Anthony walk down the aisle in July 1987. He married Mary Luna just seventeen months after a tragic auto accident left him in a coma the doctors thought was irreversible. *(Photo by James Carbetta)*

▲ Kathy Wallace won a free certificate for this 1986 portrait of her children. *Left to right:* Katy, Sarah, Molly, Gabe, and Donovan. *(Photo by Olan Mills)*

► Donovan Wallace, pictured at age 5 in 1988, eagerly sets out from his Indianapolis home for his first day at Holy Cross school. "Education is a way out," his mom, Kathy, says of their modest background. "Education gives you all kinds of options." *(Photo by Kathy Wallace)*

▲ Facing life as a newly divorced mother of five, Kathy Wallace, holding newborn Molly, is joined by Gabe, Donovan, Katy, and Sarah in this 1985 photo. "I'm just trying to beat the odds. One healthy parent is better than two sick parents," says Kathy. *(Photo by Mildred Wallace)*

▼ Sarah Wallace's 1993 high school graduation was her mom's proudest moment. "I cried for a month before and after," Kathy recalls, "because I had never been able to see that far out." *(Photo by Gabe Wallace)*

► "Never forget where you came from" is the Wallace family motto. Here, Kathy Wallace and her son Donovan, 13, sit in front of their Indianapolis home. She bought the house for $2,000 on the same block where she was born. *(Photo by Diane Medved)*

▼ With Gabe, now 17, off playing basketball, Donovan, 13, Sarah, 19, Molly, 10, Kathy, and Katy Wallace, 13, enjoy one another's company on a typical Sunday together at home. *(Photo by Diane Medved)*

▲The Hawaiian landscape is the beautiful backdrop behind the Burns family. *Left to right:* Natalie, Annie, Jennifer, Rob, and Annie's mom, Phyllis Murray. Father and daughters keep up the surfing sport around which Rob built a business and a lifestyle. *(Photo by Dan Quayle)*

▼ Rob Burns's love of surfing and entrepreneurial instincts led to the creation of Local Motion, a chain of surf and casual apparel shops he sold after fifteen years for several million dollars. *(Photo by Rob Burns)*

▲ Annie Burns stands in front of her mother's home on the beach in Kailua, Hawaii. She and her husband, Rob, helped build and decorate the house. *(Photo by Diane Medved)*

► Natalie and Jennifer Burns pose in 1993 for their mother, an avid photographer. The two girls, both of whom were adopted, are the center of Annie's life. *(Photo by Annie Burns)*

▼ A major reason Rob Burns sold his business and retired at age 40 was to spend more time with his daughters, Jennifer, 8, and Natalie, 11. *(Photo by Annie Burns)*

The Burns family, pictured in their living room, finds wisdom in the Bible. Sundays find them attending their Christian church. *From left:* Jennifer, Rob, Annie, and Natalie enjoy some family time in late 1994. *(Photo by Phyllis Murray)*

John and Caryl Cowden are living their dream as owners of Fort Lewis Lodge, a country inn in the Virginia hills. David, 14, Josh, 9, and Kelly, 11, help their parents entertain guests. *(Photo by Dan Quayle)*

▲ John and Caryl Cowden take time from a busy schedule with daughter Kelly, 11. *(Photo by Diane Medved)*

▼ David and Josh Cowden admire the season's harvest in front of their home in this 1990 photograph. *(Photo by Lee Church)*

▲ The Cowden boys wade knee-deep in the Cowpasture River to show guests the finer points of trout fishing. *(Photo by Diane Medved)*

▼ Cycling the back roads of the 3,200-acre farm is a favorite pastime for lodge guests as well as for the Cowden children, David, Josh, and Kelly. *(Photo by Dan Quayle)*

In the spring John Cowden joins guests hunting turkeys in the forests around Fort Lewis Lodge. *(Photo by Diane Medved)*

▲ "Never disrespect the eldest" is a Burtin family theme. Jackie Burtin, *center,* is pictured with her in-laws, Moise and Irene Burtin, and her parents, Mary Alice and Wallace Stanton. *(Photo by Diane Medved)*

► Continuing her higher education, Jackie Burtin earned her baccalaureate in 1983. Shown with her proud father, Wallace Stanton, she's currently pursuing a master's degree, setting an example of lifelong learning for her children. *(Photo by Dan Burtin)*

▲ Excelling in both athletics and academics, DaToya Burtin also volunteers at a local hospital, tutors cousins, and helps the extended family. Here, she is at her 1990 eighth-grade graduation surrounded by her aunt, Annette Burtin, and her grandmother, Irene Burtin. *(Photo by Dan Burtin)*

▼ Dan and Jackie Burtin believe in giving back to their community. As a Boy Scout leader in the Chicago housing projects, Dan inspired his son, Darnell, to attain the rank of Eagle Scout in 1992. Darnell was the first inner-city youth in Chicago to merit that distinction in twenty years. *(Photo by DaToya Burtin)*

DaToya Burtin, 17, aspires to be a chemical engineer or a political science professor, and studied math applications and archaeology at Oxford University last summer. The family scrimped to afford an academically rigorous school for DaToya and her brother, Darnell. *(Photo by Diane Medved)*

way she flits around the house—activity her cousin Dierdre Haufflaire calls "blowing here and there like the wind." But when Jennifer uses her imagination, it can yield extraordinarily creative results. Sister Natalie says Jennifer "likes to play with toys and imagine they're someone. She'll do that for hours. She uses her imagination really well." Annie tells of her elaborate doll setups, with involved stories and plots. I saw her in another expression of that fertile mind, dressing up in various costumes, one after the other, imagining characters as grand and diverse as a princess and a belly dancer.

Though not an outstanding student, Jennifer is academically solid, keeping up easily and relating well with her peers. She likes reading and hates math.

Jennifer just cut her hair. It makes a big difference in the life of this third-grader, since she hates to sit still. "I used to take hours to comb through her hair," sighs Annie when she recalls the long braid Jennifer formerly wore in her tight, curly hair. But now Jennifer can comb it herself, a big step toward the independence the youngster craves.

She has an impish grin. But when you want to take a family snapshot, she's the one who must be coaxed to smile.

Annie, aware of the need to give equal time to her two daughters, encourages Jennifer to pursue the singing she enjoys, at one point taking her to the Hawaiian Youth Opera Chorus at eight-thirty each Saturday morning. Jennifer likes performing, but the drilling practice and a yearning to spend weekend mornings asleep or at play caused Annie to allow her to drop out after a year's participation.

And Jennifer does receive her share of her parents' worrying. Annie frets that Jennifer is unmotivated and seeks ways to instill initiative and drive. She is concerned, too, about her youngest daughter's immaturity, but she isn't panicking. Rob is more easygoing about Jennifer's pacing. But one thing I see consistently: Annie and Rob are vigilant about their daughters' well-being. These girls will never be lacking for love.

## Influences of Culture

### *Living the American Dream: Rob and Annie's Rise to Success*

As I hear about Rob and Annie's family and the day-to-day implementation of their values, I learn the story of Rob's transformation from an unmotivated "surf bum" to a hardworking executive of an international firm. How did he develop such an entrepreneurial streak?

Rob's lineage, he says, includes both Hawaiian royalty and British nobility. According to genealogical research his mother conducted, in the early nineteenth century Robert Holt, a widower, arrived from England and married the daughter of the chief of Makaha. Before that, family lore claims ancestry as far back as the *Mayflower,* through Priscilla Alden, which was also the maiden name of Rob's maternal grandmother. On his father's side, the family says it has lineage to the poet Robert Burns. When Rob was growing up, however, all this fancy background was still undiscovered and very far from the reality of their modest lifestyle.

His father, Rob says, has always believed that "anything is possible." A naturally talented Annapolis-educated architect who served as a naval engineer and then a civil engineer, he is now living unencumbered out of his van. Despite having received superb schooling, Rob's dad was always disdainful of higher education. "He just didn't feel there was any real value in the learning system," Rob says, shrugging.

Rob points to his mother as the source of his work ethic. She supported the family with two jobs: secretary to a Hawaiian legislator by day and bar server by night. That left the three children, of whom Rob was the youngest, to fend for themselves. "You could do anything you wanted as long as you emptied the rubbish cans and raked the breadfruit leaves," he says.

Without parents who were strong motivators, he assumed he'd

turn out like an uncle, who also had two older sisters. "My uncle was an alcoholic and a hobo," Rob explains. "He went to the mainland and rode trains and whatever street people do. And I kind of felt like maybe someday I was going to be like him. He lived with us off and on over the years and he was real nice to me, and I guess I kind of related to him."

It was an experience with this uncle—and a second uncle who is a producer in Hollywood—that spurred Rob to turn his passion for surfing into a business.

The hobo uncle, after being diagnosed with terminal liver problems, had been passed back and forth between his two older sisters for seven years—but he didn't die. Finally, Rob says, they'd had enough. "It was too much of a strain because he was kind of an oddball character," Rob notes, "so they decided to send him to a VA hospital in Oregon, and for their own peace of mind, they wanted to make sure he at least got there, instead of putting him on a plane and [learning] he'd never gotten past L.A. I'd been chosen to take him." Rob was 23, just about the age he'd always expected to get serious about life. He'd been earning subsistence money shaping surfboards in order to spend the rest of his time Hawaiian canoe paddling, surfing, and playing tennis.

"When we pulled into Oregon, it was raining and really depressing," Rob recalls. "It looked sad, and I was sad. My uncle was, I could tell, contemplating something, you know. I was kind of shaken up. I took him to this old, beat-up VA hospital, which looked like the [asylum in the film *One Flew Over the*] *Cuckoo's Nest*. It was all falling apart."

On his way home, he stopped for a visit with his uncle Alan Burns, producer of *The Mary Tyler Moore Show* and other famous television series, and his aunt, whom he hadn't seen in eleven years. "They live on a one- or two-acre lot, with a pool—*Home and Garden* material," Rob says. "In fact, they've been in *Sunset* magazine. I was shocked," Rob relates. "The contrast was extremely evident. I sat around his pool. I was really sad thinking about my uncle—I knew we weren't going to see him again, that he'd probably die of alcoholism. So I stayed there for a week or so.

"It became apparent to me right off that my relatives were always buying things like shirts and sweaters. I was pretty much a shorts-and-T-shirts-and-slippers [thongs] kind of guy." But at his uncle's house, "Every day, my cousins would come home with a new shirt, or my uncle would. Everything was always new; they were always shopping for clothes. So it just struck me as odd—that people in the mainland *buy a lot of clothes*. I thought that maybe *I'm* odd, and people in Hawaii buy a lot of clothes too.

"I went home and had a dream one night. I woke up at midnight and had a vision of a little surf shop, about twelve by twelve feet, in Kailua, on the second floor of a side street I'd known as a kid. And so I woke up and said, 'We can make a surf shop! We'll make clothing!'"

Eventually Rob found an appropriate place for the shop—not the one he'd seen in his dream, but in a great location. And he borrowed three thousand dollars from his producer uncle, which he paid back from his first profits. To open the store, he "bought literally twenty decals for surfboards, which are only twenty-five cents each," Rob recounts. "And I made five surfboards. I bought three dozen T-shirts, two dozen shorts, and I didn't have much of anything else. I might have ordered some resin or something, but I do remember that my sisters brought in all kinds of plants. They filled the store with plants, and it looked almost like a florist."

The famous Local Motion name and logo were the result of Rob's brainstorming with his sisters. "Both of my sisters and myself have a pretty good eye for art," he says matter-of-factly, and one of his sisters in particular is "phenomenal."

"We sat down and were trying to figure out what we were going to do [regarding a trademark name]," he recalls. "I was a tennis player, a canoe paddler, and a surfer, and they tried to incorporate [those sports themes]. I wanted an action thing, so we started to pursue names that had that type of feel. I was looking in a

Hawaiian dictionary and came up with two names that each had about a thirty-six-hour stint. I wasn't happy with them, so the three of us sat down again. I said, 'It's gotta have action, sports.' And we wanted people here locally to be able to relate to it.

"We started writing down things, and my sister, Val, came up with the words Local Motion about maybe the tenth name, and we went up to about fifty of them. After hours and hours of brainstorming, everything sounded like junk. So I said, 'You know what—Local Motion—that's good enough.' I didn't really think it was that good of a name. It was pretty good, but it wasn't like 'Yes! I got it! We got the magic name!' Okay, good enough, let's go.

More brainstorming resulted in a unique logo that combined the words "Local Motion" with the image of a coconut tree, and within a short time, thanks to Rob's dedication, Local Motion T-shirts, surf paraphernalia, and decals were making their way to the mainland and eventually around the world.

"Hawaii is such a goal or dream for many people all over the world, and when they come here they want to take back a piece of evidence," Rob explains. "[Also, it helped that I was] a local guy from Kailua, a homegrown type of thing. Support him, you know."

By 1991 Rob's reputation for courteous service, penchant for hard work, and knack for picking locations had resulted in a thriving business consisting of seven stores. So when Minami Sports Company, a Japanese firm, made him a terrific offer, he decided to cash in.

Ironically, his astounding success was the very thing signaling him to move on. "Everything was flying," he says, smiling. "The surfing market was a worldwide phenomenon. But I knew it was a cycle, and that the cycle was about ready to come to an end." How did he know? "I always liked Hawaiian print clothing," he explains, "and talking to people, I heard that it was a twenty-year cycle, and it had hit in the sixties. Also, surfing was a look that was accepted worldwide, and I knew that when that happens, the world is going to get tired of it. It's just a phase.

"So I said, 'Look, here we have phenomenal sales. My kids are young. And I always remember when Cassius Clay/ Muhammad Ali kept getting back in the ring—it was sad to see him. He should have quit when he was on top. And I made a little mental note: 'Why not get off when you feel good about it and you're doing well?' I figured if I was right and things went bad, then I'd have to batten the hatches. I never really had any experience in crisis management—and I hate to fire people. I was thinking, 'Gosh, I don't want to do that, and if I sell it, then I'm going to have time with my kids. I'm going to have financial independence.'"

Does Rob's business story have an epilogue?

Yes. Immediately after the sale went through, "The Gulf War hit and a lot of things happened," Rob explains. "The surf market dropped completely. Overnight."

### *Giving, Hawaiian Style*

Annie and Rob both love their island home and with their wealth have tried to give back to the community, particularly with two wildly diverse projects. The first plays into their local connection: the creation and development of the music group Hawaiian Style. When he was still running Local Motion, Rob recognized the potential of some musically talented friends. He first hired them to do some jingles, but "they needed a break, and they needed some direction," he says. "So I came up with an idea where we'd Hawaiian-ize their sound. I gave them some concepts of songs to write, things to write about, and also picked some Hawaiian songs for them to redo with a different sound. And they did; they took it from there. I came up with the name, and directed the graphics on the album cover and financed it. It became a bestselling album and won a lot of awards.

"I didn't do it for the money," he goes on. "I didn't *want* to make any money. The concept was, I was bringing unknown musicians together with known local musicians. Some of them were famous and they were kind of doing me a favor by coming into this group, and these other guys were starving artists, and I thought it would be nice if they made some money. I said, 'Look, I won't make a penny on it. Just give me my money back and then that's it.' So they made a lot of money on it; it was a good seller."

I commend Rob's sense of timing. "Opportunities are in the air," he responds. "If you put yourself in a position where you have to make a decision, you'd be surprised what you can come up with." He says some of his resourcefulness also derives from his father, whom he deems an "efficiency fanatic," always trying to develop new methods that are more practical.

The second project Annie and Rob took on was a bed-and-breakfast called Haili House Inn, in the town of Hilo on the Big Island. On a visit there, the Burnses eyed the 1925 craftsman-style bungalow house, once the Main Street homestead of a Portuguese family, and visualized its potential. "It was deteriorated to the point where it was the worst building in the whole area," Rob recalls, "and it housed the most horrendous group of drunken, alcoholic drug addicts. It was a flophouse, and probably fifteen to thirty drug addicts lived under the house on plywood.

"It was the worst house, and it was a lot of money. It cost $225,000 to rebuild it, and we bought it for $150,000. It was a lot of money for the area, but it was a great thing for the community. We made it into the best building in Hilo. It was a great example of what can be done, what's possible."

The renovation wasn't without its hitches, however. The Burnses wanted to clear out the overgrown greenery but were shocked to encounter resistance. "Somebody came around with a piece of paper and said, 'Don't cut down the trees.' So I wrote on the note, 'You come over here every day and rake, and I won't cut the trees.' Here are these environmentalists telling me what I can and can't do with my property! The trees were in the phone lines and electric lines and dangerous to everybody, not only the people walking down the street. If one of those trees had fallen, the lights in Hilo would have been out, guaranteed. But I told them, 'For every tree I cut, I'll plant thirty.'"

Rob and Annie proceeded to clean up and landscape the yard, restore the house, and add a new staircase and porte-cochere entrance. Annie, with her flair for decorating, brought in much of her collected Hawaiiana and antiques, calling them in from friends to whom they'd made loans. They consider the results "beautiful." And the neighbors were appreciative. "We got a phenomenal response from the community," Rob recounts. "Guys were stopping by saying 'thank you, thank you!' just for getting rid of the tenants, number one. And number two, just for bringing back this house. The old-timers knew the house used to be immaculate."

Then the Burnses had to figure out how to get the business going from afar. Rob recalled the opportunity he was offered in his own youth, and it inspired him. "I brought in this kid, he's 23, which is the age I started," Rob explains, "and I said, 'Look, this is going to be a profit center for you and I. I'm going to give you a salary, and you build this thing up. Once it's making profit, and I get a rent out of it, you can split the profit with me fifty-fifty.'

"There was a lot of incentive for him to get the thing going, and he was a great salesman and a great host, but he wasn't into promoting," Rob says. "[Also] Hilo is a rainy town. There's not much surf and not that many girls. And this kid was from Florida. So six months after he got in, he said, 'I want to leave because there's not enough surf, not enough girls, not enough sun.' He gave me notice and I decided, well, I'm going to try to sell it, because I really don't have any great desire or passion to own a bed and breakfast and run it from over here."

Haili House Inn, with its gold-lettered wooden sign and charming aqua-and-white facade, is now for sale. It stands unoccupied, though the seven guest rooms beckon with their aloha-print bedspreads and patchwork pillows. While it's for sale, Annie and Rob make it available for vacation rental, and occasional visitors luxuriate in its decor and emphasis on detail.

## *On Guard Against Greed*

*And He said to them, "Beware, and be on your guard against every form of greed; for not even when one has an abundance does his life consist of his possessions."*

—Luke 12:15

The above was one of Rob's favorite verses "even before he came into money," says Annie. She and Rob are adamant that they not become attached to the material goods their newfound riches can buy.

They're even more zealous about teaching frugality to their daughters. "I think they need to work," Rob insists. "I think they need to suffer a little bit. If you get spoiled at a young age and get everything you want, good luck to your husband, who's not going to be able to provide it. It's going to put a damper on their marriage and it's going to take away their desire to achieve."

Rob believes strongly in the importance of individual initiative. "Two of the saddest groups of people are the very poor and the very rich," he asserts. "The very poor are usually on the dole and they look to others to give them money. The real rich get money from their parents and they don't earn it. So you have the same sad predicament, but one has a lot of material goods. The wealthy are probably more suicidal, because they have it all."

Rob voices the hopes of every loving father, regardless of income: "I believe in helping our kids develop their own fortune, and I'd love to see them get in business or help as much as I can with them earning it." Then he offers insight to a cost of success: "But at the same time, it's a struggle, because when you're rich, you're damned if you do and damned if you don't. If you *don't* give money, you're a greedy, grumpy, gripy miser. And if *do* you give it, you're not helping them."

### *Extended Family*

Where do Annie and Rob fall on the generosity spectrum? Just ask Annie's mom, Phyllis Murray, who, as Rob's business administrator, has access to that kind of information. "They're givers, is what they are," Phyllis says. Rob and Annie don't publicize it, but they've put one niece through college and a second through both an undergraduate degree and nursing school. "I scold them all the time because they give away so much," Phyllis relates. "But that's their way."

Phyllis is far more than a figurehead for the Burns family. Not only is she the valued administrator of her son-in-law's business, she also sews the children's clothes and never sits still if there's a corner to be swept or dishes in the sink. Trim and active with short gray hair and stylishly casual clothes, she lives with Annie and Rob much of the time in Honolulu, or they stay with her in her Kailua home, which Rob helped construct and Annie decorated. Insisting on frequent "reunions" and stepping in when any of her children might need her, Phyllis is the main reason her family stays close.

Phyllis tells her amazing story in a lilting accent. She was born and raised in Jamaica, the daughter of loving and dedicated missionaries. Her parents met at a church service when her mother was visiting the island on a cough-curing trip during a severe Boston winter. Phyllis had only her parents' model of marriage—"a real love affair"—since she never dated anyone or even attended school. A governess had provided in-home education for her and her six siblings. When Phyllis was 7, her father died, forcing her mother to support the children and several dependent servants by working behind the perfume counter at the local drugstore.

In 1943, when she was 17, Phyllis accepted the by-mail proposal of an American GI she'd met in a Kingston restaurant and knew only slightly. She left her tropical birthplace and was terrified to encounter an unknown substance in her new Boston home: snow. Phyllis taught her own sense of duty and propriety to her five children, of whom Annie is the youngest. Though her marriage to husband Charles Bernard, an "honorable and honest" career military man, grew into deep love, she was forced to eventually leave him after thirty years, when the influence of alcoholism drove him to uncontrollable wife and child abuse. Annie was 7.

Though she'd never worked before, Phyllis, who'd relocated to Hawaii, taught herself Gregg shorthand and, after failing twice, finally passed the civil service exam. "I had to take a job that nobody else wanted, and from there I was able to move on up in my secretarial field," she recalls. "My bosses were all wonderful—all very important people and I had very high clearances. Because of that, when the President and the cabinet came out this way, I was assigned to them. Nixon and Kissinger and Laird—I worked for all of them," she says proudly.

At the time of the separation, she was employed in Washington, D.C., but she quickly sought a transfer to Hawaii, a stop on her husband's air force tour, because it reminded her of her tropical childhood. "I knew it was small and there'd be none of the big temptations," she says. "I always used to say, 'I'd rather be poor in Hawaii than rich anywhere else on earth,'" she chuckles.

Asked the critical values she taught her children, Phyllis answers: "Love one another, unselfishly. When they were little, I never allowed them to not share," she says resolutely. "I used to tell them, 'Nothing is so valuable that it's more important than sharing.' I never had anything I wasn't willing to share," she adds, "because we're leaving it all here. It's not that important. How you feel about each other—that's what counts. And that's always with you. Nobody can take that away from you. That's the chief thing I try to tell them—to love each other and forgive one another." She says she even forgave her first husband, though more than once in an alcoholic daze he had brutally beaten her and their son and abused one of the middle daughters.

"It's not what you *want* [to do], it's what you *ought* [to do]," is a phrase Phyllis was taught as a child. Annie and her siblings carry that with them. "Ask yourself what you ought to do," Phyllis urges, "then the 'want' can come later. That's the ice cream after all the 'oughts' have been taken care of. My mother was full of clichés, but they're all *right*." Two others she mentions are "If you waste, you're going to want," and "Children are to be seen and not heard." We could sit in the parlor, Phyllis says of her childhood. "We could sit at the dining table and eat with them, but don't open your mouth.

"I'm lucky," Phyllis attests. "I raised five children in the sixties, and that was a time when the whole world was falling apart. And it wasn't easy. I had to be really tough. I had to forget about whether my kids liked me or not. I had to just make *them* likable. And that's what I did."

The key to Phyllis's success was her *consistent discipline*. "They didn't *like* the strong discipline," Phyllis admits, "but I'll say this for them, they abided by it." She gives the illustration of the time she was forced to withdraw financial support from her then college-age son who'd flunked out of the University of Hawaii. "I was dying inside," she confides. "He's the only son I had." But she stood firm, telling him, "I will not pay for failure." It took him only three months until he got a job, proved himself to the university so they'd readmit him, and worked his way up to the position of producer of the evening news in Honolulu. He's now married and a father and with his wife has built a home entirely by hand in the wilds of Oregon.

### *Religion*

Religion is clearly the center of the Burnses' family life. All of them see God's hand in their activities and directions. They speak often of their journeys of faith, and none is more moving than the story Annie relates about her late father.

In the years after Phyllis was forced to leave her husband, Annie had harbored anger and fear. "I thought about him rarely, and if I did think about him, I didn't want to be around him," she recalls. "He'd just get drunk. He had visitation, so we had to do things with him on occasion, and we were just very frightened of him." With time, he remarried and mellowed to some extent, becoming "kind of supportive later on in my adult years as a college student," Annie says.

"But then what happened was I went over to his house for dinner one night on one of my obligatory visits with him when I was in college, and after dinner, he told me he had lymphoma cancer and that he was going to die. They told him he had six months to live. I just started crying and I couldn't stop. A well of emotion just poured forth—and he was so upset. He said, 'Oh, I'm so sorry. I didn't want to hurt you. I just thought you should know.'

"I was just flooded with these thoughts—'Here's your father, this man you don't even know is going to be dead, and you don't even like him.' And so at that point I started praying and praying. I mean, I prayed for him before, but then I really started praying for him. And praying for myself and praying for the healing of our relationship.

"And he was really in search of God at that point because he was going to die. So he set about to find God, and he started looking everyplace he could think of. He was attending a Science of Mind kind of church, a lot of positive affirmation kind of stuff. He tried Unity Church for a while, and he went to swamis and he just did everything. So he decided, well, he'd go to church with me, too. And I wanted him to come to church with me. I wanted him to find Jesus.

"And it was interesting because he was such an intellectual. We'd have arguments about the Bible and he'd say to me, 'I just can't believe that you believe in Adam and Eve!' He was so argumentative, and every time I went to his house, he'd want to talk about it. I didn't bring it up. I gave him a book by C. S. Lewis, *Mere Christianity*,* that gave him a lot of food for thought and was one of his turning points. Then I took him to this healing service.

"An evangelist ex-gambler was here from the mainland and giving this revival and healing service, and I was so certain that my

* C. S. Lewis, *Mere Christianity* (New York: Macmillan, 1952).

dad was going to get healed of cancer that night. My expectations were so high. We were sitting in the pews and the man gave a little sermon and then he was talking about, 'If you're sick, come up,' and my dad went up, and he was standing in line. And as the evangelist went up and down the line to each person, he'd say what he thought their sickness was. He'd put his hand on them and say they had headaches, or they had a back problem or this or that. And I was thinking, 'My dad is the sickest one here! When he gets up to my dad, he's really going to have some praying to do because my dad has cancer. He's dying.'

"So he gets up to my dad and says, 'You know, you don't really need a physical healing, you need an emotional healing, and that's what I'm going to pray for for you.' And I was just so disappointed. I was thinking, 'Oh, this man says he's a prophet and he can't even tell that he has the sickest person in this whole church right in front of him!' So he prayed for Daddy.

"I thought that the whole evening was just a sham and that nothing had happened, and it was certainly not what I wanted to happen, and I went away very disappointed. But my dad was just kind of quiet. I mean, he didn't say anything. Come to find out, years later, that was a huge turning point for my dad in the revelation of the God of the Bible to him. Because as he sat in the pew, what he was praying to God for that night was—in fact, he said those exact words to God—'God, I don't really need a physical healing as much as I need a spiritual healing, and an emotional healing.' He had a radical childhood. He had to forgive a lot of people from his childhood. Years later, after he'd died, I found a letter he'd written to my sister, where he'd said, 'Annie has taken me to church,' and he told the whole story to her.

"He eventually became a Christian before he died. I went over to his house one day and he said to me, real matter-of-factly, 'I want you to know that I've accepted Jesus as my savior—whatever that means. I don't really know what that means, but there's just something about that man. And I've been praying and I think I should take that step.' It was a very intellectual decision. Because he always wanted to be knocked off his horse and blinded by a light [like] Paul the Apostle. He really was looking for a sign, and what he came to realize was that there were a whole bunch of little signs along the way. The evangelist was one of the signs.

"He ended up living for four years, and it was right before he died that he really felt at peace about his life and about God and his place and all that. But anyway, when he died, we were on good terms and that was a real blessing."

Religion isn't just a few moments or miracles for Annie and Rob, it's a factor in their daily lives. "The basic concepts, what God asks us to do, are all good things," Rob states. "How can you disagree with the Ten Commandments? You don't have to be a genius to know they're right, but I guess you have to be somewhat willing to be dependent on, or accept those as *rules* and concepts to live by."

There it is again—that notion of objective truth Annie mentioned in her letter. Rob seems to be echoing his wife by saying, essentially: Remember, these are *commandments*, not suggestions.

Part of Rob's acceptance came from the success he's enjoyed throughout his life. "Almost everything I was doing, I was really good at. When I was a kid, I was good at marbles and sports, and as I got older, I was good at tennis and canoe paddling, so I had a lot of time in the winner's circle. And it was fun and everything, but it just seemed a little void. I'd get there and go, 'Is this all there is? This is what everyone is making the big hoopla over?' I felt a little shallow, like I was missing something."

He started going to church with Annie when she returned from college, and "it just kind of settled into me, almost like a surrender," Rob says. "Being a Christian is not easy, but at the same time, you still know it's right. It's a process, a struggling process. Because we're human, we struggle with trying to please God. It's much easier to live the life of the world than it is to live under

God's request, because he doesn't force you to do anything. It's up to you to do, which is something that I like; I don't like to be forced into doing anything. Maybe it's an egotistical thing or a male thing, but I need a challenge."

The Burnses read the Bible regularly (Annie: "The absolute best quotes come from the Bible, especially Proverbs"), say grace at the table, and not only pray, but *discuss* their prayers. They attend Hope Chapel, Honolulu, a nondenominational church. Rob summarizes his goals for his daughters: "I think we want them to learn that we as individuals need to be responsible for our actions, but we need to be able to turn to the Bible to help us in the decisions we're going to make, to get us through the days and through the hard times. Faith and responsibility, instead of doing the blame game."

These are the messages Natalie has internalized, and she would tell other children: "To not lie. Instead of going surfing, you could study your Bible. Instead of watching TV almost every day, you could do better things like sports or go to the park and play ball. And tell your mom to read you the Bible."

### *Media*

There are good media and bad media, and lots of stuff in between. And then there's Rush. Annie and Rob talk about the influence of radio and television personality Rush Limbaugh with great respect. She started listening to his radio show during the Gulf War and attributes Rob's coming around to her conservative point of view to the following: prayer to God, her gentle nudging, and Rush.

Annie went so far as to write Rush a letter. "I don't know if he reads his letters, but I sent him an article about Rob being an entrepreneur, and I told him he helped save this guy from liberalism." The correspondence, mailed about three years ago, received no response, which seems forgivable, given the volume of mail Limbaugh receives.

Annie's such a fan that on a recent visit to New York, she went to the EIB (Excellence in Broadcasting) network office, where she soaked up the aura and exchanged a few pleasantries with the show's producer, Bo Snerdley. She tried on one occasion to become a caller on the program, but after a long wait was unsuccessful. Rob sums up Rush's impact. "What Rush Limbaugh has done has been to say, 'Yeah, the media are bombarding us, but we haven't lost yet. We just need to rally the troops.' I think that if the media would change their stance and projection, things would change."

"I'm a pessimist," Annie responds. "I think the culture war is lost. I'm glad there are a lot of people who agree with traditional values, but I don't think we can go back. I think Pandora's box was opened, and I don't think you can close it."

"But they're starting to lose money on these R-rated films that they've been producing, and they're making money on conservative value movies," Rob counters. "It's just a matter of time, you know."

Other than Rush, the Burnses have few media heroes and spend little time either listening to the radio or watching television. In fact, after the recent remodeling of their home, Rob decided that their second television set had to go. "He put his foot down," Annie says, "because he feels we should watch it together or not watch it at all." At present the family's only TV is in the living room. Rob does use it for evening relaxation and news, perhaps three times a week. He'll occasionally watch sports and public affairs programs like *20/20* and *60 Minutes,* "even though he realizes it's biased," his wife adds.

Annie says she has little time for television, though she's found *Frasier* cute the two times she's seen it. Last year she caught a couple of episodes of *Friends* but refuses to watch it anymore since the last show portrayed a lesbian relationship "on a par with marriage." Annie adds that she finds homosexuality a difficult subject for her, since she feels great compassion for the several homosexuals whose friendships she values. "It's a touchy issue and hard to deal with," she says. "I just love them, and of course I've always believed you never tease anyone for whatever they are."

Annie has a rule that no TV is allowed the girls on school nights, which is sometimes tough to enforce when she's not home or ill. But the issue doesn't loom large, since Natalie's not very interested and Jennifer prefers more easily controlled videos. Asked which shows are good for kids, Natalie replies, "Nothing nowadays. Only the science show, *Discoveries*."

Annie and Rob go to movies fairly often, but Annie says she's always "disappointed and sorry I went. The ones that are supposed to be romantic aren't. The people making movies talk down to us like we're stupid, it's insulting to my intelligence. They explain everything, and are overly didactic." Their most recent film outing was to see *Home for the Holidays,* a film they found "boring" and walked out halfway through.

Annie considers friends who allow their small children to see R-rated pictures "abusive." "To me, it's robbing them of their innocence," she states. "I am so appalled at that! A friend of mine took her four-year-old child to see *Pulp Fiction* and my jaw dropped. She said she did it because she couldn't get a baby-sitter, and used that same line that 'they're going to be exposed to it at some point so you might as well toughen them up now.' I said, 'Please don't do that again. I'll baby-sit him if you want.' She didn't call me for days. Most people feel 'All of my kid's friends have seen those movies.' It's very sad."

Jennifer's favorite film is *Pocahontas,* and the girls recently enjoyed *Toy Story,* but before that endured *Golddiggers,* a film Annie says "presented adults as liars and idiots requiring rescue by kids." Jennifer would rather just stay home and focus on a video, which she watches over and over. Her current favorite is *Heidi* with Jason Robards. She also goes for *Beethoven,* a comedy about the exploits of a Saint Bernard. Together the family favors *Ben-Hur, Rudy, It's a Wonderful Life, Fiddler on the Roof, Romeo and Juliet, West Side Story,* and *The Sound of Music.*

Rob and Annie are far more interested in reading matter. They subscribe to two newspapers, the *Honolulu Star-Bulletin* and *Pacific Business News*, as well as *Conservative Chronicle*, *Atlantic Monthly*, *Commentary*, *First Things*, *Touchstone: A Journal of Ecumenical Orthodoxy*, and the Focus on the Family newsletter. Annie's personal additions are the *Wall Street Journal*, *House Beautiful* and *Home* magazines; Rob's own interests are *Reader's Digest*, *Surfer's Journal*, and *Long Board* magazine.

Staying on top of current events has its downside, however. "Every once in a while I have to quit," Annie sighs. "Quit reading the papers, quit listening to talk radio, quit watching any kind of news. It can depress me. When I found out Clinton was elected, I just cried. When I saw him and Gore on the cover of *GQ* magazine, I knew they were a shoo-in. But the morning they announced it, in spite of myself, I just bawled."

The children can't understand their parents' interest in the news but share their pleasure in reading. Though it's tough for Natalie to read, her mother is pleased to sometimes find her engrossed in her Bible, without any suggestion from an adult. In fact, both girls often turn to the Scriptures on their own. Beyond that, Natalie subscribes to *Surf Rider* magazine; Jennifer loves *The Magic School Bus* series by Joanna Cole, Bible stories of all kinds, joke books, and fables.

I ask the Burnses if they find that the media offer America any heroes. For Rob, a couple of sports stars come to mind. He says Cal Ripken is "one of the finest, and even guys like Michael Jordan have positive things to say: determination . . . stick-to-it-iveness. And from the bottom—the ghetto—to the top. And he's humble and doesn't have green hair."

Annie and Rob lament the lack of conservative Hollywood heroes. I ask Rob to challenge his uncle, the producer, to name some conservative actors and directors. You hear so much about the virtues of diversity, but there's not much political diversity among the creative types in Hollywood. If the entertainment establishment is just choosing projects and participants based on talent, it sure is peculiar that liberals are so much more talented than conservatives.

Annie thinks that the liberal message is ubiquitous because liberals *give away* their publications, while conservatives, holding by the work ethic and free market, always charge. She cites the *Honolulu Weekly* as a case in point: "It's a newsprint kind of magazine that tells you what's going on as far as entertainment—movies, plays, etc.—but it's so liberal. Everybody reads it *because it's free*."

Rob responds that the conservative business owners who support the paper through their advertising have nowhere else to advertise, and the media's stereotyping of conservatives as "square" would discourage young people from reading such a publication anyway. But Annie maintains that if conservatives are willing to invest in their message by offering free periodicals, they can be even more effective.

## Making It Work: Lessons from the Burns Family

The Burns family is different from the other families I interviewed in several respects—and in several others it's quite similar. First the differences.

Most visibly, they've experienced enormous change in financial circumstance, whereas the other families (and many Americans) remain close to the same standard of living throughout their lives. Rob transformed from a beach bum owning a few T-shirts and slippers to a wealthy entrepreneur. Yes, he still goes to work in T-shirt and slippers and owns but a single tie—but now that's his choice rather than his station.

Rob Burns became the establishment *by ignoring it.* As an inexperienced 23-year-old who knew math only at the eighth-grade level, he set a goal and, via the simplest and most universally accessible methods, moved step by step toward it. No power lunches. No networking. No image makers, public relations professionals, or financial analysts. He had nothing and borrowed three thousand dollars from an uncle. He didn't need government offices or grants, stipends, or investors. Rob Burns literally took a dream of a small surf shop, and an observation—that people buy a lot of clothes—and with hand-lettered signs and many potted plants created a multimillion-dollar empire that still survives. Rob reminds us that in America it's still possible to be a self-made man.

Because the move from poverty to wealth is fresh in their memory, Annie and Rob want their children to understand the value of a dollar. It's a struggle to say no to children's demands when you can afford to give in, but the Burnses take the tougher route because they feel so strongly that those given either wealth or handouts lose their drive to achieve.

The Burnses approach education in their own way. Annie is vigilant about their daughters' academic progress; she's determined that they be equipped with the basics of literacy and other skills needed to guarantee a successful future; but you don't hear them talking around the dining table about colleges and career ambitions. Instead there's talk about *ideas*. Along with the usual discussion of each person's day, the family talks over current events. They talk about an article read, a seminar attended, or a letter to the editor planned. Or they talk about a Scriptural concept, an application of a passage.

Rob never attended college. Annie is glad she graduated from George Washington University, but the affiliation is not a focus for her. Rob's dad, an educated man, intentionally downplayed the value of higher education. All of these facts color Natalie's and Jennifer's attitudes toward college. Certainly, it isn't a negative attitude, but it is one that recognizes that *learning* is the really important thing.

While Annie and Rob may not have graduate degrees, they make a point to contact or meet important thinkers, often at conferences, and sometimes even bring them into their life. They hold knowledgeable people in such esteem that the girls can't miss it.

Natalie and Jennifer simply model their parents' respect for learning.

And Annie and Rob *are* accomplished students. Although there's no overt message about formal education—universities or college-prep requirements—in their home, a family theme is the emphasis on knowledge, development, and extracting wisdom from all its sources.

In many ways, however, Annie and Rob share underlying values with all of the families I interviewed. They treasure family life and desired children so much that they adopted twice. Their experiences with infertility and the adoption process contain elements of universal hope, disappointment, tenacity, and love. The close bond they enjoy with their daughters—a love that couldn't be stronger if these were biological children—is a powerful argument for encouraging unmarried women with unplanned pregnancies to offer their babies for adoption rather than follow the current trend of keeping them.

For adoptive couples the issue is not who is the parent but *who is willing to parent.* The adults who undertake the responsibility to educate, bathe, clothe, read to, and tuck in at night *are* parents because they do parenting activities. The ones who are there every night and are reliably concerned and loving have shown themselves worthy of the mission—whereas many women and men claiming a biological "right" to youngsters have proven merely their ability to reproduce rather than to fulfill the inconvenient obligations of parenthood.

Finally, a feature of the Burns family is their faith. In a country where 40 percent of Americans attend church or synagogue weekly and 85 percent identify themselves as Christians, the Burnses' level of commitment to their religion is not unusual. It's a problem, though, that rarely are religious people "good guys" in films anymore.

The film *Wings of Desire* portrays the flight of an angel as he cruises Earth, overhearing the private thoughts of everyone he sees. I'm sure that, were we to have that privilege, we'd discover Americans—in their homes, offices, on the bus, or in their cars—directing their thoughts, pleas, and gratitude to God. Prayer is far more common and useful than we hear about. I appreciate Rob and Annie for reminding us of that.

The Burnses admit that they're not experts in overcoming the perils of parenthood and marriage. They turn to teachers, psychologists, pastors, and others they respect. They look to Phyllis for guidance and learn from their own trial and error. But in telling their story, they revealed many of the methods that keep their family running smoothly and made Rob's business profitable.

Here are some wise suggestions that families should consider.

- *Don't use the "D word."* When in marital distress, you'll work harder to find a solution to your problem if divorce is not an option.
- *Keep a journal of thoughts and quotations.* Reflecting on her collection helps Annie see her own role in conflicts.
- *Recognize your stubbornness.* Then decide stubbornly to change. Rob refused to call home when on business trips, causing anguish for Annie. Stubbornness is one of the most destructive forces in marriage.
- *Consult a third party.* Just thinking about what you'll say discharges feelings and forces you to think logically. Annie and Rob consulted a therapist and a preacher when their anger reached an impasse.
- *"Time-out" as a disciplinary tool doesn't always work.* When children won't sit still or curse you when in time-out, warn them that a spanking will be the backup.
- *When asking children to clean up, participate a little bit to also teach the idea of helping others.* Rob credits Annie for teaching him this approach.

- *Let your spouse be your mentor*. Annie is learning to be firm in her enforcement of rules because of Rob. Take a moment to assess what your partner can teach you.
- *Avoid the "labeling" or "self-fulfilling prophecy" phenomenon.* Natalie copied the actions of her emotionally disturbed classmates and gained a negative label—then the teachers started expecting her behavior to be bad, and she didn't disappoint them. A new environment and new teacher put her back on track.
- *Strengthen children's desire to earn by withholding gifts and allowing them the satisfaction of self-sufficiency.* Rob insists his daughters work so they understand the value of a dollar.
- *Seek out valuable maxims and live by them*. Among the Burnses' favorites: "It's not what you want, it's what you ought," and "Waste leads to want."
- *Be firm with your children*. Phyllis Murray says she stayed tough and "forgot about whether my children liked me or not."
- *Be willing to do whatever is required.* Annie learned to put aside preconceptions about what was "appropriate for an owner's wife" and began sweeping Local Motion's parking lot. Rob's success is boosted by a willingness to do anything he assigns to others.
- *"There's always something to do."* Idle time is wasted opportunity. This is another lesson Annie learned from Rob.
- *Pray about problems.* The power of prayer provides a source of strength, patience, and perspective in resolving personal troubles. This is how Rob works through his disagreements with Annie.
- *Note the kind of behavior you want to avoid as well as the kind you want.* They're both motivating. Rob didn't want to be

like his parents, and he considers that to be his strongest impetus to success.

- *Friendliness and courtesy built Rob's business and can build families.* Sharing was the main trait Phyllis wanted her children to master.
- *Don't let possessions own you.* Use Annie's trick, and when purchasing ask yourself: "What would it do to me if this broke? Is it worth it?"
- *If you can't toss out television viewing altogether, get rid of all TVs but one.* That's what Rob did, based on the rationale that the family should watch together or not at all.

# 5
# The Cowden Family of Bath County, Virginia

*Parents, always remember that you're raising what are going to be the best friends you'll ever have.*

—John Cowden

## In Transit

The next stop on my itinerary is Fort Lewis Lodge, the country inn the Cowden family operates in rural Virginia, about fifteen miles outside the town of Millboro. Having rural roots myself, I looked forward to this trip. For me, rural America is the real America. There are no traffic jams, people are courteous, trust is high. Crime is low, so at night you don't lock your cars or your house. You know your neighbor and your neighbor knows you. Everyone gets the news from the county newspaper rather than the *New York Times*.

The setting here is strictly agricultural. Families live off the land, raising cattle and crops. There aren't many people in this part of Virginia, and though each seems to have at least one pickup truck, you won't find a single traffic light in all of Bath County.

As I arrive, the first person I meet is Mary, one of three

employees who clean the cabins and tend to dozens of other chores. Mary is from Westchester County, outside New York City. She doesn't have to tell me why she crossed the cultural ocean to come here. She left the hustle and bustle of city life looking for a more peaceful setting, and she's found it.

The area's best-known landmark is the nearby Homestead, a much larger vacation spot whose early guests included Thomas Jefferson and Andrew Jackson. The Homestead's naturally warm spring is still an attraction, but these days visitors tend to focus on leisure sports such as hunting, tennis, skiing, and golf. The latter enjoys particular popularity—fans of the sport will note that one of the game's legends, Sam Snead, lives at the Homestead.

Fort Lewis Lodge offers the same pristine countryside but caters to a smaller clientele in a more relaxed and intimate setting. Its drawing cards are the walking trails and opportunities for fishing, biking, and mountain climbing. If you want splendid isolation, the Lodge is the place for you—if you expect modern entertainment, it's not. The *environment* is the entertainment, and it's surprising how many things one can do on a leisurely walk in the hills.

## Introductions

I'm greeted by John Cowden, 44, husband, father, and entrepreneur. He's slender, taller than I am (about six feet), and has dark hair and glasses. He carries himself well and has a way of making a person feel comfortable. He and his wife Caryl, 45, have the type of personality I've heard referred to as "Midwest nice."

One of the first things I notice is a Native American poem prominently displayed in John's office. It says:

*Let me walk in beauty, and make my eyes ever behold the red and purple sunset . . .*
*Let me learn the lessons you have hidden in every leaf and rock . . .*

*Make me always ready to come to you with clean hands and straight eyes . . .*
*So when life fades as the fading sunset, my spirit may come to you without shame.*

I ask John about the poem, and he explains that it captures his feeling of closeness to the land. He's a student of Native American culture and finds much to admire in their stewardship of the land, their traditions, and even their agricultural practices.

---

Fort Lewis is part of a 3,200-acre farm, most of it forested, but also planted with 80 acres of soybeans and 50 acres of corn, used primarily as feed for about a hundred head of Angus cattle. When John and Caryl moved here, they first tried to make a go of things with just the farming and ranching. The money wasn't sufficient, so they decided to build and open a full-service country inn.

John and Caryl knew each other as teenagers but weren't high school sweethearts. They were reintroduced years later, after he'd gone to Trinity College and then Ohio State University and she'd received a teaching degree from Miami University of Ohio. They were married seventeen years ago and have three children: David, 14, Kelly, 11, and Josh, 9.

The children, who attend local public schools, are growing up in a family where both mother and father are home all the time. Work and family go together. Out of necessity, life is carefully organized and each family member has specific responsibilities. The Cowdens' cohesion and unity allows for an extraordinary independence—a theme that blends together the family's approach to marriage, parenting, and all the challenges of modern life.

---

## Marriage

Though John and Caryl live and work together, they often spend their days at opposite sides of the property doing whatever is necessary to keep the Lodge operating. They're almost always together at mealtimes, though even then both may be busy with additional chores to meet the needs of their guests.

When they finally sit down for an interview, they're quiet but relaxed. Caryl has an easy smile and an upbeat personality. She and John display deep mutual respect. They interrupt each other in conversation, but always in an easy, nonthreatening manner. When a question is asked of both, usually they'll look at each other to determine who should go first. (I wasn't keeping score, but my hindsight impression is that their participation was evenly split.) They're as comfortable together as any husband and wife could be.

Not surprisingly, the allocation of responsibilities between them was arrived at very naturally. "You need two people to run an inn," Caryl explains. "We sort of fell into the roles we have. It worked out that I managed books before, so I did that; I like to cook, so I did that too. The one that's a little bit harder is dealing with the people. Obviously, neither one of us wants to do it all of the time, so that's an area of overlap. But the other things have been easy."

"I do maintenance, building, farming, and most of the people-related tasks," John adds. "For example, Caryl will be preparing food, and I'll greet the people and show them their room and get them oriented. If they have questions of what to do and where to go, it generally falls to me, and if I'm not there, to Caryl. At breakfast I go from table to table with maps of our property asking, 'What do you want to do?' I give them suggestions about hiking, fishing, and swimming locations, and outline the time it takes to get there."

The Cowdens' enjoyment of their work translates into high job satisfaction—and helps reinforce their marriage. John shows his feeling of accomplishment by saying, "Now that we've built the buildings and have an established clientele, I deem this a success—whatever circumstances come along to help or change."

So how do the Cowdens do it? Most of the time they're focused on their roles and the execution of these roles. As an example, says Caryl, "I think about menus all the time. Every day—I just have to. And I don't plan because to me it's more of a mood thing. I do have to think of all of the ingredients I might use for a certain period of time—I have some idea of what I use, so I keep them on hand.

"Our main season, of course, is April through mid-October, so we usually have fresh vegetables all of the time. Like, today, we have watercress." As Caryl speaks, John looks on appreciatively. "You don't *plant* watercress," she continues, "it's in spring water. We have wild asparagus [too]. There are only so many people who ever have access to that. The folks around here never tell other people where they have their secret wild asparagus picking areas. Because your wild asparagus is like gold."

As the conversation continues, I learn that the Cowdens' relentless chores can seem daunting and quite repetitive but that the partnership is strengthened by their hard work, discipline, and commitment to sharing the load. Both honor work well done; therefore, each honors the other when they succeed in their tasks. "In the morning sometimes to motivate myself, I have to say, 'Get your butt out of bed,'" John admits. "There's a lot to be done. And one of us is going to do it. If I don't it's more of a burden on Caryl, and if she doesn't do it, then it's more of a burden on me. Not only do I have my list, but I have a list that she makes for me. So work roles are clearly delineated."

"My parents are different from other parents," the oldest Cowden child, David, puts in. "They cook." He continues, "They have a good marriage. Sometimes they do stuff for each other. Like when Mom's really busy and Dad puts the bag in for the trash. And when Mom's busy, Dad cooks stuff."

The Cowdens place a premium on organization and structure. They have to. Their jobs depend on it. "Many people have a career where work is off somewhere else. We're our own bosses *and* husband and wife, and we're partners in a business—all those roles have to be worked out, and we do. When the other individual *doesn't* get the job done, you tend to get mad. The problem is that the other person just happens to be your wife or husband, as well. When you take on this much land and this many hours on the job, it's constant stress. You have to be careful and recognize when it's endangering the marriage. Ask 'Where is most of our conflict coming from?' Then hopefully, if we're making enough income, we can decide to hire someone to help out."

I'm surprised by John's approach to the problem of pressure. I'd expected him to say "talk it through" or "escape for a few days." Instead, he thinks to delegate. He doesn't have the "I have to do it all" mentality. Pure practicality, with the simple goal of making the partnership work.

The business of Fort Lewis Lodge now requires three employees, each of whom works in either Caryl's or John's sphere of the marriage/business venture. One man works the farm and reports to John. Then Caryl has *her* assistants. "There are two other girls who work with me in the kitchen," she says. "The three of us have worked together now for quite a few years and we work very well together.

"We've always liked to work, I guess," Caryl continues. "To accomplish things. John and I are both like that. That's why we got into this. It's how we got down here to this farm. We knew it wasn't going to be easy. But it's nice to be always close. That's exceptional, most people don't get that. Most people don't get three or four months every year when they're off together.

"Well, it's long hours—that's why we *need* the time off," John adds. "We have a lot of time together, but when we're working, each of us is doing our own thing. And so you get home, you're tired and go to sleep—and it starts over the next day."

The family helps each other put daily stresses into proper perspective by "determining what is important and what isn't," John says. "Everything can seem *very* important when the problem first arises. Caryl controls much more of the day-to-day functioning, sees that things get done, needs are met—she makes sure that life keeps moving on. I'd say that my contribution is more of the long-range planning."

The couple says the key to their matrimonial success is communication—even though John admits he was first attracted to Caryl for her looks. They're so in sync that when asked about changes in their relationship over the years, they finish each other's sentences.

"I think there's an underlying level of trust, though you always go through phases in life," John explains. "I think you need that core, that you're in tune year after year; you're changing and maturing and, yet, you're still two individuals, sharing common ground."

John's words define a healthy union: "You're changing and maturing and yet you're still two individuals, sharing common ground." The common ground is *trust.*

When I ask the Cowdens about problems in their marriage, they speak of business pressures and the uncertainties of parenthood. They don't indicate, nor do I sense, any deep problems with their marriage. It appears quite stable and sound. I think the organizational skills that allow John and Caryl to function day to day have enabled them to lay out realistic expectations for their marriage.

Given some time to think about it, John wrote down his recommendations for spouses:

1. Individuals evolve throughout their married life. Open lines of communication are essential to keep the core of what brought them together originally alive and well. Try to be understanding (if not accepting) of the changes and needs that your spouse may have.

2. You can't take marriage for granted.

3. Differences are inevitable—develop methods to settle these differences so you can leave them behind.

4. Take time-outs to be just a couple.
5. Do what you can to stay healthy.

Wisdom from a credible source.

## Parenting

*If children live with hostility, they learn to fight . . .*
*If children live with serenity, they learn to have peace of mind.*
*With what are your children living?*

—From "Children Learn What They Live,"
Dorothy L. Nolte

The above quotation is from a poem that John and Caryl Cowden find inspiring. The couple has chosen to live in a place far removed from the hassles and complexities of urban life, in the hope that it'll be easier to teach their children the values of clean living, hard work, honesty, and responsibility. To John and Caryl, the setting has proved ideal.

John is conscious of the model of behavior he represents for his children. "No matter what, I've got to be friendly, welcoming, even if I'm not in the mood—I might have a dozen other things on my mind," he explains. "But it's part of the job. Doesn't matter if it's the social hour—or breakfast time, or lunch break—it's time to go to work. 'Plan your work and work your plan.' You can be drawn in so many different directions, whether it's a farm problem way out in the mountain, or a guest, or a mechanical breakdown, or family. You have to be list oriented. It's a fact of life."

"This is how we survive," Caryl Cowden says simply. "It can be hard on the kids. When Josh needs help with his arithmetic homework, or when Kelly wants to show off her latest artwork, and you can only give her a nod because you're juggling two frying pans and a guest just overflowed his orange juice at the dispensing machine. And now David is 14 years old and in high school, and we have to lean on him more with his algebra. But the kids see the discipline we put into our work."

"Work" is the Cowdens' mantra. Invariably, their answers circle back to the demands of the Lodge. More than any other family I spoke to, the Cowdens are enmeshed in their project. The only respite they seem to have is the three months they close down during the winter.

While a parent is working at home, children may demand special attention that the parent can't drop everything to give. Youngsters who may not immediately get the attention they crave learn firsthand about the pull of duty and responsibility. These values can't be reinforced often enough. As Caryl aptly puts it, "They see the discipline we put into our work." And since parents are the primary role models for children, observing the discipline of work at home is very likely a character builder.

John also points to the family's *guests* as secondary role models. "In essence, we've been able to take the kids to the office every day," John says. "Being around all these different people is a real plus for the children. They see a lot of different lifestyles, and they sometimes engage in conversation; other times they overhear conversations. I always point out that these people have done a lot of work to get to this position. Generally, people are coming to a country inn for a weekend; they're somewhat successful, being able to afford a weekend retreat.

"This is what you want to obtain, or at least [you want] to be in a position that you can do what you want, I tell my children. [They must] manage their life [accordingly]. Whether they go to college or not, if I can get them to the point that they finish high school and they can send in a good application, they have a choice to go to any number of colleges, whether or not they actually make that choice. At least, I consider that my job as a parent."

Another advantage to the influx of visitors, Caryl says, is that they "keep you from getting bored, from totally withdrawing into yourself, which can happen when you live out in the country." As practiced by the Cowdens, independence doesn't mean isolation—

it means *bringing the best of the outside world into your sphere.* It means selecting and allowing in the kind of influences you want for yourself and your kids.

With guests always present, private moments become integrated with normal work. "Sometimes it's unavoidable that we have to discipline our children in front of people," John admits. "If we were in a normal home, you could discipline immediately, but sometimes we might have to wait for the guest to leave. By now, the kids understand the attention we give our guests, especially Kelly, who is more social. When they were younger, it must have been difficult for them to ask, 'Why are Mom and Dad paying more attention to the people who just drove in the driveway than to me?'

"The plus is that we're here all the time. We interact with the children all the time. Caryl's not off to work somewhere; I'm not off to work. If they're out of school, we're all here, so maybe the total amount of time we give them is as much as any parent, probably more. Usually, it's a little bit here and a little bit there. But it's difficult for us because we're building this business, and we've had a certain amount of debt, and we have goals to achieve. We put in a lot of personal time [into work]—more than most people would, especially in the early years."

Raising small children and establishing a business is tough to do all at once. Caryl reflects: "We opened the Lodge in the fall of '87, when Josh was just a baby. But I don't remember it being awful, I really don't. These kids have been extremely happy, which I think is amazing. They're happy all the time. Also, most kids make a lot of trips to the doctor's, but [these kids] are extremely healthy and that's helped our lifestyle so much. The three kids have never been sick. David's had broken bones, but overall, they've been healthy—no ear infections, none of that."

What is the most important responsibility of a parent? "One role of a parent is to guide and counsel and to be an example," John responds. "That's a tough responsibility twenty-four hours a day. The other is just to be a partner and a friend. Be a friend first and a parent second. I'd say parenting is more along *those* lines. Of course, we can dictate direction, and ultimately, we're the authority."

John says he came from a lenient home, but Caryl says her parents were *more* strict than she is. "You parent just as it comes to you naturally," John responds. "Sometimes I'll have an idea that I want to perform a particular way. I'll perform that way for a month. You're always going to fall back on your natural instincts."

The Cowdens do agree that rules must be established. Says John: "We try to make the children understand that there are clear boundaries. [The kids] are going to have latitude and room to move within those boundaries, but they recognize what is going to be the line. Of course they try, they question that boundary, but we are strict and fairly consistent about it. Consistency is important. I can't say we're good at it, but we recognize it as being important."

Since consistency has emerged as an important value in each of my interviews with families so far, I ask the Cowdens if they try to follow a parenting plan or if it's more ad hoc. "It's clearly ad hoc," replies John without hesitation. "It changes every year. We're not so confident as parents that we know what we're doing all the time, and also, we might change our minds from year to year. As parents, we need to encourage our children to participate and achieve so they can develop confidence and experience the joy of accomplishment. How hard to 'push' is a tough call. It's where we use our best judgment and hope for the best."

I press a little harder. "I think a core of what we teach our children is a sense of moderation," he reflects, "so they don't take the good things or the bad things in excess. We constantly hear from parents with grown children about how fast they grow up. Our children are getting to the ages where we're starting to understand what they mean. Working and planning for the future is essential but needs to be balanced with playing and enjoying your children today."

Striking that balance is one of the toughest assignments of any parent. Pursuing career goals is a priority, but there are simply times when the children must come first.

Changing the subject slightly, I ask John what is the best way for a parent to get his or her values across. "We teach them by example," John explains. He gives an illustration of how he maintained the standard of his own behavior recently, with his children's moral education in mind. "Our car was in for repair and we had a rental car. I didn't get it in park, and it rolled through the yard fence. It didn't do a lot of damage, more to the yard fence, but it made a dent."

"Our first reaction was not to tell the insurance company," Caryl recalls. "But we both decided that no, we couldn't do that because the kids observe what we do." They state straightforwardly that honesty is the value they most want to impart to their children.

In addition to being careful about the messages they send by their own behavior, they spend a lot of time *talking* about these concerns directly. "[We] deal with things in discussions, tell them what we feel they should do, that we should behave like a family and not to treat their brother and sister this way," remarks Caryl.

"Sometimes we lecture, but mostly it's more of a discussion. It depends on the situation," John says. "It's a relief to a child to be actually punished, because then he can say, 'Okay, I did something wrong. I paid for it and we're even.' I'd say both of us probably use a certain amount of guilt. 'You know what the right thing is to do, and you do it.' We don't really discipline. I just fly off the handle every now and then."

"We don't really have to," Caryl interjects. "We talk to them a lot—and sometimes yell."

"They know if they do too much, we'll just give them a look, which means they better hop to it, because we're not going to talk to them forever," John concludes.

I nod in agreement. These parents aren't afraid to use a little constructive guilt, which is what gives one a sense of personal responsibility. Kids who never feel guilty for misdeeds have an undeveloped sense of right and wrong.

Nine-year-old Josh's summary of his parents' discipline style is that "sometimes they get mad. Like when someone doesn't call back people who might want to come here. But they usually don't get mad at each other. Sometimes they get mad at me. Like if I hit my brother. They usually sit down and talk to me. They tell me not to do it again, and to apologize. I think that's a good rule. And to say thank you. And to listen to parents."

"We rarely spank them, only when they were little," says Caryl. "We can ground them. We can take a couple of privileges away from David."

David has his own ideas on discipline. "One of my friends doesn't get disciplined hardly at all. He doesn't listen to anybody. His parents will say something and they don't back it up, and he'll just get away with it. My dad means what he says, because he'll punish me. Take away stuff like my dirt bike—take away things I like to do.

"But my real advice to parents would be to listen to what your kids want," David says, sure to be thinking of some freedom he was denied. "Parents should think back to when they were kids and how they would feel if they were the ones wanting to do something—and let them go instead of stay home. Parents sometimes get overprotective a lot, even when it's not that dangerous." Spoken like a true teenager.

Eleven-year-old Kelly, on the other hand, doesn't think lenience is best for her brothers. "I'd tell parents to discipline their kids more," she says. "Because sometimes my parents don't discipline David and Josh that much, and it doesn't really teach them much of a lesson. My parents don't want to be too mean to us. But I think parents need to discipline their children more to teach them."

Caryl suspects this problem is a matter of parental ignorance. "It just emphasizes the importance of education; certainly the importance of learning *refinement in behavior*. We were brought up with very proper behavior, and that's just not always the case around here. We were brought up to never react in anger. We try very hard to teach our children how to behave."

Caryl has hit on something important: For children to learn the lesson of self-control it's better if parents use a firm hand only when they've thought it through. In other words, use your head, not your emotions, to decide when to punish your child.

"You teach respect by showing them how it feels to be respected," John submits. "If you honor them as people, and they see that we listen to what they say—and they enjoy having respect shown to them, they're inclined to understand it and offer it to others." His statement hearkens back to "Children Learn What They Live."

Asked how he shows affection, John replies: "Winks, nods, smiles, pats, hugs. We tend to show it physically. We think it's very important."

Over and over, I hear the Cowdens return to the importance of *responsibility*—to guests, family, and outsiders. As with other families I've interviewed, one of the clearest ways John and Caryl teach responsibility is through the children's participation in sports.

Last winter—which is normally Cowden family vacation time, since the Lodge is closed—brought a striking example. Instead of the usual group excursion, John and Caryl took a romantic cruise alone, and it was only partially because they wanted time together. "That, and the other reason the kids didn't come was because all three were involved in their team sports," says Caryl. "I, for one, didn't want them to be gone if they were on a team because it's just not fair."

Adds John firmly, "If you're on a team, you can't miss practice."

"You have to be *part* of the team," Caryl joins in. "Responsibility is real important. Our children also rarely, if ever, miss school, because we taught responsibility about that too. That's what they do, it's their occupation for this stage of their lives, and they're responsible for going."

As John and I talked about his kids' participation in sports, we came up with an ego-saving idea for both parents and little ones:

"the sixty-second rule." The "rule" would limit parents' critiques of their children's performance in a game to no longer than sixty seconds. Just the right amount of time to applaud highlights and sympathize with mistakes.

I notice that the Cowdens prefer not to talk about parenting in sweeping strokes. When I ask about discipline or responsibility or consideration, they'll often pare it down to the small interactions they have with each of their children. They can philosophize about their values, but they *apply* them mindful of the needs of the moment and the child.

### *Josh*

Josh, the youngest, has the engaging smile and hopeful look of a boy completely comfortable in his environment. He's affable and eager to please, but not too forthcoming when I talk to him, a typical 9-year-old, a little uneasy with being asked so many questions. The main thing on his mind today is sports. "I'm on the soccer and baseball teams. Little League. Last year I played T-ball. When I'm home, sometimes we play ball, or soccer and ride bikes. In the summer we swim down at the river. I fish down there a lot," he says, pointing. "I catch trout and red-eyes and big bass. In the winter we go sledding, on the hill over there.

"The most fun for me is riding my bike and going in the hot tub. I play with my friends—one's close and the other lives farther away—they come over a lot. We play basketball and ride bikes together."

I ask him what his parents teach him, and you can tell he's trying to come up with something good, but answering such questions just isn't something he's called on to do every day. Lots of shrugs and smiles. But one thing Josh does know is responsibility, and it's easy for him to enumerate his chores: "I take out the trash and feed the dog," the enormous chocolate Labrador, Max, who lumbers up to newcomers with welcoming slobbers. "I show people around, where they can fish or hike or ride bicycles. I teach them how to do stuff, like play baseball. I play with the kids who come to visit."

Talking to John and Caryl about their kids, I note a real adult-child connection, the crucial ability to sit back and listen rather than plow ahead with preconceived parenting rules. "Josh is a lot of fun. Probably a little more cocky than the others," John notes. "Academically, he repeated the second grade because he had a language . . . "

"Deficiency," Caryl finishes. "Back in kindergarten he had a speech problem pronouncing certain letter combinations."

"He's very bright in math. But he had problems with the reading," John continues. "The alphabet took us forever to teach. It was a big decision to keep him back. We're confident about it now, but we were wary of that initial conversation with him. But he was fine. He said, 'Yeah, you're right.' So of course he has had a great year now. He's really on top of things."

Josh is entering fourth grade (and his sister Kelly sixth grade) in the public school twenty minutes away. "The elementary education so far has been really good," says Caryl. "Most of the teachers have moved into the area, and they're very devoted, very supportive. A lot of the teachers go to the same church; a lot of them live on the same road. There just happened to be some open land, and the teachers all happened to build there. The closeness makes it a real good experience for the kids."

John agrees. "For most of the teachers, our school is their entire career. They move in and raise their families, so it's not just two years and then they're moving on. Very stable."

It's reassuring, after hearing so many sad tales about the state of the nation's schools, to hear the Cowdens speak confidently about theirs. Talking to them, I sense that their satisfaction is rooted in the ongoing communication they've had with Josh and his teachers and the strong sense of community that is fostered by their children's school.

Also significant: They haven't waited for the school to discover the problem with their son; instead, on their own initiative, they've investigated and monitored Josh's progress. It rings a bell because I remember that this proactive approach was also taken by the De La Rosas, Kathy Wallace, and Annie and Rob Burns.

The Cowdens also make it a point to carefully hear and observe their children. Says John, "Josh will wade right out in that river and then he'll watch the guests fish. And the second they leave, I've seen him go right over that hole where they made a big catch. I've also seen him listening when people have conversations about fishing. He'll just act like he's fooling around somewhere else, but he's listening about the bait they're using."

That day I have the chance to watch Josh with his older brother fishing in the green Cowpasture River. The two boys, intently casting their lines in the gentle thigh-deep current, might have stepped out of a scene frozen a century ago. That's one of the beauties of the Cowdens' independence—their activities, values, and directions are timeless.

## *Kelly*

In my interviews, I'm trying to discover not just methods parents use to transmit important values but the type of kids who best accept these values into themselves. In Kelly Cowden, a freckle-faced girl of 11, I see a beautiful example of a thoughtful, well-behaved child. She's the most verbal and outgoing of the three children, contemplating her answers to questions and framing them in precise phrases.

I ask her how she spends her time. "My friend doesn't live that far, and we usually play together. She comes over almost every weekend, or sometimes she just comes over and then Mom takes her home after dinner. Most of my friends I can talk to, and we share a lot in common. They're always there for me, and they just comfort me a lot. They make me feel loved.

"If we have lots of kids, we play hide-and-seek or capture the flag or tag. A lot of time I like playing outside or doing artwork. I have an art shop downstairs. I like to make pictures and cards and different designs. I usually make them up. I can show you one brochure—it's for 'Silver Thatch Inn.' I've got the beginning and half of the second page.

"I'm on a softball team, and I'm planning to be the pitcher. It's girls' softball. I did Brownies, and cheerleading is kind of like an organization. And I did the computer club. I have a Macintosh, I think."

Kelly is aware of the skills she's gained living at Fort Lewis Lodge. "Our life is different from my friends," she says. "Other kids don't meet as many people as I do. My parents teach me to be kind to other people who come, and to meet them." Concerning her future she says, "I want to go to college, maybe the one my mom did, Miami University in Ohio. I don't really want to go to one very close; I'd like to go farther away, just to see more of the world, I guess. I haven't heard about very many colleges yet, but I know I'm going to go. That's something my parents taught me is important: to work hard. To be disciplined." I'm impressed. How many 11-year-olds can so easily cite the values their parents most want to teach them?

Caryl and John talk about their daughter with pride. "Kelly's really an exceptional person," Caryl says. "She is so thoughtful and considerate of other people. Here's an example, and it's not even about someone who's her friend. Sort of a heavy girl, who had glasses for the first time, who we don't even know. Her mother called me up and just wanted to thank Kelly and us, because everybody was mocking this little girl, and Kelly is the only one who told her she looked nice. She's real sweet and caring."

Her disposition stays sunny even in the face of the usual brotherly hazing. "She's so forgiving of them. How she puts up with them . . ." John says, shaking his head.

As for Kelly, "She comes right through it; nothing gets her down," Caryl confirms. "Another example of this was this last year in her class—she has a very bright class and Kelly is in the fifth grade. But in the second or third grade there were three girls and one boy whose parents are involved with the school system, who'd gotten into the gifted program. Kelly was not originally in that, because she didn't peak in anything when she was younger.

"But she's taken the challenge—she works to be up there with those kids. She's [developed] a lot of confidence and she's achieved. She does as well as the kids in that gifted group. It's really neat because she's tried, she has that goal and she's succeeded. She's very, very motivated."

"She handles a situation," John concludes. "She's very pretty and she's a good athlete too, so a lot of the girls are jealous. A lot of them are critical, but she understands where that is coming from. She's still very nice to them rather than being rude."

### *David*

When I go to interview David, he's wearing a Fort Lewis Lodge camouflage cap. He's a clean-cut boy and still displays a bit of childhood innocence. At 14, he stands a head and shoulders taller than his brother as they return from fishing in the Cowpasture River.

"I like to hunt deer; I've tried turkey hunting," he tells me. "I shoot squirrel, then I eat 'em. It's good. I shoot groundhog, but I don't eat 'em though. Throw those away. They dig big holes in the cornfield and it messes up the tractor."

David, too, has his chores. "I work in the cornfield raking. In the summer I cut all of the grass behind the lodge and the house. Sitting on the mower, it takes all day. I get paid for it. No allowance, but I get paid for doing things. I do odd jobs, if my dad needs help. I don't get paid for shooting groundhogs, though, because that's fun."

Like most boys living on this mountain, David has easy access to firearms. "We have a bunch of guns. I shoot the groundhogs with a .22. Hunting's real big around here. We get out of school for hunting season because so many kids would miss, just skip school. Instead, they just let us out. This year we got all week, because it was combined with Thanksgiving, so we had two days for Thanksgiving and the other three for hunting season."

David's just completed his first year, eighth grade, at the county's high school. Says his father: "It has about 250 kids and [they're from] a lot of families we don't know." John has the usual fatherly concerns as his boy enters adolescence, and he wants to be sure David doesn't get in with a bad crowd. Like Kathy Wallace, whom we met earlier in the book, he knows that *associations matter*.

Another of John's major concerns is David's preparation for higher education. "We want our kids to go to college, and at the high school there's a lot of vocational emphasis," John says. "Many of the kids have no intention of going to college." He sees this as the result of economic factors. "There's only a small middle class in Bath County. The economy of a rural mountain area just doesn't have many jobs to offer. Without the Homestead hotel area, where a lot of retirees have built large homes with the money they made elsewhere, there wouldn't be many people who are well-to-do. We're part of that small middle class. With few exceptions, kids with more potential who were raised here are forced to move away if they want college or a career. Unfortunately, that leaves many local families who don't place an emphasis on education. Beginning with elementary school, too many kids just don't get help with their homework."

David is aware of the differences. "A lot of kids around here say 'ain't' and stuff and just don't talk very well. Just have poor grammar. My parents correct us whenever we say something wrong. But in general, my parents aren't too strict. Some kids' parents *are* real strict, and won't let their kids ride motorcycles and stuff, or go hunting by themselves. My parents let me do those things."

The generational conflict is just beginning to affect the Cowdens. "As kids get older, there are more problems," John reflects. "They get harder to communicate with. We're finding that with David."

"He's unmotivated but he's a very hard worker," Caryl adds. "Once you get him going on a task, he'll take charge of it. He has a lot of success in school, though he's not worked real hard at it."

John continues, "It's a real hard age. It's not that he's turning off—he's just not turning on. We're his motivation. It's just him getting bored and wanting excitement. Not wanting to do the dirty work."

The perils of adolescence scare John justifiably. There are problems to contend with whether you're rural, urban, or in the suburbs. Hearing his concerns, though, I reflect that at least his family has the advantage of independence, which I see as a form of partial shelter against the outside world. The enemies to David's development are boredom and lack of motivation, which, while significant, are certainly less threatening than gang membership, hyped-up sexuality, drugs, and other direct challenges to parenthood control and authority. The Cowdens have made their task easier by choosing to live where these most dangerous of influences are minimized.

If you ask David, there are both benefits and drawbacks to living in the country. "We sometimes get called rednecks," he says. "It's just a term [to imply] that you ride in big trucks and chew tobacco and all that. I don't chew, but a lot of people at school think it's cool. When kids get in trouble it's usually vandalism. Or if you talk back to the teacher. You get suspended for a couple of days.

"I like living here because there aren't gangs or anything. Nobody out here has ever brought a gun to school, even though everybody has them. If you do something around here, the whole county knows about it. Anything around here spreads fast; everybody talks to each other. Out here things are a big deal because nothing else is going on."

The Cowdens make a big effort to keep open lines of communication on social issues. I ask them how they handle the question of drugs. "We haven't really talked too much about that," Caryl admits. "We've [spoken] a little bit with David, being 14, but we haven't really talked about that too much as a family. They've done that at school, with the DARE [drug education] program. Even the younger kids in elementary school have that, so we feel for the time being that is good initial support."

"I'm planning on going to college," David says when I ask about his ambitions. "I want to try to get into [the University of Virginia], but I don't know if I'll be able to. I want to be some kind of businessman. Maybe run this place. It's not an easy job—I've watched my parents. We have a guy who works the farm, but my dad actually runs it. He tells the guy what to do and he could run the farm if he didn't have the Lodge. So, I guess he's running two things at the same time. Most people only do one. I'd keep it as a hunting lodge, too. I'll probably get married. I'd like to have three kids, two boys and a girl."

This is one 14-year-old who has a pretty clear sense of what he wants out of life.

## History and Cultural Influences

"I always wanted to go into farming," John admits, "but it never crossed my mind to be an innkeeper. I was interested in agriculture from the beginning. My father was an attorney; farming was his hobby, I guess you could say. Some people play golf, or do this and that—but his relaxation was to go to a farm. We lived in Ohio, so he invested in a farm there that we went to often—and he bought this Virginia farm a little later, in '59 when I was 9 years old. We made several trips down there.

"Dad died when I was 18, and by then I'd decided to major in agriculture. Afterward, I got a job with a farm management firm. We'd handle property for absentee owners, similar to what [the] situation was here with this farm at the time."

Caryl continues their story. "Even though we'd been in the

same class at Oakwood High—that's in a suburb of Dayton—we didn't really know each other. We were reintroduced after we both finished college. I got a teaching degree, then I moved to Lexington, Kentucky, to take a job, but I didn't last long in education.

"My mom became real sick, and she went into a coma. I moved back to Dayton—it seemed like I needed to go back home then. I moved in with my dad—I was upset and not focused and it was already into the school year. I just needed a job. There was one available at Winter's Bank in Dayton. It was the largest bank there at that time. . . .

"My mother was in a coma five years before she died. That was real hard for me, but I stayed in banking the whole time. I liked it at the bank. As it turns out, my grandfather had worked at that bank also."

"When we met and got serious, we talked about moving to the farm," John explains, then jokes, "I didn't tell her that she'd have to cook for a crowd every day. Truth is, the operator my family had working this farm was about to retire, and it was an opportunity for us. We decided when we were engaged that we'd give farming a try.

"We tried different enterprises—growing Christmas trees, cattle, and adding row crops. Soil type dictates what you can do. Some fields are suitable for row crops, but a lot of land is just not suitable from an erosion and productivity standpoint. We were unique because at that time this area was exclusively livestock. Our crops were on a small basis, about 130 acres. In Ohio terms that's one field, but here, there are a lot of small farms—locals came out and marveled at this big Fort Lewis farm where we put all that corn. But when you go and sell it, it's 130 acres of corn just like Ohio's 130—and it's only going to be worth so much. It got to the point that the farm wasn't going to generate the income we wanted.

"When we first moved here in '78 it was uncanny, the number of people in our age group. It was the sixties back-to-the-land type of thing. It was wonderful. This house and the other house, getting together was so easy. We always had picnics. We did that a lot, but then, as economic demands came in, it got tougher. Some of [the families] were employed by Virginia Power, they'd get better jobs, and move. Then one by one, this friend and that friend moved away and all of a sudden things were changing. That's about the time we got the idea of a lodge, so our efforts kind of [transitioned] into that."

Given that the Lodge is the focus of their existence, I ask what drove them to make such a demanding choice. "In land management you always step back and let the land tell you what it can do—you just can't force an enterprise," John answers. "So we looked at our tract and what it had to offer. The county itself was already known for recreation, through the facilities at the Homestead and Warm Springs—historically, people have come to this area to 'take the waters.' In some of the old country stores you can go in and see pictures of a three- or four-story resort with two hundred rooms, and they'll say, 'Yeah, that used to sit over on the hill.' It was amazing, the number of people the trains brought to the area—all the steamer trunks loaded up for the full summer season. This was when politics and gambling and medicinal claims to the water, with its minerals and warm temperature, made this quite a high-society area. Now, the Homestead and the Greenbriar hotels are the only remembrances of that era. . . .

"Since recreation was already thriving here, we needed to expand on that. And the fact that we were so remote required us to have full service and provide meals. There's just not very much opportunity in agriculture now; people raised on farms ask, 'What's my career opportunity?' Most farmers are counseling their children not to go into farming. I've bucked the trend and now I have a country inn."

I note this further example of Cowden resourcefulness. John assessed the land's capacity and, instead of going full speed ahead with what he might've liked to do, laid out careful plans. It's the kind of lesson that parents can generalize for their children—for example, it's better to select a career based on your strong and weak points instead of just taking the first job that comes along. And when choosing a mate, it's wiser to give your head a chance over your heart.

Another shaper of the Cowden lifestyle is the historic corner of earth they had to work with. John Lewis, "the father of Bath County," deeded his land in west-central Virginia to his only American-born son, Col. Charles Lewis, who in 1754 built a stockade to protect the southern pass of Shenandoah Mountain from Indian raids. "Col. Lewis went on to die a hero's death in the 1774 Battle of Point Pleasant, now widely regarded as the first conflict of the American Revolution," reads the Cowdens' brochure. "His 3,200-acre mountain farm, once known as 'Fort Lewis Plantation,' has remained relatively unchanged over its 200-year history."

That has been one of the Cowdens' great blessings. They never forget that they live on land that has been cherished and worked by many generations of predecessors. Of course, it's easy to capture that feeling in Bath County, one of the truly historic parts of Virginia, but it strikes me that even in the most crowded, modern city, families profit from a sense of attachment to their corner of the world.

## *Religion*

Religion is, as we've seen so far in this book, vital to many cohesive families, but it doesn't figure in the Cowdens' lives on any regular basis. They express little desire to affiliate with any organized religious group. Only Kelly shows a natural inclination in that direction. Says her mother, "Kelly prays every night and she's influenced a lot from reading the Bible. She likes to go to church. She doesn't get there all of the time, but she has a lot of friends who go there. When she was in the second grade, her teacher was very religious, and somehow even though it's against the law, they did pray in school. The teacher was very supportive of Kelly, and religion is just part of her now. She prays all the time and she tells us about it. She explains the meaning of everything in terms of a religious side of it, and we're kind of amazed because we don't push that at home a lot. Our boys aren't like that, but Kelly is."

Though the family doesn't practice any particular religion in the home, John and Caryl do have some religious background. "John was raised Episcopalian and I was raised Presbyterian, so we attended church—but we didn't have a strong religious sense in our families other than attending church, I guess," Caryl says.

"I think that a lot of our family values and how we run our own lives are rooted in the church, in the Ten Commandments," John adds. "But we haven't been inclined to join a church here. They tend to be too conservative for us." Still, Caryl and John are not only accepting but actually *pleased* with their daughter's religious inclination, volunteering it as one of her virtues, and respecting her enough to deliver her to church services they personally decline to attend.

### *Media*

As you drive through any remote part of the United States, you see a huge number of satellite dishes planted near homes surrounded by woods. No one really lives that far from the popular culture.

Given what I'd heard from previous families—especially the children interviewed—on the impact of media, I'm curious to know how David Cowden weighs in on the issue.

"There's just not too much to do here," admits David. "The high school kids get in a car and go to Staunton, to the movies. It's an hour away. The only video store with new movies is there. We have a little one about forty minutes away, but they only have old movies.

"We have a satellite dish. If you don't have one, there are just two channels. I like comedy movies and action. Comedy and

MTV. I have a lot of CDs up at the house—all the popular groups. We have a radio station that's up-to-date."

"It's true that there's not too much going on," his father affirms. "David doesn't have the desire to initiate activities. He needs things laid out, so television fills in the time for him. Kelly and Josh don't watch much TV."

Caryl notes, "They never have. They've never talked about commercials or any things off the TV. That really hasn't affected them. They just play; they do a lot of artwork, they play with other kids outside a lot; they keep busy doing stuff. David's more reluctant to interact with guests than the others, but he was a little older when the Lodge started. Kelly's very social and organized. She'll get the kids together."

Kelly prefers other activities but admits to taking in an occasional program. "Sometimes I do watch TV, but my mom doesn't really like me to watch it because it doesn't have very much appropriate stuff. Sometimes I like to watch [*Beverly Hills*] *90210*."

"Sensationalism seems to be an essential ingredient for the media to be competitive in sales," her dad points out. "Hopefully, consumers' interest will reverse this trend."

So far, all of the families I've interviewed seem to be fairly discriminating when it comes to TV viewing. Still, if statistics can be trusted, the De La Rosas, Wallaces, Burnses, and Cowdens are decidedly in the minority. That leads me to believe Congress made a wise move in early 1996 by requiring that all future television sets contain a V-chip. Nonetheless, it is still critical for parents to teach their children to be both discriminating and disciplined when it comes to media.

What about the influence of other forms of media? John Cowden's current musical preferences are country and bluegrass, in which David has little interest. "I don't like country," the 14-year-old says. "More and more it's like rock and roll. Adults think they should listen to country music because they live in the country."

The local newspaper, *The Recorder*, serving Bath and neighboring Highland counties, is highly regarded, John says. "People really read it. They like the community interest stories. Actually, we've had some editors who've been very good, and editorials on various topics have covered government controls, unfunded mandates, and local issues."

What kind of news causes a stir? The Cowdens quickly recall that Elisabeth Kübler-Ross, an author known for her work on death and dying, at one point intended to build a home in the area for children with AIDS. "There was a lot of conflict with that," John notes, "so the paper had to take a stand. She's since moved [the project], there was so much opposition. I don't think the opposition was from [the board of] state health. I think she had even greater obstacles—neighbors. There were a lot of hurdles that sort of got the community in an uproar."

Another provocative news story Caryl and John mention is one I envision under the banner: BUS DRIVER, FORTY-SOMETHING, DATES NINTH-GRADER. The event became a major scandal partly because it occurred at the same time as a second incident. "We have practically no crime here," John explains. "Doors open, windows open, keys in the car. It's a safe and secure environment. There was a violent rape, and this other story, the bus driver dating the ninth-grader, back-to-back."

Though there are, of course, many areas where the scale of crime—and scandal—is far greater, it's clear that places like Bath County aren't completely sheltered from the more unpleasant aspects of life.

### *Extended Family*

John and Caryl feel they're unusual in Bath County because they're separated from extended family. Most of them are in Dayton, Ohio. "I'm the youngest; I have two sisters and a brother," John explains. "My brother's a lawyer, married, living in Boston. One sister's married and in Dayton; my older sister, she's about 52, is not married and she's blind.

"She had limited sight through maybe 10 years old. She lives independently in an apartment around the block from her mother, and she has a guide dog. She's had a dog most of her adult life. She does a lot of artwork. She's with a group of artists, a gallery in Dayton. She does weaving, pottery, works with clay," John says with clear respect for her.

The Cowdens go to Dayton during their yearly winter hiatus. In the summer, family members visit the Lodge. "We always try to get together at Christmastime," Caryl says. "We communicate on birthdays, and through letter writing." Though they agree that Dayton is a nice place to visit family, the children wouldn't want to live there.

"I'd never want to live in the city, even Dayton, where we go to see my cousins, grandfather, and grandmother," David says. "Every time you turn around, there are too many people standing there. It's loud; always noisy. It's got background noise wherever you go. Here there's more room." But David does admit, "I like to go *visit* the city. I like the idea of just being able to walk around the corner and be at the movies and stuff. Here it's so far away."

Kelly is also drawn to travel. "Sometimes we go to Cataloochee Ranch in Maggie Valley. It's where my grandmother has a house in North Carolina. There's horse riding and I think they have other animals like goats and cows."

One of the traditions that seems to have gone by the generational wayside is letter writing. "We use the phone a lot," Caryl comments. "John's mother writes letters; sometimes my dad does it. We've gotten really bad about that. We do talk on the phone."

While parents and relatives have been the primary source for the Cowden's values, others, by their inspiring examples, have also contributed. John says, "My role models are those I live and work with rather than people in public life." Relationships formed through shared experiences "give strength to the principles I believe in." Besides his parents, John cites as role models:

John Holden, director of Camp Kooch-i-ching.
Floyd Madden, president of Stroop Agricultural Co.
Garvin O'Cull, a contractor who taught me the building trades.
Vader Sutton, who taught me to know and love the mountains.
Tom Alexander—[In my mind, I see him with his] deep tan from the hay fields, sitting tall at the head of the Cataloochee Ranch table. I thought he was king when I was a boy.

These are *real* American heroes. All of the families I've interviewed seem aware that public relations is a thriving industry and that many of the stars of our celebrity culture deserve little admiration. Better to seek models of self-discipline, compassion, responsibility, friendship, work, courage, and other ideals in familiar people than in misleadingly polished images produced by publicity machines.

## Making It Work: Lessons from the Cowden Family

The words opening this chapter, "Parents, always remember that you're raising what are going to be the best friends you'll ever have," come from a father whose three children treasure their home. All of the Cowden children aspire to their parents' kind of marriage, a family with the same configuration as their own, and careers running the same farm and country inn their parents have established. I see in John and Caryl's family a special attribute, something few people have talked about. They've *set themselves apart*, in a positive way, from their peers and the popular culture, creating a support system of self-sufficiency. The more I visited with them, the better sense of their true independence I felt and heard.

There's an old saying that "a man's home is his castle." That sounds rather old-fashioned and even a bit sexist now, but there's a germ of truth in that cliché. It suggests that no matter how tough and challenging the outside world can be, no matter how small you feel in facing it, the confines of the family bring safety and security. The Cowdens have their satellite dish. They have guests traipsing through their lives from all over America. But at Fort Lewis Lodge, they've created their own separate comfort zone.

Independence as a family means acting as a family: It means *individuals* living and working *interdependently*. Each relies on the other, indeed cherishes the other, for the unique contributions they bring to the family as a whole. Each person needs outside interests, and no child should grow up in a vacuum. But in conducting the interviews for this book, I've found that the *first priority* of the strongest families is always each other.

In surveying more than a thousand people with my questionnaire on family values, I discovered that 37 percent of responses to "What do you think is the most important ingredient in maintaining a healthy family?" mentioned some variant of this theme of independence as a unit.

"People today are so busy—we seem to go off in separate directions too many times," writes a middle-aged chemical salesman in Louisville, Kentucky. Like many others, he concludes, "Families need to do *more* together." Edmund Burke, the great British political philosopher of the eighteenth century, emphasized that the great battles of life are won not by mighty armies but by the "little platoons" of family, neighborhood, and local institutions. Increasingly, Americans seem to be realizing that they can, and should, fortify themselves against hostile forces by creating their own platoons.

The concept of "family independence," as practiced by the Cowdens, hasn't been much discussed in the broader "family values" dialogue. In a sense, a homeward focus goes against the popular wisdom that it's *good* to have lots of outside interests. Kids are considered enriched when they take ballet, piano, computer class, and gymnastics. They're considered socially advantaged when they're on the go to friends' houses, birthday parties, forays to the mall, and basketball practice. Of course, these activities *are* worthwhile and assist in the development of well-rounded children. And they're consistent with raising a strong family.

The problem arises when these activities *take over*. Before you know it, the soccer is back-to-back with homework and the piano lesson. The birthday parties go one after the other. Meanwhile, the parents feel like chauffeurs—or they themselves are off to the gym, the golf course, the office, or the factory, and everyone is passing like rushing traffic.

While the Cowdens spend large chunks of their days in separate pursuits, it's important to note that there is a difference in the underlying priority.

The Cowdens' *activities are rooted in their home* and common interest. Kelly's art talent is expressed in creating brochures for made-up country inns. The children do their part to be hospitable, playing with visitors, helping with chores. They know they must wait for Mom and Dad if the parents are busy with Lodge tasks, so they plan their free time around their parents' availability. Meanwhile, John and Caryl Cowden are dedicated to meeting their children's needs while *at the same time* seeing to their own ceaseless work demands. They never emotionally shut the children out or designate any part of the property off-limits. Instead, they draw their children into their world and include them in accomplishing their innkeeping obligations. When Josh plays baseball, he includes the guests in his games. David goes to the forest with visiting hunters.

As a family, they *touch base frequently*. They consult regularly, checking up on each other's contributions to the common enterprise. The children are keenly aware of their duty to continuously respect, if not directly assist in, the running of the Lodge. Josh takes visitors to the fishing hole and exchanges ideas on bait, Kelly rides bicycles, and David's off deer hunting with separate groups of guests. All later converge at the grist mill for lunch. They're available at a moment's notice to help their mother and father with anything they're requested to do on top of the assigned chores. The key is that each person *feels drawn back* for information and status reports often; each stays conscious of the other's location and activities. Home is where the action is.

The Cowdens' values are simply part of the way they conduct business, instruct their children, and set their priorities for spending time. It occurs to me that a useful exercise is to ask whether an objective observer would deem *your* family focused *inward* or *outward.* Would your family members say they feel clubs, get-togethers, and moneymaking tasks are an equal or stronger pull than home? A full plate of external activities might be a diversion from the family's priorities.

The concept of individualism was perversely redefined as the freedom and rights campaigns of the late 1960s broadened in the early to mid 1970s. You might remember the best seller *Looking Out for #1*, by Robert Ringer. Here are just a couple passages.

> If you've accumulated a lot of excess baggage in the way of friends who contribute more to your discomfort than pleasure to your life, by now you should be convinced that you can't afford the extra weight—not if you're going to succeed in looking out for Number One [p. 278].

> Charity is fine, so long as you can afford the time and/or money to engage in it. I must again emphasize, however, that the best way to help the poor is by not becoming one of them [p. 139].

This landmark book characterized the era's ruthless pursuit of personal satisfaction. It was a time of unparalleled egocentrism, perfectly described by Tom Wolfe as the "Me Decade."

Though trends often don't last long, the principles of '70s narcissism stuck. In certain cases "feeling good at the expense of others" even became institutionalized. Marriages, for example, crumbled as "staying together for the kids" and "sticking it out through the tough times" were lambasted as martyrlike rationalizations for lack of gumption. Yes, it was a deep hole we dug ourselves into, and we're not out of it yet.

Seen from the new perspective the Cowdens give us, it can be appreciated that there are times when individualism is the *opposite* of family devotion—the *opposite* of putting family first. If the members of this Virginia farm family have anything to teach us—and I believe they do—it's that it's time to trim back the *Looking Out for #1* psychology and give more of ourselves to shared activity.

Certainly, a family needn't be plunked down in the isolated setting of a country inn to manage an inward focus. All of the other families interviewed for this book accomplished it. For example, the De La Rosas create a haven for themselves amid large, multigenerational homes, apartment complexes, and gangs. A day off begins with Mass at the local parish, then brunch, then visits by extended family, welcomed within Tony and Carmen's chain-link-fenced yard with friendly card games, sharing of the week's news, and plenty of homemade food. The De La Rosas create their own inward focus by simply expecting each member to be there and through the parents' own model of behavior.

Happily, some scholars have identified family independence as an encouraging new trend. Barbara Dafoe Whitehead describes its best attributes: "It is a shift away from an ethos of expressive individualism and toward an ethos of family obligation and commitment. It's a shift away from the assertion of individual rights . . . and toward a recognition of individual responsibility. It's a shift away from a preoccupation with adult needs and toward greater attention to children's needs. It's a shift away from a calculus of happiness based on individual fulfillment and toward a calculus of happiness based on the well-being of the family as a whole."

### *Being There*

The essence of family independence is simple: *You've got to be there.*

One of the hopes of parents who must spend a large chunk of their time away from their children is that a small amount of "quality time" with the child is equivalent to, if not better than, a great deal of time where attention is not focused directly on the child. Unfortunately, studies have shown that children whose parents work are *less likely* to have Mommy's undivided attention than those whose mothers stay home.

I found in my own survey widespread recognition that time together is central to strong families. This was offered 21 percent of the time as the number one ingredient for creating a healthy family. And a representative national sample of fifteen hundred women in 1995 found that 18 percent list time at home as a primary family value.* That's a significant number—it followed not far behind religion, unity, and morals as the main quality selected.

A special category of time together is sharing meals. Several studies show that four or more nightly meals shared together per week improves children's school performance as well as feelings of family cohesiveness. *Reader's Digest* tested 2,130 high school students to determine their academic achievement. "One of the most striking findings in our poll," writes Rachel Wildavsky, is that "sixty percent of students who said their 'whole family sits around a table together for a meal' at least four times a week got high scores."

How does family dinner translate into school success? It's the underlying sense of support expressed around the table that gives students motivation and affirms the importance of their studies. Having dinner together was cited by educators and therapists polled by Delores Curran in *Traits of a Healthy Family* as one of the crucial determinants of family success. This is a direct, relatively easy method of improving many aspects of family life—communicating, pulling together, teaching values in the context of daily events. Marilyn and I have always made it a point to eat with our family whenever possible. Admittedly, it gets more difficult as the children grow older.

* Families and Work Institute, *Women: The New Providers*, Whirlpool Foundation Study, Part One, May 1995.

Family independence has some benefits to marriage as well. Wallerstein and Blakeslee in *The Good Marriage* found that husbands and wives with the same family-centric goals had the happiest marriages. So "putting families first" benefits not only the children but the adults' relationship as well. Healthy marriages put the children second to the spouse, but both spouses *shared the priority of their family.*

Based on the Cowdens' experience, here are some concrete steps any family can put into practice:

- *Spouses: Appreciate your joint daily triumphs as a sign of marital success.* Grand moments are fleeting; achievements built up over years bring deeper, more satisfying rewards.
- *Parents: Regarding sports activities, remember the "sixty-second rule."* Critique performances for no more than a minute. This counters the temptation to live vicariously. Remember, these are only games being played.
- *Chores are important character builders*, and help reinforce the notion that all family members are pulling together as a team for the common good. Lists help to organize each family member's tasks.
- *Parents need to stay attuned to individual differences among their children and not assume that blanket expectations in every area are appropriate.* The Cowdens, for example, are sensitive to Josh's academic pace and respectful of Kelly's inclination toward religion. They're also aware of each child's strengths and allocate chores based on competencies.
- *Parents: Be conscious that children follow what you do more than what you say.* The Cowdens consider the messages they send their children with their behavior, even when it comes to little "white lies."
- *Touch base with other family members.* The more contact you have with each other, the more you're pulled together.

- *Seeking a sense of history in your home can pull family members closer and make home feel more valuable.* The Cowdens are proud of the pioneer history of their Lodge, and this deep sense of connection to the past is one of their many gifts to visitors as well as their own children.
- *Even if you are not openly religious, show respect for the positive values religion imparts.* John and Caryl encourage Kelly's developing faith and thereby reinforce the basis of their own beliefs—which are rooted in the Ten Commandments.
- *Cultivate letter writing—even if it's just a quick E-mail.* The Cowdens, like many busy families, rely on the telephone but appreciate the letters they receive from the grandparents in Dayton.
- *Look close to home for heroes; identify people you know who exemplify basic virtues.* John Cowden's list of personal heroes was a reminder that there are role models all around us.
- *Family members: Maintain the proper balance between "outward focused" and "inward focused."* Are outside activities a greater pull for family members than events at home? If so, reorganize and get creative so that home is the most desirable place to be.
- *Be there.* Especially for family meals, which can be the hub of communication and stability.

# 6

# The Burtin Family of Chicago

*A word fitly spoken is like apples of gold*
*in pitchers of silver.*

—Proverbs 25:11 [quotation often cited
by Jackie Burtin's mother]

## In Transit

To find the Burtin family, I only have to take a forty-five-minute plane ride from Indianapolis to Chicago.

After arriving at Midway Airport and picking up my rental car, it's on to the Burtin home on Chicago's South Side, right next to Cicero. The drive up Cicero Avenue is slow and crowded.

The Burtin family is African American. They live on a city street that is impressively clean and neat. The first thing a visitor notices is the orderliness of the neighborhood. The yards are well kept; the litter that is so common to cities is absent here. It's the picture of a secure, proud middle-class neighborhood.

## Introductions

The Burtins are an intact family whose foundation has been a long-term marriage and the stability of living on the same street for twenty-three years. Upon entering their home, I'm quickly struck by their familial closeness. I admire the rows of framed family photos on the fireplace mantel and surrounding bookcases. There's a shot of daughter DaToya as a little girl riding on her tricycle. And a high school photo of son Darnell, looking ready to take on the world. Also front and center is a wedding picture of Dan and Jackie.

As always, the first few moments are "get acquainted" time. The conversation segues from how my flight was to family matters to sports, and it doesn't take long to get comfortable.

---

Married in 1969, Jackie and Dan Burtin have raised their son, Darnell, 21, and daughter, DaToya, 17, on their cohesive block on Chicago's South Side. Dan, 46, and Jackie, 45, both come from large families with strong and respected parents. Dan, a computer specialist for the city of Chicago, is the third of nine children; his parents have been married forty-nine years. Jackie, a substitute teacher, is the second of six daughters; her parents have celebrated forty-eight years of marriage. The members of their extended family, all in the Chicago area, are daily participants in a lifestyle that has reached far beyond blood relations. For twenty-two years, the Burtins have volunteered services to the Salvation Army, the Boy Scouts, the children's schools, and a myriad of community organizations.

---

The Burtins epitomize my philosophy of "*putting family first.*" Here are a few examples of what that commitment means to them:

- When Darnell called from college with an edge of nervousness about an upcoming doctor's appointment, Dan took off work and made the drive to the campus to accompany his son.
- Though they drive modest cars and shun frequent nights out or other expensive pastimes, four years ago the family

invested in a lakeside cottage in rural Michigan. There on weekends Dan and Jackie have quiet time, Darnell decompresses, and everyone visits the aunt and niece who live nearby.
- Yearly vacations are an extended-family affair, with the grandparents joining in—because, DaToya says, it's more fun that way.

In this family, *communication* is one of the bases of success. They speak directly to me and to each other. Though they'll interrupt one another, they do so respectfully. The parents let the children speak freely, signaling an underlying comfort. The conversation is rapid and freewheeling. When Jackie's mother, Mrs. Alice Stanton, cites the Bible and its proverb about words "fitly spoken," she's broken the code for this family. Its members are well educated, well spoken, and insightful.

In a world where urban dwellers tend to move often and keep their neighbors at arm's length, the Burtins live in an uncommonly close community. Residents of their two-block row of homes practice a highly effective "neighborhood watch" to protect children and homes. Most have lived there many years; the Burtins are considered "junior" residents. In the evening, as the day cools, generations of families gather on the sidewalk and grassy parkway, sharing jump ropes, friendly greetings, and news of their families. This mutual caring, Dan says, is one indicator of the "extended-family values" his family enjoys.

Another indicator is the fact that the Burtins' house is always open to any and all relatives. During my visit, Jackie's and Dan's parents plus an uncle stop by for visits. This is routine. The Burtins take it upon themselves to motivate—and provide a second home to—many of the cousins. Given the number of Dan and Jackie's sisters and brothers, the house can quickly become packed with relatives.

As in any large family, some members have had struggles. However, the Burtin family provides via "roundtable discussions" a method of airing concerns and seeking advice. The formal structure of the family unit, and the communication fostered by strong parents and grandparents, helps sustain goodwill.

The Burtins have their priorities, and education tops the list. Darnell is currently completing his bachelor's degree at the predominantly white Illinois Wesleyan University at Bloomington-Normal, about an hour's drive from Chicago. He's also a management intern at Pepper Construction Co. DaToya, a senior in high school, takes advantage every year of a "Summer Opportunity of a Lifetime" program through her high school, Providence–St. Mel. The summer of '95 took her to Oxford University in England.

Education doesn't stop with the children. Both Dan and Jackie are lifetime learners who often take one or two courses at a time. In fact, Jackie is in a master's program now.

The Burtin family's themes—communication, neighborhood, extended family, social awareness, and education—are the foundation of their success in marriage, parenthood, and relationships with others.

## Marriage

She thought he was "a playboy," so she kept her distance. It was 1967 at Chicago's Lane Technical High School, and Jackie Stanton, a nose-to-the-grindstone student of 18, formed that early impression of her future husband. They were part of a large, loose group that "hung" together, and "a friend of his was interested in a friend of mine," Jackie recalls. Through casual encounters and eventual double-dating, their acquaintance bloomed.

Dan admits that initially "when she saw me I was always talking to another young lady," but after a few dates he managed to convince Jackie that "I wasn't the type of person she thought I was. I had a plan in life, I wanted to be somebody [and] not just hanging in the streets. I had a conscience about things I did and what I said around people I respected."

Dan's determination to succeed, coupled with his sense of humor, won Jackie over. "Laughing a lot," she says, has always been a part of their life together. "I was looking through my bridal book last night," Jackie confesses, "and I thought, 'He *was* handsome, wasn't he?' Sure, he's got a little weight on him now, but both of us do. Yeah, I still love him, probably more. In fact, I *know* I love him more."

At ages 19 and 21, after almost two years of dating, they went right from their parents' homes into marriage, with a lavish ceremony—six groomsmen, six bridesmaids, a flower girl, and a ring bearer. In addition to attending Loop Junior College (now Harold Washington College), Dan worked full-time at Sears, Roebuck. He'd started there as a clerk while in high school and stayed twenty years, eventually rising to the position of internal auditor.

Just a month after the wedding, Dan was drafted. "I got the notice one day, and the next day I went and signed up for the air force," he remembers. "I said, 'No, no army!' . . . and still wound up being a security policeman." Six months later he was discharged due to a flare-up of an earlier injury. "I got lucky," he says in retrospect. "I had a lot of friends who didn't make it [back from the service], or who came out and haven't been right since."

By 1974 they'd moved into their present home and Darnell was born. "After that," Dan recalls, "I busted my shoulder playing semi-pro football." He'd played with the Chicago Eagles for nine years, practicing two nights a week and playing Sundays while working full-time and attending school.

The young marriage had its share of challenges. "There were a lot of early problems, basically because I was away from home a lot," Dan admits. "I'd work all day and go straight to class until nine-forty-five or ten."

Then there were those nights out with the guys. "Sometimes you realize that in a marriage there are those things that you can't do all the time," Dan says. "You can't just hang out with your friends and go those places. I'm hanging out with some fellas and they'd want to go out and have a beer, and I'd say 'Yeah, I'll go.'

And I may just call home and say, 'I'm hanging out with the fellas,' you know?" But Jackie wasn't so pleased. For her, "It was a big deal," Dan confesses. "It was like, 'You didn't call—I didn't know where you were. You could have at least let me know.' Those things are important," he adds. "We learned that communication is important."

The worst obstacles, Jackie recalls, were financial. "Both of us were still in school," she says, "and just learning how to manage." Yet none of their hurdles have ever been large. "Well, we've argued. But we've never had any type of pushing or shoving," Jackie assures me. "I'll never forget what my father told my husband before we got married: 'Do not hit my daughter. If you feel you have to hit her then you send her back home.' We've never had any problems like that. We do a lot of talking; we just talk and we have our disagreements. I guess both of us can be stubborn and opinionated at times.

"Our disagreements can range from a political issue to a religious issue," Jackie continues, "but we've always been able to sit down and discuss it and usually we come to a consensus. Neither one of us really changes the other's mind or opinion, but we just agree that we can't agree and leave it like that."

They do agree that even after twenty-six years, their love is still strong. How do they do it? "I enjoy doing things spur of the moment, out of the air," Jackie responds. "He likes things planned out. So sometimes I'll wake up in the morning and say, 'You know what? I think this will be one of those Jackie days!' And we'll just take off."

A "Jackie day" is spent fulfilling her whims. Often it's eight hours together browsing malls, garage sales, or thrift marts. She's teased by her friends because she spends the day shopping and usually returns with only a bag of peanuts to show for it. But Dan pays attention. "She'll see something she likes," he says of their forays to the stores, "then we'll walk away and I'll go back and get it another time."

He also surprises her with perfume or special clothing. "You'll probably never wear it, but here it is," he tells her. "She'll laugh and say 'okay.'" He's quick with sincere compliments as well: "Like I'll tell her she's pretty, she looks good, and I'll buy her something really feminine and say how nice she looks in it."

They don't mind showing affection in front of their children ("Sometimes at home we'll look at each other and just walk up and hug and kiss," Jackie says) and they "play a lot" with good-natured wrestling and chases. They also plan getaways without the kids, whether brief ("a play, have breakfast, stop for a little dinner or a cup of coffee," says Dan) or a little longer, such as weekends at their Michigan retreat.

Of course, the years have brought major changes, mostly for the better. "I've grown to trust him a lot more," Jackie says. "I loved my husband when we were first married, but I guess I was kind of independent, strong willed, 'I can do things for myself,' that type of mentality. And I had to learn to trust him to do things, to have faith that he could do it as well as I could or better—maybe differently, but with the same outcome.

"With the kids we've learned to really enjoy each other, and that takes time," Jackie continues. "It's not something you know after five or six years of marriage. And one more thing—I noticed a change in myself when I turned 40, it's a self-growth type of thing [that she brings to the marriage]. We're independent but we're also interdependent on each other. We enjoy doing a lot of things together. I think we're probably best friends." Jackie is caught by the truth of it. "We're friends! *We're friends!* It's just grown—the marriage has matured along with us."

A big part of that came from rising to the responsibilities of parenthood. "When you come up with a bunch of sisters and brothers you think you understand and know—until you have your own," says Dan. "There's a lot more to it than just being [physically] there for them—a lot of emotional things; you have to be there in spirit, and guide and teach them right from wrong. Children, you tell them one thing and then they see what you do, and they'll emulate you."

I nod, recalling how many times this same point has come up in my previous interviews.

From their vantage point, what do their children most need to understand about marriage? "We talked to our son a lot," Dan reports. "And we'd say, 'Look for somebody you respect, and who respects you. Someone you want to spend the rest of your life with. Not just the physical part of it; you've got to remember that individual is a person. She has her opinions and a mind of her own.'"

Jackie concurs. "You need to find a person you really like as an individual," she cautions. "Marriage is not easy and it's something that takes a lot of hard work—you're going to have problems, but as long as there's open communication, then one partner can say what they feel without worry that someone else will be hurt by it. Also, in our relationship, neither one of us 'outpowers' the other. I may be stronger in some areas and Dan is stronger in some areas—you have to expect that."

Dan calls the union "a partnership." It's demonstrated by the chores. They've both handled the bills, in five-year stints, and everyone pitches in with the rest. "He cooks, he washes dishes, he mops floors," Jackie says. "One thing he won't do too often is clean out the toilet. I usually get stuck with that job—but then, I don't change oil. He says, 'Well, you change the oil,' and I say, 'You clean out the toilet," and so we usually say forget it, we'll stick to our own job there."

## *The Burtin Grandparents: Marriages of Example*

I had the opportunity to interview both Dan's and Jackie's parents, whose combined years of marriage total ninety-seven! They represent a marital standard that seems to have lost ground over time in black America, because today two out of three black children are born to unmarried mothers. This wasn't always the case, of course: Professor Eugene Genovese and other historians have documented the amazing resilience of the black family, which survived cruelties in slavery (in slave states, marriage was even forbidden by law) and other disadvantages over almost three hundred years.

The Burtin grandparents married in a very different time. In the mid-1940s, African American rates of illegitimacy were only slightly higher than those of the larger society. By 1965, however, in the aftermath of the Watts riots in Los Angeles, then–assistant secretary of labor Daniel Patrick Moynihan's *The Negro Family: The Case for National Action* sounded the alarm that nonwhite out-of-wedlock births had risen to 23.6 percent (compared to 3 percent of white births).* He asserted that the man's position in the black family was eroding, marginalizing them and undermining the strength of marriage in the community. For this revelation, Moynihan was blasted as being racist and insensitive. The controversy was so intense that the issue was not seriously debated until a generation later.

America can at this point only hope that rates of illegitimacy will return to their 1960s levels. Since 1960, when 91 percent of white and 67 percent of black children under 18 lived with both parents, percentages of intact families have plummeted. In 1993, 77 percent of white and 36 percent of African American youngsters had both their birth parents in the home, drops of 14 percentage points and a whopping 31 percentage points, respectively.†

In light of the reaction to Moynihan's warnings thirty years ago, it was too risky politically to challenge the popular wisdom—that children suffered little from living in a stable single-parent home; that divorce was a desirable option for unhappy spouses; and that marriage, given the opportunity for sanctioned cohabitation, was superfluous. While data demonstrating the negative consequences of illegitimacy gathered in academic journals, there was little public debate about it until relatively recently.

*Daniel Patrick Moynihan, *The Negro Family: The Case for National Action* (Washington, D.C.: Office of Policy Planning and Research, U.S. Department of Labor, March 1965), discussed in an excellent paper by Mitchell B. Pearlstein, "From Moynihan to 'My Goodness,'" publication of the Center of the American Experiment, Minneapolis, Minn., August 1995.

†U.S. Congress Committee on Ways and Means, *The Green Book,* and U.S. Department of Commerce, Bureau of the Census, "Marital Status and Living Arrangements," March 1993.

After so many triumphant years, the Burtin grandparents, Mr. and Mrs. Moise Burtin and Mr. and Mrs. Wallace Stanton, are deservedly content. Not only have they honored the institution of marriage, they've enjoyed it; not only have they raised a total of fifteen children, but these children have without exception grown to lead productive lives. In fact, the children have excelled far beyond the parents professionally, most attaining college degrees. And, like the parents, they're raising exemplary children of their own.

Both families consider religion indispensable to their success. Moise and Irene Burtin centered their marriage and family of nine children around Mount Olive Baptist Church. They gained guidance from the Bible and still regularly read it at home. Theirs has been a self-sacrificing life of devoted service to family, church, and neighborhood. And it continues to be so: Though Mr. Burtin spent thirty-two years driving a delivery truck and seventeen years in the gasoline business and is now officially retired, he excuses himself this afternoon to get to his part-time job issuing supplies in the streets and sanitation department. He is also the "handyman" at their church. Says Mrs. Burtin, "He helps everybody. Whenever they call—to take them shopping, run an errand for the church, whatever. And in the neighborhood, and for my daughters-in-law and sons—everybody—when they call, he never says no."

Mrs. Burtin shows pride in her husband's charity; he is equally supportive of her in her role as mother and grandmother. They share and relish their role as magnet for the grandchildren. They recently bought a large house in anticipation of the youngsters' frequent return. They have an amazing way of communicating:

Mrs. Burtin: "We did practically everything together, whatever my children were in, I was always involved. One thing I used to always tell my children: 'I love you, you're my child, whatever you do, whatever problems you have, bring it to me, and I'll help.'"

Mr. Burtin: "Tell the truth."

Mrs. Burtin: "If you're right, I'm with you, and if you're wrong, I'm with you. I'm going to tell you you're wrong, but Mama will be there. It don't get too late, it don't get too early—they call me because that's my time. Kids got to know that; they have to know that they got their parents behind them. . . . *It's good to know that you always got a home.*"

Jackie's parents, like the elder Burtins, both grew up in the segregated South; her father, Wallace Stanton, lost his mother at age 3 and he "never knew" his dad until he was 15. He raised himself, aided by the charity of two kindly women in Birmingham, Alabama, a long time before there was a civil rights movement. He shares recollections of riding in the back of the streetcar—a policy that he says was abruptly shifted when, as the result of a crash, it was decided that the black passengers should ride in the front so as to absorb any impact.

While on a military stopover in Chicago, he met his future wife. As with the Burtins, church is central in their lives—"We joined the Armed Soldiers of the Salvation Army" through their children's interest about two score years ago, Mrs. Stanton explains, and they've volunteered their services extensively in its Home League, Sunday school, and youth programs.

The Stantons hold up work and character as essential to family viability. Mary Alice Stanton's favorite quotation is: "Go to the ant, thou sluggards, consider her ways and be wise" (Proverbs 6:6). She explains, "That ant works all summer storing up for the winter. You have to work for what you want."

## Parenting

The Burtins' style of parenting is an object lesson in traditional values: respect, loyalty, self-sacrifice, hard work, charity.

It's significant that the Burtins practice these values in inner-city Chicago, where within a few minutes' stroll, thugs peddle crack, gangs threaten violence, and girls await their welfare checks while their impregnators "hang" on the streets rather than work for wages they consider not worth the effort. The Burtin children have seen all of this, but they've *never been tempted toward it.* In fact, they work actively with those who don't have strong families to help them resist such traps.

Dan and Jackie tell how they immunized their children from the perils around them.

## *Respect*

Respect, especially for elders, is a Burtin family tradition. "It's what we call 'respect straight across,'" Dan explains. "My grandfather, I respect him. And my father—I always say 'yes, sir, no, sir.' It's just the way I was brought up—I respect him as my father. I'm a grown man, I have my own family, but he's still my father, and we taught our kids that. I don't care how you feel, or how angry you are, you respect your grandfather because he's what we call the head of the family. He is the patriarch. He's there. Never disrespect the eldest."

The Burtins are equally strict about those outside the family. Dan admonishes his children: "When you meet someone else's parents, show them some respect. We know it's hard, especially today with the young people. They want to be cool and at times, they'll forget. We see a lot of kids—'Yeah, what's happenin', how ya doin'' and all that. And it comes out—and I say 'All right, watch it,' and they'll usually go back and say, 'Okay, I didn't mean to be disrespectful, I'm sorry.' It's a line of respect that we have to give our elders. If we lose that, then we've lost all control."

This is what Dan Burtin has instilled in his own children. He also demands it of the teenagers he's led in his sports teams and the Boy Scouts. "That's the way I talk to the youth," Dan says, "They come in and say, 'Hey man, yo yo yo, you know.' I say, 'Excuse me, time out. In this program, I am Mr. Burtin. Your name is—?' and I say, 'You are Mr. Smith. I am an adult. You are a young man and I will treat you as such if you treat me as such in return. Now, what is it that you want?'

"And we'll talk. I'll say, 'You got a problem, let's sit and talk about it. I'll give you respect. You show me respect and I don't care how tough you are. When you walk out the door, you can be as tough as you want. But right here, when you're with me, or within this building, or within this program, you show respect to every adult.' And I have put young men out of the program. I say, 'You can't come in tonight with that attitude, until you show some respect.'" So what happens? "They go, 'Yeah, okay, I'm not coming back.' So fine, the door's open."

Jackie interjects, "They're back the next week. They're usually back."

And what of the others, I want to know. "There've been those who've come in the program and then left," Dan goes on, "but they return—or they may have left and didn't return, but yet, if I see them on the street, they'll stop and talk to me. And I've been told 'thank you.' They say, 'I didn't turn out the way I know you wished I had, but thank you, you did help me.'"

Jackie mentions a kid named J.J., a Boy Scout. "Oh, he was a little rough one," Dan acknowledges. "But he was smart. He was quick. You give him something, he could figure it out. We go to camp, and he could put up a tent—he was good, but he just wanted to hang with the crowd, and I just kept trying to pull him away. Eventually, he moved out of the community.

"The Scouting troop I worked with wasn't here, in this area—I worked in the projects, in Rockwell Gardens," Dan explains. "We [he and Jackie] took our kids into Rockwell so they could see—with all apartments—kids from everywhere. I said, 'You can go anywhere. Don't be afraid. But you have to respect, and then they respect you.'" Dan volunteered in the housing projects for twenty-two years, for the Salvation Army, Midwest Corps. The Boy Scout troop proved especially rewarding because of the changes he observed in boys like Marvin Robinson.

"He was the shortest, the toughest, the hardest little guy that came," Dan recalls, shaking his head. "He wanted to beat up, to jump on everybody." What was his problem? "He just had too much free time, because he could come and go at will," Dan surmises.

"He had a brother, but supervision wasn't strict. He could come and go and just ran wild. In the projects, if you want to do better, if you want to do right, you got this environment saying 'If you do this, you're a nerd. You're not cool.' So you try to be cool and be part of the group. Plus the fact that Marvin was only about five feet tall at the time, so he was short. We call it short man's inferiority complex, where he felt he had to be tougher than anybody. He had to be tougher and stronger and badder than anybody else. So that's the way he came in."

But Dan had a strategy. "I made him a student leader. Right away," Dan explains. "I said, 'Okay, you want to be bad. You're in charge.' I said, 'You're responsible. Make sure they act right. . . .' Sounds too good to be true? . . . Yeah, he resisted it. But I still told him, 'You're the assistant patrol leader. If they don't do the job, I'm getting you.'"

Marvin finally took on the responsibility—because Dan kept him in a respected position of leadership. "I would go to the unit, and if they weren't doing what they were supposed to do—you know, patrol wasn't neat or they were kind of acting up—I would come to him. And we'd get a command for attention, and if they didn't jump to attention, I'd walk up to him and say, 'Mr. Robinson, you got a problem with your unit. If you want to keep your rank, either they shape up or somebody else will get the rank. You have a patch and rank on your sleeve of your uniform.' I said I would 'take it off right here in front of everybody else. Not to embarrass you, but to show you that if you don't want it, I'll give it to somebody else.'

"He didn't want nobody taking it off. He kept it," Dan reports. "He kept moving up, and he finally made assistant senior patrol leader. And he just missed making Eagle Scout. He made Star, and he got too old. He didn't fit the age requirement. We had one boy make Eagle, and we had three almost make Eagle. The one boy, the first boy on the West Side of Chicago to make it in twenty years."

The "one boy" who made Eagle was Darnell Burtin. Marvin

Robinson graduated from Grant High School and is currently studying to be a paralegal, working part-time with a law firm.

## *Extended Family—Neighbors*

The Burtin children, by their own accounts, were raised by *two sets* of extended family: their kin and their neighbors on the block. Both reinforced the same values, demanded the same standard of behavior, and made themselves available for guidance whenever the children needed it. "Everybody on this block had something to do with Darnell Burtin being raised," the young man acknowledges. "That goes from that corner"—he points up the street—"all the way to the hospital." He gestures in the opposite direction, referring to the health facility two blocks away. "I'd get in trouble. I'd get a whupping down there. I'd get a whupping down *there*. I'd get a whupping here. I got a whupping everywhere. I got more whuppings than I can count. I can't remember how many times I got hit. That's how it was with every kid, you know. I think there's one kid out of the whole group of like thirty of us that may be in jail. That's an unbelievable statistic. It takes a whole block to raise one child."

Darnell's experiences reflect those of his father's youth. Recalls Dan, "When I was growing up, my whole block, when I'd do something they didn't like, someone would grab me and say not to do it. I'd be guaranteed if someone saw me doing something when I was growing up, that before I got home, my mother would know. And she would get me, and she would yell up the stairs, 'I'm going to tell your dad!' And it was like, man, I got to wait the rest of the day—my dad's going to kill me."

Dan knew he wanted that kind of monitoring for his children, and the isolation ("We don't have more than one crosswalk") of this block has been a buffer against urban problems and against the "none-of-your-business" mentality in much of modern life. Jackie had known about this house throughout her youth, since it had been owned by the Salvation Army for use by its officers. "By working there and by going to their church, I knew the officers were getting ready to move and they were considering selling it," she says.

The neighbors were proprietary even then. "They felt we would fit in the community," Dan notes. Meaning that the Burtins shared the local values, and the young couple would participate in the unwritten mutual protection policy. "The kids play up and down the street, and every family watches what everybody else does," Dan begins. "If and when kids get to fighting—" Jackie cuts in, "Which is very little. They don't fight a lot." "But when they do, you leave them alone, you see how far it goes," Dan says. "Eventually somebody will intervene and say, 'Okay, stop it.'"

### *Extended Family—by Blood and Marriage*

It's the same way in their extended biological family. The Burtin children respect their grandparents and are kept in line by them. Both sets have strong views about child rearing. Mr. Moise Burtin summarizes the lessons he and his wife taught Dan and his siblings: "Taught them to read, listen, and be obedient." Their method? Passages from the Bible, and a strong hand when necessary.

Mrs. Irene Burtin concedes that it's tougher now. "It's a whole different generation. When our children were growing up, [it was] like: You say it, and they listen. Now they say, 'Don't spank children,' and I don't understand that because I spanked my children. I love my children. I didn't beat them, but I would hit my children. And they know that I would do it now!"

"You're talking right from wrong," adds Mr. Burtin. "And I feel if you're parents, it's your right to do what you want to do—not what society tells me I can't do. I'm raising this child. I give birth to this child. This is *my* child. And I have to do what I think is right to raise this child. Because if you don't raise them, the state and the city will raise them for you.

"Some of the parents—I know they really don't need to hit because they don't know how. There's a way to hit a child. When they do something wrong, you tell them, 'Don't do it.' And if they keep doing it, you're supposed to show them you're still in control. When you get tired of telling them, then you have to show them who's in control."

Mrs. Mary Alice Stanton, Jackie's mother, in a separate interview, repeats Mrs. Burtin's recommendations almost exactly. "You start teaching them at a real young age, and then as they grow older, you have to think of different things to do." She pauses, then brightens. "When they'd fight one another, then they'd have to hug and kiss one another and a lot of time they didn't appreciate that because they were angry. That would be a punishment. Then I'd spank. I mean, I had an old switch. I'd always get the legs—that's what I dealt with.

"And, like I say, we taught the kids concerning the Bible, and told them to always keep Christ in their life, and I'd teach them the Bible is a guide for a good life, for a healthy and a righteous life. And I'd often remind them also, when they'd do little things out of order—'Remember what we'd talked about, what we've agreed about, concerning the Bible.' And they took the Salvation Army—they also taught them the same things concerning the Lord Jesus, you know. And so, I can say they've done real good."

Dan and Jackie were also vigilant about their children's behavior. They were unyielding about curfews, for example. Recalls Darnell, "When I was in high school, I was an athlete, and I'm a good athlete and I wanted to go out and stay out. When we won a big game, I wanted to stay out until two o'clock in the morning—I was 17 years old. All my other friends' parents seemed like they didn't care. And I'd try to come in here at two o'clock in the morning and my parents were sitting on the front porch. You know, that's embarrassing. So it was kind of rough, you know. When I was that age, I was like, 'Man, this is wrong. Dad, this is wrong.' But now, I'm almost 21 and I can see."

Darnell, self-described as "different" from the rest due to his daring and mind of his own, took a bit of shaping. "My father told me—I don't want to curse—my father told me, if I ever joined a gang that he'd kick my ass. And that didn't really scare me, but just that thought stuck in my head, of me hanging out with these guys that are supposed to be tough, and seeing my father walk down the block and trying to come get me." A second push to stay straight was the experience of peers in his "little bad crowd" at age 10 or 11 who "were going to juvenile homes. One guy got shot in the leg. Another guy got shot—I knew him. I was like, 'I don't want to get shot.'"

Still, Darnell sometimes deserved punishment. "The belt? Oh yeah. But I loved it. I mean, I don't want to say I loved it, but I love it now. The thought that I really did something—it makes me sit back and laugh, and say, 'If I was a parent, I'd have whupped this child too.' And it's just funny to sit back and take a glimpse at some of those things and say, 'Man, I can't believe I did that.' When I got to a certain age, Dad made me think. Dad said, 'Now, you know what you just did. Think about it. Think about what you really did. Why don't you sit down and *really* think about it?' And then this made me feel bad, and so I'd sit down and think about it."

DaToya avoided the need for discipline simply by learning from Darnell's mistakes and their consequences. But on the occasions she deserved it, she received "a spanking sometimes. A slap on the hand. A spanking if I really got out of hand and if I really deserved it, but most of the time, my parents just yelled 'Toya, don't do that!' I'd cry, like 'I'm sorry.' I'm kinda that kind of kid. But I didn't get too many whippings. That's the kind of person I am—I do what I'm supposed to do and that's it."

Darnell received a variety of punishments. For example, one time Dan and Jackie cut off car privileges for a week. "I had to get back and forth to work, back and forth to school—work was downtown, school was in the suburbs." I suggested to Darnell that perhaps his parents were strict. "I don't know if 'strict' is the word," he replied. "They were *hard.* I know people's parents who were strict who didn't let them do anything. My parents got to a point where, 'If you want to, make your mistakes. Go on. Don't kill yourself, but make these mistakes and you'll learn from them.' So they weren't strict; I think they were hard. I thank them for it. Too many kids that I know whose parents weren't hard aren't doing anything. Nothing—sitting at home, watching TV."

### *Roundtable Discussions*

The Burtin family is so cohesive across generations that one child's missteps are the concern of them all. Any family member can call a "roundtable discussion," and everyone appears. No social engagement takes precedence. There, a child not performing up to potential is guided with words of concern and caring. Mr. Stanton: "Bring them in, and 'Let's sit down and talk about it. What's your problem? Why can't you do it? Your mother did it. I did it.'"

After repeated efforts to assist one family member over something Mr. Stanton calls "a little too deep, and I don't want to tell you about that," it was decided that there was no choice left but to ostracize him. Mrs. Stanton, however, is a softy. Scoffs her husband, "She's overprotective, see. It's not that bad, but it's still what I don't want. But she'll pet him."

"Talk and tell him to do right," Mrs. Stanton corrects. "At least be praying, encouraging."

The family meetings sometimes have another purpose. "Just recently we had Father's Day," DaToya says. "We all got together. My cousin set up a program because she wanted to express her feelings for the family. She's like 22 [years old], in college, and she wanted to express how hard it's been and to give her thanks to those who've helped her.

"First, she wrote a story that explained being grateful and things like that, and then she took a quote out of the Bible. Then we went from age, children first, and you just told what you were grateful for, and you gave thanks to those who helped you. And everyone did it, and the tears flowed. And we had friends who came by, and they were just sitting there, crying. You know, it's kind of a unique thing—we're very open about our feelings. Usually in the family, we tell each other, 'You helped me out—thank you. You've been there when I've needed you,' and things like that."

Jackie mentions another facet of that Father's Day gathering. "I think Darnell was really surprised and shocked to learn that so many of the kids saw him as their role model. He was totally blown out. His mouth just dropped!" Jackie says. "They told him how much they admired him with track and college—they just went on and on. He has a lot of confidence anyway, but he told them, 'You know what, I'm going to have to rethink things before I do them now, because I wasn't aware of how much you were watching me, and how much you all love me.' They just expressed this to him, which was good."

### *Setting an Example*

Jackie Burtin has one of those positive outlooks on life. Everything comes up roses. (Of course, her mother, Mrs. Stanton, is known never to frown or speak an unkind word.) On every topic—crime in the neighborhood, the decline of African American families—Jackie is always minimizing the negative and playing up the positive, repeating in several contexts that "if you go in looking for the negative, that's what you're going to find. If you go in looking for some positive things, [you'll find that] as well."

This upbeat attitude characterizes the "I can do it; I *am* doing it" approach with which the adult Burtins conduct their lives. Dan and Jackie Burtin don't just talk the talk, they walk the walk. The recommendations they offer their children aren't hollow pronouncements but *descriptions* of what works for them and for their parents.

But there's no coasting for the Burtins; their positive attitude is the motivator for constant *striving*—for self-improvement through education; for the success of their nuclear family. The Burtin children were fortunate to have parents insistent on cheering—and coaching—them in sports as well as academics. Members of the extended family strive for regular contact and formalized roundtable discussions. Then there's the effort to make a difference for others, exemplified by the charity work that each of the Burtins undertakes. DaToya staffs the office at a nearby hospital; Jackie was a Cub Scout den mother for three years and consistently volunteered to be a school room mother and field-trip chaperon; and Dan has coached the USA Track Club for thirteen years.

The Burtins' core values—respect, education, and making family a priority—are constantly reinforced at home. DaToya claims flat out that she absorbed her values "by observation. I saw what they did and I took it in. I say, 'That must be the right way because other people feel good or other people appreciate when you do it this way.'"

The Burtins live life to the fullest, especially when it comes to family and neighborhood. You walk up to their front porch, where the Burtins await you, hear them call hello to Mr. Verge and admonish a five-year-old on a rickety tricycle to stay out of the street. You sit in their living room for, say, twenty minutes, and you're likely to see cousin Augustus, 14, popping by to shoot baskets and three neighbor boys scampering through to the TV room.

Afternoons often find Dan coaching and DaToya playing (or running, since she's excelled at volleyball, basketball, and track). For years at night, you'd see Dan hitting the books with his children, checking over both his graduate coursework and their math. (Now it's Jackie's turn to finish term papers on deadlines.) You might come by one wintry day to see Darnell two doors down, shoveling his fourth front walk, unable to quit "once he got going with the shovel." And then the family comes together for the evening meal, pitching in to get the food out buffet-style, sharing conversation around the table, and cleaning up, with rotating assignments of chores.

I ask the younger Burtins to define what a good parent should be. They echo the same sentiment of *self-sacrifice.* "A parent is someone who gives you more than they have," Darnell replies. "They give you so much of themselves that sometimes they can't do for themselves. They sacrifice what they don't have to give to you. If you watch animals, lions and tigers, they do more for their child than they do for themselves; they'll go hungry." Also, Darnell adds, a parent is someone who teaches you "how to grow so that when you reach that age you can go out on your own."

DaToya says "a good parent will care for you, give 110 percent for your life. It's a person willing to sacrifice to give you the necessities to go on to become a person by yourself, an independent person."

Jackie's view similarly holds that "a parent is one who loves you more than life itself really. He instills in you the tools to prepare you for survival in the world—[a parent is] someone who's nurturing, caring, dedicated to [making] the child the best possible person he can be. Teaching him to care not only for himself but for other people."

Finally, Dan adds, "Also a parent is one who is willing to stick by their guns on an issue and be able to say, 'Yes, I'm wrong' at times. To sacrifice. To give to your children what you probably didn't have, or to give to them so they can survive in the world, so they can be an adult. From experience, you know that it's hard out there; life is rough, and if you're not prepared, it will eat you."

### *Darnell*

Darnell is tall and athletic. He's confident, well spoken, and a straight shooter. There's a certain presence about him that would probably make him a successful politician if he chose that path.

He talks candidly about himself and his family. "My sister's more of a straight-A, honor-roll type. Goes to school, follows Mama's rules, does what Mama and Daddy says. I was never that way. Me and my parents were always into it. I always had something to prove." Whenever I ask Dan and Jackie for their take on Darnell, they defer, telling me to "ask him yourself." They clearly respect their son, stepping back as if giving him room, expecting him to make the splash he does.

"I'm always looking for my own answer," Darnell admits. "Whatever they said wasn't good enough until I found out the truth." He recalls a time in high school when he ignored his father's warning not to go out one evening and, as a result, suffered a slight concussion in an auto accident. Another time he disregarded their warnings and ended up with a speeding ticket.

"I think making those mistakes has helped me to be the person I am," he says. "I'm very outgoing and I always have to find the message to something," which refers back to their religion. Darnell is tentative about "their" faith. "I always fought them over going to church because I had so many questions when I was younger. I didn't believe the Salvation Army was church, and I wanted to go to a Baptist church. The Salvation Army just was where they served food and everything. We didn't have a choice, and I thank them for not giving me a choice—I became an Eagle Scout because of the Salvation Army. I know a lot of people through the Salvation Army and it helped me grow as a young man. Without Salvation Army, I think I might have been in a lot of trouble. Friday nights I was playing basketball. It kept me off the streets."

Darnell freely expresses gratitude. He's a young man who can look back and admit his mistakes. He's especially contrite and objective about his teen years, not something you'd expect from someone in his early twenties. In our culture, it seems that adolescence—that is, limited accountability, permission to goof off, lowered expectations of behavior—has stretched into the late twenties. I've seen youths who continue school (usually at their parents' expense) solely because they don't want to grow up. I've met young adults who don't think at all about the Fifth Commandment

[Honor thy father and thy mother], yet they expect money from their parents or speak disdainfully about their folks' honest efforts to instill good values. At the same time, I've met others like Darnell, whose respect and dedication to their families never make it into the newspapers and whose daily activities don't show up in government statistics. These young men and women are the real hope for America's future.

At the time I talk with him, Darnell is on summer break, living at home temporarily while working at Pepper Construction Co. in Chicago. In the fall, he returns to Illinois Wesleyan University, a place he calls "a white school" where many of the students from rural farm communities gain their first contact with African Americans. Darnell doesn't mind being a role model. He often declines invitations from "the guys" for late nights: "I tell them that I'm working and I'm almost an adult." Darnell doesn't have much free time. The commitment to work and school doesn't allow it. He's extraordinarily focused.

Asked to describe the main values his parents taught, Darnell—like the rest of the Burtins—first answers "family." Then he adds: "independence and responsibility." He confesses, "One thing that really killed me this year was that I had to ask my parents for money. It's the first time in three years that I've ever asked them. It's a rule of thumb that I never ask anybody for anything because I get it myself, not illegally, but one way or another. And I had to ask them this year, and that hurt me, but that shows they taught me something: independence. They taught me, 'Son, you can't ask all the time. Sometimes nobody is going to be there to help you.' You know, I have my own apartment. I pay my own bills."

Darnell defines responsibility as "being able to take care of what you *have* to do before what you *want* to do" as well as prioritizing purchases. "I see a lot of young guys driving around with these new cars, but they have no houses," he laments. "Driving around with new cars and they have no jobs. I *will* have a job, so I'm not worried about getting a new car. A new car is going to come. And I'd rather have a house than have a car."

Darnell has his priorities straight. We don't give enough credit to people who can forgo the immediate gratification of a new car in favor of the difficult and deferred rewards of saving and sacrificing for a home.

Darnell is aware that his community has deteriorated. "Twenty years ago you had black men in the community working, [you] had jobs. Now, you got waste dumps—where the blacks are located you'll see landfills. Also, if you look at the percentage of people on drugs—given that blacks are only 12 percent [of the population]—there are more blacks on drugs. There are more black males that don't have jobs or are in prison than white males. I mean, there's so many people on drugs, and there's violence. It's just getting really bad."

Darnell continues: "I think it's just a nonchalant, not-care-about-life attitude that I'm seeing a lot in the black community. . . . I see it so much here, and it kind of hurts my soul because people are supposed to surpass their parents, and I don't see too many people surpassing their parents. I think I'm surpassing my parents, you know—that's only because that's what a parent is supposed to be. He or she is supposed to set their child up to where they can do better, or try and help them do at least the same. You're not supposed to do worse, I don't think."

### *Darnell on Success*

Darnell has seen that cycle of dependence on the government and believes blacks don't break out of it because "they don't know what success is. Nobody's told them what it is." Darnell does his best to educate his friends. "I mean, I can come in four days a week, but they see me coming in my suit and say, 'Like, what you doing over here? You from the neighborhood?' I always have to show them, 'Hey, I live right here!'

He's a man bent on success in its highest form. "If I see something and I want to do it, I'm going to get it. I say that about anything. I tell people that all the time, and they call me sarcastic, conceited, stuck up. In the black community they call me that, and in the white community, they say that that's good. That's determination. And I think that's so stupid to say you're stuck up because you have a goal to attain and you're going to attain it. I can never understand it.

"That's why I think I've lost a few friends," Darnell adds. "I talked to a friend of mine today. I happened to have five minutes free time and I called him from work. And he was like, 'Man, I haven't seen you in a month! I haven't talked to you!' I said, 'Let me get settled first, and I'll come back and get you and help you all.' He says, 'Come back and *get* me, *help* me? What do you think, you're above me?' I say, 'I'm not above you, but I've moved past you.'

"I think success has a stigma in the black community," he says. "Young black men sometimes believe sports are their only way out. When I came out of high school—I could show you—I got letters from Stanford, University of North Carolina, University of Nevada, whatever, for track. I didn't accept a track scholarship. I don't want to be a piece of meat. I can go to school on academics and graduate and be successful in that, and not use sports as my crutch."

Darnell is saddened by the sight of acquaintances who've become "winos just sitting on the corner" wasting their talent. "I don't know, [maybe] they're scared to be successful because when you're viewed as successful, you're viewed as trying to be white. I'm going to tell you that, but I don't care—success is success, it doesn't have a color. And now I know that, working with Pepper Construction. I've been really successful in what I do, and it doesn't have a color. Not to me.

"So, I think in the black community, some people are scared to be successful—and I don't understand why. The high school I went to stresses that success is what you go to school for—what you work all your life for is to be successful. Success can be defined as graduation from high school. Success can be defined as graduation from college. My success isn't defined as that. I haven't defined it because I don't have a ceiling yet."

He does have definite ambitions: "I'm 21 this year. I want to graduate—no, *I am going to* graduate in May. I plan to work next year—I want to say Pepper Construction Co. I'm talking about going back to get my master's, my MBA. Me and some friends are talking about opening up an engineering consulting firm in the next three years. By that time, hopefully, I want to get married—around [age] 25. I want to start to raise a family, around 25, 26. Same age as my parents. They got married and they had time to themselves and then they started raising a family. I think some people wait until like 35. You can't grow with your kids. I want to grow with my kids. And for the long shot, I want to be my own boss. That's the main thing. I want to be my own boss and I want to see my sister graduate from college."

Both Darnell's mom and dad told me about the watchful eye Darnell keeps over his younger sister. Their relationship is so close that DaToya says her brother is almost like a second father. "She's my baby, that's my baby girl!" Darnell says with pride. "When I was [living] here all the time I could really see her doing well, and now I'm not here. And I call and it's like, 'How you doin', baby girl? How's school?' 'Darnell, I'm so tired.' It's hard, you know. She'll call me: 'I'm so ready to go to college!' And I'm like, 'Just slow down! Relax! Have fun!'"

He wants to help pay for DaToya's education. "You gotta help each other out," he says. "Family is your base. I don't want to say that if you don't have a strong family, it won't be good, but a strong family is like—it's the world. *It's the world!* You've always got something to lean on."

### *Darnell Talks Family*

Darnell's description of "family values" displays a wisdom beyond his years. Here are his words:

"'Family' is a word that can branch off into a thousand different things. And my family can branch out into a thousand different things. Strength might be the name—strength can branch out to responsibility, penance, and hard work. We lean on each other when we need help, and even when we don't need help, we just talk to one another.

"My family is like no family I know of amongst my friends. My father's always been there for me, which I can't say for most of my friends. My mother has definitely been there, especially in my teenage years when my father and I couldn't get along. They're still there because they're supportive. I say, 'Oh, don't come watch me run track. Don't come watch me play basketball.' And no matter how many times I say 'don't,' they're still there. They've always instilled that family is going to always come, because family is always there. And I guess that's instilled in *them* by their parents."

Darnell adds, "If your family is strong, you can overcome anything. If your family is a rock then nothing will ever push it over. I've always been able to run back to the family and my family always reaches and snatches me up and says, 'Look, boy, you are doing the wrong thing.'"

### *Darnell on the Value of Communication*

Communication and roundtable discussions have kept the Burtin family together. Here's Darnell's assessment of the benefits of such openness:

"Of all my friends and associates, my family is the only family I know that consistently sits down and just talks about just anything. My friends' families seem cold toward one another. They just don't talk like we talk. We come in the house and every day I can remember from fifth grade, my mom came home—as soon as I got in the house: 'How was your day?' I'd say, 'okay.' She was like, '"Okay" is not going to cut it. Let's talk about your day.' Even now, when I come home from work, [it's] 'How's your day?' And I'll sit down and tell her something about what I did at work today, or I'll call her from work, and say, 'Mom, how you doing? Work is hard. I'm tired,' and so on.

"In other families, I don't know if they want to talk. Some families, where young kids have children—they just shut it away. We try to talk about everything, get it out in the open. I guess that's what makes us a real close family, not only amongst the four of us, but having as many family members as we have, that extends out all over the place.

"If I wasn't able to talk to my parents, I was able to talk to my aunts or uncles. Talking is so strong in a family—and in a job. In class in college they stress communication skills. They stress looking in the eyes like you do to me. Communication is what can win you and lose you in a job. People always tell us [Burtins] we talk way too much, whatever that means. That means we're articulate, it means we know the difference between *A* and *B*."

That's not always the case with some of Darnell's friends. "My best friend—his father has ten kids. He and his sister have the same mother. And his father is what I'd call like a friend of mine now, but his father wasn't there for him when we were growing up. And he wasn't able to have that father when he messed up in basketball or going through puberty. He came down and talked to *my* father.

"A couple of my friends who do have fathers, their fathers are always working. Most of them, their fathers weren't willing to spend time with them, just coaching teams or anything else. My father's always been the kind of guy who was willing to coach or help out. I mean, he's given so much time, sometimes I have to tell him to stop."

Darnell's appreciation of his dad, and willing recognition that others are not as lucky, provide another example of his ever present humility and gratitude.

Darnell has a girlfriend, a young lady his age who has a daughter ("She's not my daughter, though"). Darnell was selective in choosing her: "We were friends for four or five years before we even started dating," he explains. "Then, before we started dating, I'd look—I don't want to say I watched her, but I watched her parents and I watched her family.

"I don't think I'm old enough to be looking toward marriage, but at this point I want somebody I can talk to. I can't come home and be like, 'Well, what did you do in work today?' 'Nothing.' You know: 'How's school?' 'Well, I didn't go to school today.' I like to come home to 'How's school?' 'Well, today was statistics, I learned about building bridges' or, even if she wasn't doing that, she'd be in law school or she'd be in business—you know, 'I learned about slopes, or about the market,' or something like that. I'd like to hold a conversation besides sports; I like to talk about something that's going to open my mind. I like to learn new things every day."

His current girlfriend is studying civil engineering and is an accomplished computer programmer. Darnell says she "turned a bad thing [having a baby out of wedlock] into a good thing. She's had support from her family. Her parents help her, and that's the kind of thing I like."

I ask Darnell to summarize his advice to parents: "I think the belt solves a lot of problems—and I think kids are crying way too much about 'My parents beat me!' What these kids call a beating, I used to call nothing. And not only that—I think parents need to spend time with kids talking to them. My parents talked to me. I was always able to talk to my parents; I was able to talk to my aunts or uncles. I think that my parents, raising me, have helped me just be the person who I am. I'm not bad, I'm not great—but I'm somewhere in the middle."

### *DaToya*

I've known some terrific young people, and I'm fortunate to be the father of three of them. But if you asked me to describe the ideal child, I'd say DaToya Burtin comes pretty close. And part of her charm is that she would strongly deny it. But it's all there:

beauty, brains, athletic achievement—and, more important, consideration, humility, compassion, and competence. She says she likes to "do, do, do"—taking her cousin Augustus, the 14-year-old I mentioned earlier, out to shoot baskets, and then helping him with his homework. Tutoring kids in her school. Helping out, in any way asked, at Loretto Hospital.

And when she participates in anything, she doesn't just join in, she leads. Her track teammates gave her a unique nickname because "I get everybody together. I know what everybody's running, where they need to be, when, what time—do they have the entire uniform? Do you have this, do you have that?—I'm just like the mother goose. Go drink your Kool-Aid now—drink some water before the practice! Da da da da da! So they call me Mother Goose."

## *Education—First Priority*

DaToya is a tall girl, strong and pretty. Her face is the image of her mother's. As with most 17-year-olds, school is the center of her life. She attended grades one through four at Franklin Fine Arts Academy, a public magnet school, where she studied piano and sampled the offerings in dance and art as well. But two long teachers' strikes in a four-year period disrupted classes in the public schools and greatly disturbed the Burtins, who felt the strikes were "a thing of making more money," so they looked at other educational options.

A friend told them about a private school, Providence–St. Mel. After the family visited the school, DaToya was tested for admission and was accepted for fifth grade. Darnell visited on a day off and, according to Jackie, "fell in love" with the place. He transferred there as a sophomore. Says Dan: "The [school] wants to make sure the kids are at the level they should be for the grade they want to go into—or above," Dan says. "It's challenging—I don't want to say *competitive* because I don't know if I like that, but it's challenging; and I appreciate the challenge it offered my kids."

One of those challenges is the "junior contract" that commits each student to an attainable GPA for senior year. If you don't fulfill the contract, Darnell reports, "You get kicked out." "The school picks your GPA depending on your work from past years," DaToya explains. "They give you an average. I have to make a higher GPA than other kids because my grade-point average was higher." Darnell's contract stipulated a 2.5; DaToya's required a 2.8.

That's just one of the standards set for the students at Providence–St. Mel. "You can get kicked out for anything—hair, earrings" that violate school rules, DaToya notes. Another stipulation: no jewelry, and no baggy or tattered jeans. Principal Paul Adams patrols the halls, vigilant about all sorts of infractions. Darnell was once fined twenty dollars for jumping over the grass. For most violations, there's a discipline court made up of both students and teachers—and the peers are the ones meting out the worst punishments. For example, if clothing is missing and not returned, either a whole class or the at-fault individual will have to buy a replacement. Dan Burtin says it's a child-centered school for those who are "involved, willing to learn, and willing to sacrifice. In a safe environment. The school itself is no-nonsense." Later he smiles, "The kids say they can't stand it. But they love it."

DaToya said she was intimidated at first by the admissions director's warnings that "this is a power school; two to three hours of homework a night," but credits her success to her fifth-grade teacher, Mrs. Rita Caruso. "She worked individually with each student, picked up the bad points, showed you how to get beyond that and how to work harder, taught you how to go home and how to study. She was really like a mother figure in school; she kept you in line. And she's still there and whenever I need her, I still go to her class, 'Mrs. Caruso—it's hard.' And she just gives you those encouraging words—you know, 'You gotta keep going.'"

And she does. The key to it all, DaToya says, is self-discipline. "I schedule myself: I have so much time for this, and so much time for this. I have to say, I'm a bookworm. I have to hit the books a lot of the time, and then from there I go to my sports and friends and social life. I try to balance everything out. We had a class in sophomore year on how to schedule study time and other time because they want you to be balanced."

This school has no tolerance for guns, drugs, or bad behavior. DaToya says, "Our school is so strict, if anyone sees you with a gun, they call the police and the officer will take you to jail."

The Burtins arrange their budget around the $3,000-per-student tuition at Providence–St. Mel. "Education was our main priority for our children," Dan says. "I could have gotten a brand-new flashy car and said 'Skip the education'—but to me, their education comes first." The school does have scholarships for students who score highly on their tests, as well as need-based financial aid.

One reason education has always been the "number one priority" for Dan and Jackie is that their own parents insisted on it. And, interestingly, both Dan and Jackie are products of single-sex high schools.

In Detroit an experiment of all-male public schools in the inner city was challenged as unconstitutional. The schools were formed after surveys discovered boys could learn more without the distraction of girls and vice versa. I visited one, which was a model of discipline and high standards. The notion that single-sex schools violate the Constitution is absurd. The criteria should be the academic and social success of children and what is best for their future rather than some pointless notion of gender balance.

### *Winning the Big Race*

Another major focus for DaToya is sports. When she got to Providence–St. Mel, she plunged immediately into just about everything: "I did cross-country. I did volleyball, track, basketball. Anything the school had, I tried." She's currently on the volleyball team. "I've been all-conference, all three years of school so far. So it was kind of nice. Varsity squad freshman year and everything." She started volleyball in elementary school—in fact, it was sports that displaced piano and overtook her desire to be a pianist.

A big part of DaToya's success in sports is the example set by her father. After his semipro career, Dan says his reaction was, "Well, I'm tired, I'm finished." That didn't last long. DaToya's dad explains how he was drawn back to the field. It started with Darnell: "I said, 'Oh, God, here's my son. Next generation.' We looked around for a program to put him in, and there was nobody out there working with the kids. So we sat down. We talked about it. I said, 'What would you think if I got out and helped coach Little League baseball?' Jackie goes, 'Well, at least I know where you'll be, and you and my son will be together.' So [Darnell and I got involved in] Little League baseball, tae kwon do, basketball, and Boy Scouts for ten years—he made Eagle Scout. And from there into high school, I helped him with basketball, cross-country, and track. He won a few state medals. Then I wound up coaching JV basketball at Providence–St. Mel. And girl's varsity track. I just feel I should work with kids and give back what somebody gave me. That's my philosophy and we try to teach it to the children."

The USA Track Club Dan organized had met the Saturday before our interview—and DaToya had qualified for the regional championship. "I really like it, and I like the family unity you can get on our team," she enthuses. "Everybody on my team I have a love for, and I'm always there for them whenever they need me." Throughout the years, DaToya has gained from her sports participation: "I met my best friend through volleyball, and she and I have been tight ever since. It's helped me academically. When I started sports, even though my grades were good, B average, they went up to straight A's because I knew I had to be on top of both [athletics and academics]."

Interestingly, DaToya never chose to enter athletics. "My parents forced me because I was quiet, and I was shy because I was five [feet] seven [inches], she remembers. "And so my parents figured if I joined sports I'd meet people, because I didn't hang with anybody. I started playing volleyball, and I started liking it, and I started to meet people and everything. I'm a competitive person. Not only in sports but academically." I asked DaToya to name her sports heroes. Her answer? "Myself." Move over, Michael Jordan.

### *DaToya on Life*

This straightforward self-confidence makes DaToya willing to take risks. When she enrolls in the "Summer Opportunity of a Lifetime Program," DaToya says she "always tells my counselors that I want to be the first person to go [to a new location], or to go by myself, to make an image for the school. I want that job. I want them to see how hard I can work and how good the school has prepared me to go into the world. That's kinda like my thing, to be the first person to pave the way for others."

That leaves the world wide open to her, with lots of options for her future—for both college and career. "I've got ideas in my mind, but I'm willing to go wherever they give you some money," DaToya notes pragmatically. "But, if I had to choose, it would be between Spelman College, which is my grandmother's old school, and Georgia Tech, because I have an idea to go into chemical engineering, and they have one of the best engineering programs in the world."

Unlike many high school seniors, DaToya knows her potential major and is already focused on what that major may bring her in life. "In your junior year at Providence–St. Mel, you're required to write a sixteen-page paper on your choice for the future and the steps of going about it," she explains, "and so, when hunting for a career choice, I came upon chemical engineering. I read about it and it seemed interesting—it's a big field, but it has different branches.

"That and politics, those two. The ideology part of politics, I really enjoy that," DaToya continues. "The concept behind the formation of government. Like Thoreau and Locke, things like that.

It kinda gets you to think just how it's supposed to be, but it didn't get that way. I really want to study it and see where I can go with it. If I couldn't become a politician, I'd actually like to teach it because I get so involved in the ideas behind it. It excites me." As she speaks, she reminds me of my own youthful zeal for this challenging career. As is the case with Darnell, DaToya's enthusiasm and energy would make her a natural in politics.

DaToya is sensitive to others, a quality acquired from firsthand experience. "I went through a lot, especially because I'm different than all the other kids in school," she admits. "I was in fourth grade, five feet tall, so I was a giant to them. I would get teased and sometimes I wasn't happy with myself." She was fortunate to have parents who knew just how to handle it. "My parents told me, 'Everybody is going to be different, but if you don't love yourself, of course other people aren't going to like you.' They talked to me and they just said, 'Be DaToya and be yourself, and see if they come back and be your friend then.' And you know, I learned—just be myself and love myself and be happy with who I am, and whatever goes from there, goes from there."

DaToya had a great predecessor to learn from—her hero, Darnell. "Yes, Darnell is like a role model," she confirms. "Not too many girls have their brother as a role model, but although he did his bad dirt, everybody loved him. I don't know why. Like in school, Darnell was chosen for everything—he was the speaker at every big dinner. He's a great personality and people like him. And I was envious because of his self-love. Darnell loves himself; he is happy with himself, [with] who he is. So of course, people can only be happy with him and like him.

"And also, he's an athletic person, my brother—very athletic, and I really am proud," she says, nodding. "He had the best times in everything; I try to follow behind in his footsteps in track. For example, I tried hurdling. I'm a Class A hurdle champion, but I found out that's not *my* thing, that's my *brother's* thing. I learned to separate myself because I wanted to be just like him. But then I'm a girl—I *can't* be just like Darnell."

Sometimes he's a bit too protective. "He tries to take over my daddy's job because he might not like the privileges that my daddy gives me," DaToya grouses. "Especially now, because I'm a teenager, and he goes on and on and says, 'I know how I was then, and I know how these guys are.' So he's very protective, *very* protective. I mean, it's good. Sometimes I get angry at him because he scares some of my male friends away, saying, 'I know how he is, because I was like him.' And things like that."

Ask DaToya about teen sexual mores, and she'll shrug. "Well, I don't know because that's not a subject I talk to my friends about. I mean, if they feel they should do that, then that's their business. I really don't try to get too personal. If they tell me things, I listen and I don't try to give them advice, because sometimes they just need someone to listen to their problems. So I listen and I just accept what they're doing, and I don't turn them away because they're doing something that I may choose not to."

Many parents would like to know how Jackie and Dan inoculated DaToya against pressures for sexual activity. They gave her the "birds and the bees talk," she says, but adds that she's simply one individual who has no need for a relationship right now. "Sometimes I feel that my friends just want attention, and that's why they go to boys so strongly. Where me, on the other hand, I have all the attention I need. And not just at home, but also in school, because I do everything in school. I go travel for the school. I give talks for the school. I'm in different programs and I spread my attentions to other things instead of just boys. Right now, I really don't look for boys—and when the time comes for me to have a boyfriend or whatever, it will come. But my parents always told me, 'You might not find true love until college, so why look for it in high school?' I want to have fun right now. I don't want to be tied down with nobody asking me where I've been and who I've been with. Because the only person I should be answering those questions to are my parents, not anyone else."

In fact, DaToya's not even sure if she wants a family at all.

"Right now, I'm really not looking to having kids, [because] I think it hurts," she admits. "And so I don't want to go through the pain. And I know kids are heartache—not a heartache, but you know, it's tiring. My little cousin, who's 9 years old—we all pitched in to help raise him. So we had to take him with us and it was like, 'Man, this little boy is wearing me out!'" DaToya says that right now her goal is to get her own future set, and perhaps then she'll change her mind.

She summarizes her feelings about the most important aspect of her life: "Family comes first to me. Without my family, I don't know where I'd be today, because they have been my support through everything I do. Especially my parents. And my father—he's been my coach in high school. And I mean, you always don't agree with them, but you know that saying, 'Parents know what's best.' So, I might fuss and everything, but my family—they *do* know what's best for me. And if I try something, I usually get to like it. If not, I just do my best at it all the time."

## Cultural Influences

Crime. Unwed mothers. Welfare. The judicial system. These are some of the topics that come up repeatedly as I listen to the Burtins. That they're an African American family is never far from their consciousness; race is a significant backdrop to the values by which they live their lives.

For some of the families I interview, though, the topic of their race never arises—in fact, it seems silly to imagine, say, the Cowdens prefacing a sentence with "For white families in America . . ." the way the Burtins frame many of their thoughts. For the vast majority of white Americans, race plays little or no role in their routine. For the Burtins, though, it's something they can't avoid.

For example, when I arrive at the Burtins', I wonder about their location on the map—I'd seen "Cicero" on a sign near where I exited the expressway. Offhandedly, Darnell says, "We can't go to Cicero, no black people there," referring to the community Dan notes is "right at the corner from us," just a few blocks away. There, Dan adds, he can "feel the old stigma from the fifties and sixties," prior to advances in civil rights.

The October 1995 Million Man March in Washington, D.C., "was fantastic," Dan says. "It was something that was needed by black men trying to get together because we just don't seem to have a good cohesiveness. It was like an awakening.

"I wasn't able to go," he notes, "but I took the day off and sat and talked with some friends and we discussed some issues and tried to come out with our goals and objectives, and ask what we were going to do to carry on what the march was about. With me it's not too much, I'm already doing a lot of the things that they were bringing up. But I was telling the other guys that they need to get more involved. And they keep saying, '*You're* doing something about the problem!' I say, 'Well, I can't keep doing it by myself, I need more support from the other men to make it worthwhile.'"

Dan had to coax the men, mostly neighbors, into change. "Most of these guys were married, two were single," he reports. "They kept saying, oh, their jobs—you know, they took that day off, but they'd say they work and they don't get off until eight o'clock. We had that discussion again—you know, 'You have to determine a medium, what's important.' They kept saying, 'The job, the job, the job!' and we'd never get around to discussing what's important to us individually, as people. So we need to push the job back.

"If you look at [why] industry has come about," Dan adds, "supposedly it was to give us more leisure time with our families, but in fact, instead of giving us more leisure time, we're spending more time at the workplace. It's very ironic." Dan's friends came around. "They started agreeing and said they'd make an effort to do more with their families, and in their communities and schools, and with their children, than what they'd been doing in the past. And we've decided to meet like once a month and discuss what's been happening and what they've done. We're going to monitor each other."

The Million Man March was a topic of discussion at Dan's job as a computer specialist for the city of Chicago, where many of his co-workers are women. "We'd been discussing [Nation of Islam leader and march organizer Louis] Farrakhan and his comments," Dan recalls. "Some agreed, some disagreed. Some didn't like him at all; they say it was a farce that he backed the march. I said, he came up with the idea, but the people who went weren't just from his background or his religion, they were all different beliefs; the march was for everybody. I don't agree with everything he said, but he makes some good points. If I make a comment, it's my opinion, I'm not telling you to follow everything I say or do, but listen to what I'm saying and make your own decision."

The impact on the nation, Dan asserts, was positive. "The march brought together some of the younger men, who realized the importance of unity, with the older men who'd done it back in '63 with Martin Luther King, and in some instances have lost contact with what they remember about the way they were brought up. And it gave them a chance to reunite themselves back with what they know is right."

Jackie supports Dan's enthusiasm for the march. "I think it was good, something needed for the black male; a sense of unity, a building of self-esteem. I have mixed reactions to Farrakhan," she admits. "Some of the things I understand, am in agreement with, and some I'm not. We're not followers of Farrakhan, but some of his statements are true, not all of them, but some of them—like the [need for] unity for economic development in the black community. I disagree with the racial hatred. I know he's made a lot of derogatory remarks about white people or the Jewish community that I'm not in agreement with, but I can't quote it because I can't remember. The *feeling* about the racial thing is what bothers me about some of the things he says."

Also splashed across the news has been the O. J. Simpson double-murder trial and its aftermath, unavoidably intensifying the issue of race. Darnell is up-front in his belief that Simpson "did it, just because he really loved her [ex-wife Nicole] and she was with somebody else, and I don't think he could take that." But he describes the effect of the yearlong trial as "a double-edged sword. It was good for the black community because it shows we've come a long way. But I thought the racial ties wouldn't be as bad; they have actually gotten worse."

Jackie says the not-guilty verdict "was correct" because the prosecution "did not prove without a doubt" that Simpson committed the murders, though she thinks it's likely "he has some privileged information" about it. The larger lesson, she believes, is the power of money to buy a defense: "Some black people have gotten to where they can pay for these attorneys and research people and investigators, whereas at one time it may not have been possible for so many black people to—not actually attack, but to fight the judicial structure. We do know that money is justice."

Dan agrees with his wife on both the Simpson trial's outcome and its lesson that wealth brings a better defense. The "media circus," Dan feels, has served to highlight problems with jury selection that have always irked him. Jury selection should be based on a candidate's ability to be impartial rather than events in his past, Dan insists. It annoys him that a law-abiding potential juror at jury selection is denied the benefit of the doubt when it comes to impartiality, while a convicted felon at a parole hearing is given every benefit of the doubt—and not only paroled long before his sentence ends but "furnished money and education to give this person another chance."

### *Prison: "Make Them Want Not to Come Back"*

Dan Burtin speaks of crime and punishment with an authority born of direct experience. He volunteered for two years in the federal prison system, teaching real estate to the inmates, and has concluded that parole and plea bargaining make the crime problem worse. "I figure, '*You do the crime, you do the time*,'" Dan insists. "In our system, there's no deterrent for crime. Most of them know the system. Say I'm a 13- or 14-year-old. I can commit a crime and I won't go to jail for it because I'm a minor. Society will say, 'He's young, he doesn't know any better.' But he knew how to commit the crime." Dan holds that "once you commit the crime, then you've surrendered your rights as a citizen."

Capital punishment, Dan believes, can deter future criminal acts. "If you look back to years before, crimes were committed, but people always thought twice about it, saying, 'I could hang, or I can be electrocuted or get a lethal injection,'" he declares. "Most criminals would go in there and rob a place and then leave. They'd say, 'I'd never use a gun; if I go to prison, let me go for robbery, not for murder.' Now you hear a lot of criminals say, 'Hey, I don't care one way or the other.' Our prison system is like a country club."

Dan has strong feelings about the luxury he's seen our government provide convicted criminals. "They have cable TV, they have television in the dayroom. They have gym privileges, they have vending machines," he recites. "They can have candy and pop, they eat well, they have a library where they can study. They sit there and write briefs, trying to get an appeal of their cases. They have lawsuits, they have visitation, and the people bring them money they can use in the vending machines.

"They get half a dozen cards to send home for birthdays and Christmas. They dress well, *and they complain about it!* 'It's too cold in the wing!' they say, and they protest so they'll bring in more heat. They have basketball teams, volleyball teams, Ping-Pong teams. They give parenting classes for the women—they give them diplomas, they get awards. They got great living conditions—air-conditioning. The Federal Metropolitan prison downtown is air-conditioned!

"It's *better than the street!*" Dan asserts. "You eat real well. For graduation I went there for some of the students that we taught. We had graduation cake, coffee, tea, soda, lasagna, chicken, pie—everything!—pasta salad, potato salad!

"They should eat, but they should *not* have filet mignon, steak, potatoes," he maintains. "I look at some of the meals for kids at school, and *they* don't eat that well. They have hot dogs, they may have hamburgers, chicken, milk, apples—but they don't eat that well. They don't have pasta salad, or a choice of three different meats. These are *kids that are going to school,* yet they don't eat as well."

So what *should* prison be like? "Tough. Real hard," Dan replies firmly. "I don't believe in air-conditioning—maybe fans, keep the air circulating so they're comfortable. But they should make it as hard for an individual as possible, so you won't come back. Instead of having gym and sitting around, they should work. Give them something to do, make them earn it, make it hard for them, make it tough. Cable TV—out! No TV, no radio. Make them want to have that life back again. Maybe they could all go see a movie once a week, but take away the TVs and radios.

"Give them the option to use the library to expand their minds, but no, they can't have all those color TVs, radios, CDs, choice of gym shoes. You know, they wear nice gym shoes! Take away the vending machines and stuff. Make it hard, make them think while they're sitting there, about why they're there."

## *Community Challenges*

The Burtins could have moved to the suburbs years ago, but they've chosen to remain in the inner city. This is their choice despite the media's insistence that it's "dark and gloomy. [In their reports] the first thing you see is the young fellow walking, hungry, on drugs," Dan says. "[The images projected are of] fellows walking around with the hoods on their heads. They want to rip you, snatch your purse, jump on people, shoot people." The media exaggerate, he asserts, but admits, "It's all around us, it's everywhere."

Darnell talks about the changes he's witnessed in his own life. "I used to be able to walk," he recalls. "I used to be able to ride my bike all through the neighborhood. I did the thing where the guys used to chase you, through different blocks, but it was different then. Now you worry about getting shot. The neighborhood has changed to the extent where you just see more drugs. The drug thing is really bad.

"In our neighborhood," he goes on, "you don't have to tell [a given] person to go sell drugs, because it's in his mind—not all blacks but a lot of younger blacks—that [doing it] is the only way to make money. I know a lot of guys who'll say, 'Man, Darnell, you're going to college—that'll cost you four years, and I'm out here making $20,000 a year!' I guess $20,000 is a lot for somebody when you don't have to pay taxes. But it's not worth getting shot at when you're getting paid for stuff like that. But that's just the mental slavery [they're in]."

Darnell sees easy money as a trap that has snared some of his friends. "It takes a strong family like ours to break away from that, and there are a lot more black families like ours that *have* broken away, but there are a whole lot of families that haven't," Darnell contends. "And when I talk to them, they think that some of the stuff they do is the right thing to do. Sometimes, some mothers will say, 'Oh, yeah, I know my baby does that [sells drugs], but it's the only way to make money.' That is the stupidest thing I've ever heard."

Jackie's father, Mr. Stanton, agrees. "I know lots of young men today who say they'd work if they could find a job," he says. "Why *don't* they have jobs? It's because they feel the jobs don't pay them enough. And why don't the jobs pay them enough? Because they don't have anything going up here," he says, tapping his head with his finger.

"That's the whole problem. The pay is too little for them, and that don't make sense," Mr. Stanton goes on. "They'd rather not work. The mentality is that 'I can sit on the corner and sell drugs and make more than I make on the job.' But *I* never got any higher than ten dollars an hour, and I raised up six children, sent them to school. Music—I gave the children lessons; it was costing me fifteen dollars for fifteen minutes at the time they were taking music. I had three take music, and I wasn't making nothing." Mrs. Stanton corrects, "*Four* took music." Her husband continues, "My wife and I would do without lots of things just to make sure our children had a good foundation." So, what can we do now to eliminate the drugs? "I doubt if we'll ever do it now."

Dan recalls asking a drug dealer about his lifestyle, and the response he received was: "'I get my checks, go out and buy drugs and sell it to make more money, and I get by all month. And then I get my next month's check, and I do the same thing.' He said, 'I don't work, I get a check. Why should I work?'

"And that's all they do," Dan laments. "They just sit out there and say, 'Why should I go to work at McDonald's and make four dollars an hour when I can stay home and get a check and food stamps and medical care? And I don't have to do anything?'"

Also fresh in the Burtins' minds is a tragedy that befell a friend of Darnell's just last summer. Dan relates: "Some friends were hanging. They were out, driving around. They were going slow about one-thirty, two in the morning. They just graduated from high school, this whole group of them. The guys [perpetrators] mistook them for another group of guys, and they shot through the car and killed him."

"He was a good kid," Jackie notes sadly. "He got a scholarship," adds DaToya. She carries a cellular phone to keep her folks apprised of her whereabouts and to use in an emergency.

"The violence and drugs are obvious," Dan says. "You can stand on the porch and say, 'It's right here, right there, right there,' and point to it and know where the drug activity is. And you'll say, 'Well, *we* see it—how come the police don't see it?' And the police say, 'We don't have enough manpower.'"

Darnell thinks the police "just can't handle" alcohol and marijuana cases since they're overwhelmed with more serious problems like crack use.

"The police are there to enforce," Jackie says, "but if you're not complaining enough, they're not enforcing."

### *Watching the Neighborhood*

Rather than complaining, the residents of their two-block area have created their own mutual-protection network. "Ladies who don't work look out the windows," DaToya says. "They can tell you anything that's going to happen." And indeed, when I first approached the Burtins' house, I noticed several faces peering through curtains.

"When I come home at two, three o'clock in the morning, they jump me the next day," Darnell adds. "'What you doing coming in late when you gotta go to work?' I say, 'How did you know I was coming in at two o'clock in the morning?'"

"I appreciate them!" Jackie smiles. "I appreciate the ladies. And like we said, we do get on the phone when we notice things and we'll call the police."

"We turn the porch lights on," Dan continues. "We walk out. We'll see them and we'll stand out on the porch."

The concept sounds similar to Neighborhood Watch, a police program that has been successful in combating crime in both urban and suburban areas nationwide. Just setting up the plan is a positive step, a signal of mutual concern among neighbors. Beyond that, there's the deterrent of cardboard signs in the windows and posted warnings to intruders on the street. Typically, a block captain organizes the effort. On the Burtins' block, it's less formally organized but comparably effective; *everyone* takes equal responsibility.

Dan describes a recent example of the neighbors' nonthreatening style of heading off trouble. "Some kids left the fire hydrant on down at the other end of the block and it wasn't hot, so we walked down there and said, 'Hey, how're you doing?'" Dan relates. "'Why do you have the hydrant on?' They said, 'Well, it's hot.' It's not *that* hot. We talked to them and said, 'Would you mind cutting it off?' They said, 'Okay—who in the world are you? Straighten it up—no problem.' We just talked to them. 'Where do you guys go to school?' They didn't get upset. They just started laughing and talking with us. Then they cut it off and left."

A large part of the problem of bored, prowling kids is lack of parental limits and supervision. It's a *parental* move for a group of friendly looking residents to give outsiders the unspoken message, "We care about our area and we're going to make sure that everyone here behaves right." At such times, residents become de facto father figures, stepping in and setting boundaries—in a firm but positive way.

### *Welfare and Unmarried Mothers*

But many families in the black community are father*less*. "Women," Dan claims, "say they feel they can't handle these young men, you know. And they say the streets, the environment is a little bit too tough for them."

Darnell says he knows "kids from the community" whose "parents have three or four kids with three different fathers, stuff like that. The mothers think, 'Don't you get more welfare if you have more kids?' A lot of them think of it like that."

Dan Burtin believes that the prospect of even a modest boost in welfare is incentive for girls to get pregnant. "You know, that black mentality, that attitude where, when the child hasn't been born, they think, 'I'm going to get away from this, get out and do my own thing. I'm going to try it,'" Dan explains, "and the next thing you know there's another child, more money. Before you know it, they're caught up in it. Some of them want to break away, but some of them don't."

In every aspect of these tough conversations, Jackie Burtin is charitable—she looks for something positive to say. "I don't think they know *how* to make a change," she asserts.

"I think over the years what happens is it becomes a crutch for most people," Dan says, referring to welfare income. "They depend on it; they look forward to it. Instead of being a tool to help them be self-sufficient, now, 'It's all I need. I don't need anything else.' The welfare system in its original state was a good idea, but today I think there's a misuse of it. Basically, it needs to be shut down and restructured so it will work the way it should. They should be told to go to school and learn a trade so that in six months or a year you can be off the welfare roll and become part of the working population."

### *Religion*

Every child needs guidance, and the Burtins know that there's no better guide than religion. Both Dan and Jackie, as I've already discussed, were raised in religious homes, where Bible verses remain guides to daily behavior and "we all sat at the table and ate together, and we had a prayer," says Mr. Moise Burtin.

"There was no choice until I was about 16 years old," recalls Dan Burtin. "Every week, I was in the Baptist church. It was like Sunday, automatic. I was in choir, you know. Whether you could sing or not, you always became a member of the choir. It was something you did as a youth. Junior deacon in the church—I automatically did it because my father was a deacon. It was something I learned to do every Sunday: Get up, Sunday school, Sunday worship, and then there was evening programs. The whole day. If you were sick, you stayed in the house. You didn't come out and play, and that was it."

The values that Dan ascribes to his church are easily summarized: "Family . . . Somebody in the church always was responsible, watched over you."

Jackie adds that her experiences growing up with the Salvation Army taught "loyalty, commitment, dedication."

"It's that unity again," Dan responds. "Like in the church you weren't an individual, you were part of a family, just like our extended family here."

Did Dan ever question his upbringing? "Oh, I questioned it," he answers. "I went to Catholicism. I went to some Catholic churches with friends of mine just to see what it was like. I was in catechism, I went that far. Because a lot of my friends on my block were Catholic. It was like okay, they got to a certain point, and I said, 'No, I think I'll stay where I am.'"

Jackie's early religious training was in the Baptist church, but the social programs at the nearby Salvation Army attracted her three older sisters, and the family gradually became involved. Like her husband, she went through a period of doubt. "I think as a teen, it really came about when I got into science courses," Jackie confides. "The theory of evolution, and then you have your belief in Adam and Eve, and they kind of begin to contradict each other. Whereas with the Bible, you're going on faith—and now here's a supposed scientific proof of what happened. So, yeah, I questioned it for a while, but as I got older, I remained in the Christian faith."

Darnell isn't afraid to question anyone, even religious authorities. "I always ask," he reports. "I'm the type of guy who'll come up and say, 'Well, you said this in church—will you explain that to me?' And they'll sit down and explain it to me, but it seems like we're going in circles. I never get a straight answer, and maybe it's not straight to me. So I've never been able to completely satisfy my need to go to church.

"My grandfather sat down with me and said, 'Well, if you don't feel the need to go to church, why don't you sit down and read the Bible?' So I've tried to make it a [point] to at least sit down and read. The Bible is just another book. It's history. And the Bible is the word that is supposed to be taught from God to man. And man makes mistakes. That's why I believe the Bible has mistakes as does religion," Darnell asserts.

His sister does attend church with her grandmother, "willingly" accompanying her to the Salvation Army Midwest Corps. But DaToya also has uncertainties. "At the moment I'm at that stage in life where I believe in a higher being and things like that, but somehow the church for me has problems as an organization. I have no question about the laws and guidelines in the Bible, and how they represent themselves to the community and what they do." Still, she prefers to remain unaffiliated. "I would like to belong to a church, and maybe I will one day. But at the moment—no."

"In our church we had a problem," Dan concedes. "We're looking for a new church currently."

DaToya admitted that a particular incident turned her off. "The pastors got mad at me because I was late. I told them I had homework and I had to leave early anyway because I have school. They told me the church always comes before your school. Nothing else matters."

"Right," chimes in Dan.

"And I never went back," DaToya concludes. But her life is far from religion-free. Prayers are said at Providence–St. Mel, she says, and there are meaningful religious discussions at the family roundtable. "We'd talk about what laws we should follow in life," she says. "Things like that, not only in the Bible but law that comes from the heart. I have a lot of questions; I ask my friends why they do certain things. And they say, 'Because it's in the Bible.' I say, 'Is that your only reason, because the Bible says you should do that? You don't do it because you actually want to do it, or because you know that it's right—but because the Bible says you should do it?' I get a lot of anger on that side because they think I'm an atheist because I don't do what the Bible says. I don't believe every single word."

"*We* believe that the Bible is the word of God," Jackie says.

"They question," Dan nods. "We try to give understanding."

## *Media*

The Burtins agree that media stereotyping has been a major influence on attitudes in the African American community. "Through media, you see so many negative things in the news, in the paper," Dan says, and it provokes anger. "And [people] figure the only way they can get over it is to try and play this role," a tough-guy stance. He claims that a message drummed into television viewers is that "the only thing that's in this [inner-city] area is gangs and drugs."

Mr. Stanton contends that values of African Americans are the same as those of the country at large—despite an image that sometimes suggests otherwise. "So many feel that all black people are the same. . . . It's not true."

"Like we've got a girl from Alaska in our school," says DaToya, "and kids come asking her, did she live in an igloo? I mean, they just don't know any better. That's the problem: People don't know better. They stereotype, they assume, based on what they saw once, on what little knowledge they have."

"You've just got to try to educate, make them aware of what they're saying, which is not always true," Dan comments. "Maybe they need to go and start educating the Ku Klux Klan," Mr. Stanton interjects, and Dan mentions a rally of the racist group in Chicago that week that "got out of hand."

"A lot of people don't look past the headlines, or they don't look past even the newspaper article itself," Dan says. "A lot of news media will say one thing and you'll get another news station and they'll say something else. Sometimes the information is contradictory. A lot of people on the average probably read one newspaper, or watch the news on one channel. So that's what they're believing. . . .

"I read the *Chicago Tribune* on the job, I read *Time* and *Newsweek* magazine, the *Wall Street Journal,* and the *New York Times*. I'm interested in what's going on worldwide. I take the same story everyone's writing about and I'll pick out the commonalities, the same thing, and say that could be closest to the truth. But still, I take it with a grain of salt."

"I stopped reading the newspaper," Jackie admits. "When I was in college I really got turned off reading the newspapers because of all that grotesque stuff that was in there about Vietnam, so I don't read them. I do listen to the news and read *Newsweek* or *Time* magazine," she says.

Dan's also hooked into electronic media. "On my lunch hour I'll go to the library and sit down at the computer just to get some information on something I wasn't sure about; I'll research it. I'll go, 'Okay, I remember this discussion we had? Now I've got some information,'" he says. "The last time was a sports item. It just came up on the job: 'Where are minority athletes in sports?' They wanted to know what happened to a quarterback named Sonny Sixkiller after college. And I found out that he tried out for pro ball with the Washington Redskins and then he got cut, and right now he's back there on the reservation working with youth programs."

Though the Burtins are heavy sports participants, they're moderate fans. Dan is vocal on the steep increase in ticket prices over the years. "I could go to a game and pay a dollar a head," Dan recalls of his childhood visits to Chicago ballparks. "The people who enjoyed the sport supported it and cheered the teams on."

Now, it's a matter of economics. "As bad as the Bears are, they're two-thirds sold out for five years. They'll never lose money regardless of how bad they are." As for the rest of them: "Now, to go to the Bulls [basketball] game, you're talking about $20 to be in the upper balcony, $7.50 to be in the nosebleed area." With $10 to park and $2 for a hot dog, a dad can't take his son to more than a couple games a year—even less with several children in the family.

"I read a lot of books," Jackie says of her preferred pastime. "I just finished *The Middle Passage* by Charles Johnson, and I'm currently reading *The Chamber* by John Grisham." I ask her which books in retrospect seem most worthwhile. "I read [Alex Haley's] *Roots*, and that's a book my kids had to read; I gave it to each one of them when they turned 11 or 12.

"*The Pelican Brief*, also by Grisham, was a very good book," she continues. "I read a book and take in what I want and I pass that along to my children through verbal discussion. The only thing I insisted they read was *Roots* because I think it had a lot of valuable historic background information that they need to know. Darnell—one of his favorites was *Stride Toward Freedom: The Montgomery Story* by Dr. Martin Luther King, Jr. So when they bring back books, they tell me and I'll usually read them behind them. Then we discuss them. There's a book named *Billy* that one of Toya's teachers gave her to read last year and she was really interested in that. A couple weeks ago we were discussing *Canterbury Tales.* She [also] enjoys Shakespeare."

Dan has been doing mostly technical reading, he says, since the city is changing to a new computer-programming system. Other than that, he recommends *Stride Toward Freedom,* the book brought home by Darnell. Also, "I read the novel *Blood* that was about black Vietnam veterans and what their stories were. I wanted to experience more what these guys went through. *Roots. Soul on Ice*, I read that in high school. And recently I ordered a book for DaToya about Angela Davis, her autobiography, it's out of print."

The Burtins have a cozy den off the kitchen they've turned into a television viewing nook, but it appears the main beneficiaries are cousins and neighbors. The couch touches wall-to-wall and faces the television; a shelf overhead holds their small video collection. They switch on Walt Disney's *Aladdin* to entertain three visiting youngsters.

With all their activities, the Burtins have little time or interest in television, other than some occasional PBS programming for Dan. They had cable TV for two and a half years, but "we were paying for it but nobody was watching it so we took it out," Dan says. The shows they do cite as watchable are *The Cosby Show* and *Home Improvement.*

They've always limited TV consumption for kids in school—their own, and now 14-year-old cousin Gus. "We just turn it off," Jackie says. "No TV until the homework is done."

It's the same rule Jackie followed as a child. "You've got to have certain guidelines," her dad, Mr. Stanton, attests. "If you don't have it, quite naturally, the kid's going to watch everything on TV."

"Like when our kids was coming up," Mrs. Stanton continues, "they didn't watch TV until after homework was done. And then the TV would go off at our bedtime. That was nine or nine-thirty. The homework comes first."

Mr. Stanton has no use for television, he says, except "Channel 11 [WTTW, Chicago's PBS station]. I love Channel 11," he enthuses, "and I watch it. I just wish I was able to contribute, you know, but when you're on a fixed income, there's a few things you can't do."

The Stantons don't rent videos, though "the kids got all kinds," says Mr. Stanton. "I get Channel 11, I'm happy. Why should I have to get movies?"

Mrs. Stanton agrees that television fills her need for entertainment. "Channels 11, 32, 38," she recites. "We watch *Oprah* in the morning. *Donahue*. We don't watch too much." The Stantons seldom go to films in the theater. "What was the last one?" Mr. Stanton asks his wife. "Two years ago . . . "

"More than that," she responds.

They favor "the old musicals," old black-and-white movies, *The Godfather*, *Star Wars*. "Anything that's decent," Dan replies.

## Making It Work: Lessons from the Burtin Family

In everything they say or do, in every action, the Burtins are involved with extended family. As Darnell puts it: "Family is your base. A strong family is—the world. *It's the world*. You've always got something to lean on."

And the "leaning" is never casual or taken for granted. Family is actively revered, respected, and celebrated. It's recognized and appreciated. "Instead of voicing it or emotionally showing it, I might go bake you a cake," DaToya says of her style of gratitude. "I might get out the vacuum and clean the whole house. I'm a kind of 'doing person.'" Each one of them is also an openly *thankful* person.

That attitude is evident when Dan is asked to name his heroes. They're not sports figures or politicians but individuals in his past to whom he feels a debt of gratitude. There's Mr. Brock, who "was like a father" to all the kids who played ball. And Mrs. Twine, Dan's fourth-grade teacher, who "was an inspiration." And of course, Dan cites his father as someone he admires. "He always told me I could do whatever I wanted to do."

The Burtin family is uniquely self-reliant. When a child is out of line, he's not referred to some government-funded hotline for advice. When he has trouble with his homework, he doesn't hire a tutor. When a major decision comes up—which college to attend, what direction to take a floundering career—it's not the school counselor or personnel officer who goes through the options. Roles that have increasingly been parceled out to agencies and service professionals are handled with confidence and a personal investment impossible to match elsewhere, in several family venues. There's the heart-to-heart talk with Jackie or Dan, the bike ride over to the grandparents', the phone call to the sibling, and then, if necessary, the "roundtable discussion" where "thirty or forty heads are better than one."

Children don't "get in trouble" in the Burtin family. Dan has eight siblings; Jackie has five. None of the many cousins has had brushes with the law, experienced out-of-wedlock birth, or become involved with gangs or drugs. The main reason is the family's "preventive medicine." A child slacking off in the most minor way—disrespectful of elders, earning C's when he's capable of A's—is caught in a net of concern, by family members individually and collectively.

A lot has been made of the widened racial gap in America, a phenomenon some say merely reflects a three-hundred-year-old wound that has never healed. A front-page story in the *Los Angeles Times* recently quoted University of Chicago political science professor Michael Dawson as saying: "There is substantial support among all African Americans for building *independent* [italics mine] black institutions—from schools to political parties to businesses that would favor the hiring of black people."* Clearly, the Burtins have no need for separate, preferential institutions. DaToya considers it a drawback that her school is all black, since her goal is to meet a wide variety of people. Darnell brushes aside black co-workers' accusations that he "talks white," since he knows

* Sam Fulwood III, "Black Attitudes Shift Away from Goal of Inclusion," *Los Angeles Times,* October 30, 1995, A1.

his effective communication style has brought him to a position of authority in a white family-owned construction company. Though the Burtins enjoy a marvelous cohesiveness within their all-black residential enclave, the homes, with their well-kept yards and neat brick facades, would offer the same comfort in a middle-class neighborhood of any color.

Shelby Steele writes eloquently about the need for the African American community to work for the "nexis of a new identity" that is a "meeting of black individual initiative and American possibility." He blames black leadership for "keeping the larger society . . . feeling as though they haven't done enough for blacks." He warns that "the price they pay for this form of 'politics' is to keep blacks focused on an illusion of deliverance by others, and no illusion weakens us more."

The Burtins exemplify the message of accomplishment Steele lauds, as he instructs black leadership to "tell us what they tell their own children when they go home at night: to study hard, pursue their dreams with discipline and effort, to be responsible for themselves, to have concern for others, to cherish their race and at the same time make their own lives as Americans."*

A study of "Characteristics of Strong African-American Families Cited by Community Leaders" in 1983 found the following values most prevalent: strong kinship bonds (54 percent), strong achievement orientation (46 percent), parenting skills (46 percent), strong religious-philosophical orientation (32 percent) and intellectual-cultural orientation (31 percent).† Sound familiar? Jackie, Dan, Darnell, and DaToya exhibit all of these strengths. But I would submit that these are not only attributes of strong black families but the hallmarks of *all* stable, cohesive homes.

The Burtins offer useful tips for improving marriage, parent-

* Shelby Steele, *The Content of Our Character: A New Vision of Race in America* (New York: HarperPerennial, 1991), 174.

† Andrew Billingsley, *Climbing Jacob's Ladder* (New York: Simon and Schuster, 1992), 333.

ing, and community and cultural life. Here's a summary of lessons you can incorporate into your family's routine.

- *Adult education is important on two counts: as an example of seriousness about school and as intellectual stimulation to keep your mind and your marriage fresh.* Both Jackie and Dan see education as a lifelong endeavor, and they take turns pursuing their degrees.
- *Phone home.* Especially in early marriage, there's no such thing as too much attention and reassurance. Touching base during the day reconnects the loving bond.
- *Take a day off occasionally to spend time with your spouse.* "Jackie days" may be spent browsing at a mall, but more important, they're a chance for hand-holding and talking with no other pressures pending.
- *Attention to small wishes brings big payoffs.* Dan checks out which clothing items Jackie admires, then returns to buy them as a loving surprise.
- *Don't be afraid to hug and kiss in front of the children.*
- *Have an "open-door policy" to encourage kids, grandkids, cousins, and friends to visit.* This is the essence of Burtin closeness. Whenever DaToya needs someone to listen, she knows Grandma and Grandpa—who bought an extra-large house to welcome extended family—are eager to help. And from the elders' point of view, there's no greater wealth than their family.
- *Insist on respect for elders.* Not only in addressing them face-to-face, but in honoring them by talking of their accomplishments, recalling their wisdom, and following their successful methods of child rearing. The Burtin family venerates the wisdom of its elders.
- *Curfews underscore both parental caring and authority.* Dan noted that the worst "toughs" in his Scout troop had

parents who let them run wild. He and Jackie were known to sit out on the porch until 2:00 A.M. waiting for a late and embarrassed Darnell.

- *Force your children to talk.* When they balk at describing their daily events, insist. When Jackie asked Darnell, "How's your day," and he responded with a shrug, she declared: "'Okay' won't cut it."
- *Organizations such as Boy Scouts teach family values and are worthwhile time investments.*
- *"Roundtable discussions" among family members are a safety net for catching problems before they grow.* The Burtins have dealt with problems from slacking students to broken marriages in such a context.
- *Neighborhood Watch programs enhance neighborhood cohesiveness and individuals' sense of security and well-being.*
- *Keep the neighborhood clean.* Little breakdowns in order lead to bigger ones. Graffiti and broken windows invite further crime.

# 7

# Preserve, Protect, and Defend: Advancing the Values of America's Families

*In general . . . upward mobility depends on all three principles—work, family, and faith—interdependently reaching toward children and future. These are the pillars of a free economy and a prosperous society.*

—George Gilder

You've just met five admirable families. Each family is maintaining robust "health" while confronting and dealing with a wide range of challenges. These families are quite different, yet their stories share themes that cut across geography, race, and religion.

The most important feature of these families is that they're *not* remarkable. In fact, they're *usual.* They are, like many American families, doing a great job maintaining their ideals, quite apart from all the problems our society faces.

What's their secret? To them, there is none. They simply practice the values that make families strong. These values aren't new or revolutionary; rather, they represent the foundation of any successful family. They teach their children by both word and example the importance of honesty, industry, morality, courage, respect, faith, compassion, humility, and duty. Though our culture often undermines family values, these families are continuing to thrive. Yes, crime statistics have been alarming, but these families act responsibly. Yes, teenage sexual activity is rampant, but these families counter the temptations of the world with frank discussion. They work to *insulate* their own youngsters as much as possible from risk. Yes, many children drop out of high school, but these parents instill a respect for knowledge and a commitment to continued personal development that inspire their children to achieve.

## The American Family: Commonalities and Differences

Tolstoy wrote that "happy families are all alike" but that "every unhappy family is unhappy in its own way." As you have just read, these happy families are alike in many ways. Yet, contrary to Tolstoy, each is also *happy* in its own way, too. There are many ways the De La Rosas, Wallaces, Burnses, Cowdens, and Burtins are alike and yet unique. Though the problems of life are similar, the means by which each family tackles these concerns are different.

The commonalities in these families, though they are from Virginia to Hawaii, can be broken down into ten areas.

1: *Respect*

Tony De La Rosa considers respect "the most important value" he and Carmen teach their children. This trait is not particularly popular in the media. TV families seldom show children respectfully rising for an elder or calling neighbors "Mr." or "Mrs." Yet, these and other signs of respect are second nature to these five families.

A national devaluing of the virtue of respect began with the vicious taunting of the President of the United States during the Vietnam War. "Hey, hey, LBJ/How many kids did you kill today?" was the angry chant of demonstrators in the late 1960s. A slogan of the time was "Don't trust anyone over 30." Members of the "establishment" became the bad guys while dissident youth emerged as heroes. Since then, the "question-authority" mentality has eroded respect for the very men and women we should be looking up to: scholars and elected officials, teachers and clergy, professionals and entrepreneurs. The De La Rosa, Wallace, Burns, Cowden, and Burtin families don't permit such an attitude; all are passing along the importance of respect and honor.

2: *Discipline*

In each of the families discipline is a central issue of parenthood. Each understands that it is the parents' responsibility to punish their child in order to reinforce the principle that certain behavior is not just inappropriate; it's not tolerated. For the most part, they approve of spanking a child for flagrant disobedience as a means of asserting control over the child's well-being. However, they're apt to use it as a last resort after trying alternative disciplinary methods. Kathy Wallace tries communication and explanation, which usually works. Her children's built-in desire to "take care of Mom" makes them even more inclined to listen.

The consensus on discipline is that *children require limits,* and parents are acting properly and lovingly when they spank their children with fair warning. It teaches them that "actions have consequences," as Rob Burns says. Spanking is not seen by most of these parents as teaching violent responses to disliked behavior, a theory advanced by some prominent child experts. Rather, experience tells them it's a way to shape behavior toward respect and obedience. And, significantly, each of these families balances firm discipline with great love.

3: *Attentiveness*

"Communication" was one of the words that appeared most frequently in my family values questionnaire. And a prerequisite to good communication is attentiveness. A common trait of all the parents I interviewed was an intense interest in the moment-to-moment progress of each person in the family, especially the children. The parents observed their children for signs of distress, fatigue, illness, or other problems, as well as for indicators of success and happiness.

Caryl Cowden is alert to 9-year-old Josh's school difficulties. Kathy Wallace, even though she is pressured with financial and logistical problems, puts highest priority on time with her children and gathers them together nightly for an exchange of information around the dinner table.

Central to the idea of attentiveness is that each child is unique and has personal idiosyncrasies and requirements that demand differing responses. Parents who speak their minds plainly but don't take into consideration the special personalities of their children are not communicating fully.

4: *Education*

Without exception, all five families believe strongly in education as the key to advancement. There's great anxiety in America today about the deterioration of our educational system. Violence and mediocrity have become the norm. Such fears spurred the Burtins to select the rigorous Providence–St. Mel, where their children could excel academically under stringent standards. Kathy Wallace sent some of her children to Holy Cross School, thanks to Pat Rooney's Educational Choice Charitable Trust. The Burnses have gone to a great deal of trouble to find the school and program that meets Natalie's needs.

Given the level of these parents' involvement in their children's schooling, it's not surprising that all of the children have attended college, or plan to. Even the De La Rosas, who had no higher education, and Rob Burns, who grew up hearing negative messages about the usefulness of college, strongly encourage their children to pursue degrees.

5: *Media Curtailment*

Our five families spend an extremely small amount of time in front of the television. Nationwide, the average adult watches twenty-six hours of television and the average child twenty-three hours per week. None of the adults in these families watches anything near that number of hours—in fact, some of the families interviewed say they don't bother with TV at all. The most TV-interested parent is Rob Burns, who watches news programs an hour or two three times a week. Kathy Wallace says she can't watch the tube because "it puts me to sleep." The others say they don't have time for it.

In fact, many of the parents like the idea of a TV-free home. They feel that having no television is even better than owning one, despite the few "good" programs occasionally available. They seem to agree that no television show is as good for their children as reading a book, finishing homework, or playing outdoors. Television is the boredom killer of last resort.

By minimizing time spent in nonparticipatory entertainment, especially TV, we can spend more of our precious time communicating with our families instead of withdrawing from them.

6: *Financial Prudence*

Regardless of their financial situation, all the families emphasize to their children the virtues of thrift and frugality. Families on either end of the income spectrum were the *most* concerned about it. The Wallace family counts out change for the big treat of a McDonald's meal. They balance the need for new shoes with the need to fix a hole in the roof. Kathy says her fondest dream is to be able to relax about the family's finances. Her children understand the hard work and sacrifice that is required to provide for them.

Rob and Annie Burns also worry about their children's attitude toward money. Their girls know the family can afford what it wants and balk when their parents attempt to teach them the value of a dollar by refusing to get them everything that catches their eye in a store. But Annie and Rob know they're doing the right thing.

The lesson universally conveyed to children in these healthy families is that nothing should be taken for granted. The value of money lies not in what it can buy but rather in *what it took to make it.* Money, in every case, is linked to work, and each family makes it clear that they owe everything they have to their work ethic. Children are given chores, not only as a normal contribution to the family but to remind them that rewards come only from work.

7: *Self-Sacrifice*

The concept of self-sacrifice is regaining its due. In the "Golden Age of Selfishness," from the late 1960s through the 1980s, a popular message was, "If it feels good, do it." If you don't like the confining vows of marriage, ignore them in favor of this new invention, "open marriage"; if you don't like requirements in college, agitate until they're relaxed.

But each of the families I interviewed conveyed the notion that self-sacrifice not only benefits others but is personally rewarding as well. Tony De La Rosa flatly declares that his purpose on earth is to build and serve his family—when that's done, just "throw the dirt over me." The Cowdens sacrifice for their family project, Fort Lewis Lodge.

The common denominator of the families, though, is that while they may be self-sacrificial, they don't really see it that way. They're not "giving up" a personal desire in order to serve; they're doing their duty and gaining joy from their services to others. If Carmen De La Rosa needs a ride to the market, Michael is there without hesitation. If daughter Denise needs help folding envelopes for her consulting business, Mom is eager to pitch in. I heard two families (the Burtins and the De La Rosas) talk about lawn mowers—sons who automatically mow others' lawns and fathers who reciprocate without a second thought. The families *give* and *do* and don't stop to consider what is "in it for them." They find happiness in giving of themselves.

8: *Commitment of Faith*

Four of the five families were committed to their personal faiths. A *Newsweek* feature notes that 57 percent of the population regularly attends church or religious services, and 80 percent of baby boomers consider themselves religious and believe in life after death. The Burtins had backgrounds in the Salvation Army and the Baptist church and volunteered for twenty-two years in youth programs and other activities several days a week. Their grounding in their faith doesn't waver, owing largely to the biblical values instilled in their youth.

By teaching their values to their children, each of the five families looks to a supreme authority beyond themselves. When parents display their own belief in God, children learn that a life based on faith provides a firm foundation. Parents are more credible when setting rules and goals if they can offer a grander scheme, a source of comfort, and a sense of the eternal. And children who see their parents submitting to a God will be more willing to submit to their parents' rules as well.

9: *A Sense of Place*

All of the families I met are deeply rooted in their communities. Two of the mothers, Carmen De La Rosa and Kathy Wallace, live on the same blocks where they were raised. Two families are actually dependent on their locations for their livelihoods—the Cowdens of Fort Lewis Lodge and the Burnses, whose Hawaiian-themed surf shops couldn't have existed in any other setting. The Burtins, twenty-three years in a house on their very protective and cohesive two-block span, are the next-to-newest residents in that area, a year ahead of the newcomers on the block. For the Burtins, Wallaces, and De La Rosas, relationships on their streets are not just nodding acquaintances with friendly neighbors—they're surrogate-parent arrangements where children are entrusted to their care and discipline.

Some people change their residences every other year. But the families I spoke with do not. Their communities form the bedrock of their lives, and their children will return for holidays with their own children. Such stability helps make families and communities healthy. Children need to know that they are loved and supported. When the community they live in is interested in them, supports them, and encourages their successes, they will thrive.

10: *Optimism and Gratitude*

"I love you; I appreciate you." You read how difficult these words are for many people to say. Not so with our families, who are equally ready to recognize the good things in their lives. When I first spoke with Jackie Burtin on the phone, she impressed me with her positive spin on negative news. "The antidrug ads you see on TV are usually awful, trying to scare people," Jackie notes, "but the other day I saw one that took a different tack, that actually presented a positive approach to a negative condition," she says. "That's what we try to do—to take life as optimistically as we can." Each of the Burtins says that when something that seems bad happens, it always turns into something good.

These families are grateful for life's blessings. Annie Burns wrote Jennifer's birth mother in gratitude that the young woman didn't choose to have an abortion. Darnell Burtin was moved when his cousins, gathered at a "roundtable discussion," each expressed their appreciation to him for being a good role model. The Burnses say a moving, personal grace before they eat, thanking God not only for the meal but for the circumstances that allow them to be together as a family. *The most needed value in America now is gratitude*—because there is so much to be grateful for. Grateful to our Founding Fathers, to our families, to our friends and neighbors. And most of all, to God.

America knows what family values are because so many Americans live them. The five families I observed are healthy and happy; are raising fine, achievement-oriented children; and are contributing to their communities. It's not a matter of obeying some obscure list of rules or following the lead of some strangers in Washington. They're doing what they think is right.

Does that mean government actions are irrelevant to family life? Far from it. Though the fact went unnoticed for a good many years, families are affected, both for better and for worse, by the policy choices we make.

The phrase "It takes a village to raise a child" has validity only if the "village" is friends, extended family, neighbors, and other privately assembled groups who can reinforce the lessons of home. But if the "village" is government, then the endeavor is doomed to fail. Governments don't raise children. Parents do.

Any agenda for families, therefore, must be rooted in the modest understanding that government cannot fine-tune the health of our families any more than it can fine-tune the performance of the economy. Government doesn't have the answers.

Unfortunately, government has acted for many years as if it did. As a result, in areas from taxation to welfare, from education to crime, from divorce to adoption, public policy has undermined the family unit. The real problem in our society hasn't been so much that families have failed but that government has failed to act in the best interests of families.

Here is a partial list of what public policies have done to the American family.

- Taxes have increased dramatically, across the board and for all income levels. This requires parents to work harder just to stay in the same position economically. For many families, the option of one parent staying at home with the children has been lost.
- There is a tax penalty on married couples: jointly filed income taxes are higher than they'd be if the couple were still two separate taxpayers.
- For many years, the personal exemption for children did not keep pace with inflation. Thus, it has greatly diminished in value.
- "Antipoverty" programs supply economic incentives for illegitimacy: The more children born out of wedlock, the more money comes from the government.
- Divorce laws often allow the dissolution of a marriage—even where children are involved—with little more difficulty than a simple name change.
- Virtually all religious expression has been banned from the public square. In the most recent bizarre example, a public school student was assigned to prepare a research paper on a historical figure and chose to write about Jesus Christ. The paper was rejected as a breach of the "wall of separation" between church and state.
- Parents, unless they can afford it, have been denied the opportunity to choose where their children go to school.

The message is that parents' wishes are irrelevant and the needs of the child don't matter.

- Though violent crimes occur at rates once considered unimaginable, government has failed to give police and prosecutors the tools they need to imprison the perpetrators. For every 100 violent crimes in America today, only one criminal is put in jail. The rest continue to take their toll on a growing number of neighborhoods and homes across the country.

There's little question that each of these policies has had a negative impact on families. We must move quickly to repair the damage.

We must pursue policies that take the side of the family, which has been referred to by many as the first department of Health, Education and Welfare.

Keeping in mind that this is not a book about policy, here are a few things we can do to strengthen the family unit:

1. *Taxes*

• In 1948, a median-income family of four paid just 2 percent of its annual income in federal taxes. Today it's 24 percent. We probably can't turn back the clock to the 1948 level, but we can at least point ourselves in that direction.

• Repeal the marriage penalty.

• Increase the tax exemption for children and index it for inflation.

• Repeal regulations that prohibit employers from paying "family wages." If an employer wants to pay more to an employee who is raising a family, there should be no legal barrier to doing so.

2. *Divorce*

• States should consider overhauling "no fault" divorce laws, at least where children are involved. Children's interests should come first.

3. *Welfare*

• Welfare should be reformed, in President Kennedy's words, to "stress the integrity and preservation of the family unit." That means ending economic incentives for illegitimacy and giving states the authority to find the best ways to encourge the most effective antipoverty programs the world has ever known: work and marriage.

4. *Adoption*

• There are fewer than 100,000 adoptions annually—and a smaller number today than there were twenty-five years ago. But consider these two numbers: More than a million parents are waiting to adopt; there are a million abortions in America every year. Aren't there ways to bring these numbers together, toward zero?

5. *Crime*

• According to crime expert John DiIulio, Jr., "About 1 in 3 violent crimes is committed by someone on probation, parole, or pretrial release at the very moment he murders, rapes, or attacks." It is time to end the revolving-door justice that keeps known violent criminals on the streets rather than in jails.

There was very little discussion of political philosophy during my interviews with the families in this book. There were times, however, when public policy–related issues drifted naturally into the conversation. The Burtin family, for example, had pointed words on welfare. The De La Rosa family spoke about crime from firsthand experience. Rob and Annie Burns, with their two adopted children, have strong feelings about the social value of adoption.

There was one issue, however, that brought out the strongest feelings in every single family. After traveling thousands of miles, spending several dozen hours interviewing families, and reviewing hundreds of pages of transcripts in preparation for writing this book, I discovered that education, above all else, dominates the attention and concern of these families.

They are not alone. In late 1995 the *Wall Street Journal* reported that poll respondents mentioned education as a top priority nearly twice as often as they had in the same poll a year before. Other recent surveys show similar results.

To improve education, parents must be empowered to select for their children the school that best suits their values, whether that school is public, private, or religious. Unfortunately, our public schools today are beholden to big labor unions and education bureaucrats. Too often, the education debate gets bogged down in turf battles. Far more time is spent talking about spending levels, union rules, and tenure privileges than about what is in the best interests of children. Reforming our public education system will require parents and concerned citizens to take on some very powerful special interests. But it can and must be done.

There are, of course, many self-anointed education experts. The real experts, however, are the people who can always be counted on to concentrate single-mindedly on the needs of the children: their parents. To remind ourselves of whose opinion should be sought first in any discussion of education, recall the words of some of the individuals interviewed for this book, both parents and children.

Kathy Wallace:

"If my kids want to stay [in our neighborhood], I want them to choose to stay here, and not just be here because they have no other choice. Education is a way out. Education gives you all kinds of options. And if they choose to stay here, they stay with the option of leaving."

Darnell Burtin:

"The high school that I went to stresses that success is what you go to school for. Success can be defined as graduation from high school. Success can be defined as graduation from college. *My* success isn't defined as that. I haven't defined it because I don't have a ceiling yet."

Dan Burtin:

"Education was our main priority for our children. I could have gotten a brand-new flashy car and said 'Skip the education'—but to me, their education comes first."

Rob Burns:

He says his wife is prone to "worry all night" about their daughters' education. Both say they would leave Hawaii, if necessary, to meet the special educational needs of Natalie, their oldest.

John Cowden:

"For most of the teachers, our school is their entire career. They move in and raise their families, so it's not just two years and they're moving on."

Michael De La Rosa:

"There was no question that we should do well in school. . . . We were always looking ahead toward some goal or objective. We came home and did our homework before anything got done. Everything was attached to a responsibility."

Manuel De La Rosa:

"I think the biggest reason my father worked so hard was so we could get our education. Wherever we wanted to go."

Comments like these are undoubtedly echoed by families across America who view education as the key to their children's future. Theirs is the true wisdom on the subject.

Two years ago, a *Time* magazine essayist wrote that "We may be stuck with the family—at least until someone invents a sustainable alternative." No one ever will; no "sustainable alternative" to the family exists. Whether you place your trust in Scripture, history, science, reason, or common sense—all evidence suggests that strong families are the only earthly hope for the future of this or any other civilization. Try as we may to improve our society, our efforts will be in vain if we ever lose sight of that central truth.

That means we can provide the best education in the world, but only if parents remember that they are the most important teachers of all. It means we can control crime, but only if our sons and daughters understand their responsibilities and their own worth as children of God. It means we can reverse the cycle of dependency, but only if our homes are places of discipline, self-respect, and hope. In the words of my good friend Michael Novak: "One unforgettable law has been learned painfully through all the oppressions, disasters, and injustices of the last thousand years: If things go well with the family, life is worth living; when the family falters, life falls apart."

Preserve, protect, and defend the family: This is the first order of business for our civilization. It should be the first order of business for our political system as well. Let us make it that way.